As populist parties increasingly enter government coalitions we need solid academic research rather than received wisdom [...] truly empirical systematic study on the topic, shattering nice, comforting 'truths' and raising uncomfortable new issues.
Cas Mudde, Associate Professor, University of Georgia, USA

When mainstream parties can't prevent their populist rivals doing well in elections they can always take comfort in the fact that, if they ever do so well that they get into government, they're bound to make a mess of things, right? Wrong. In this fascinating book, McDonnell and Albertazzi take a look at all the available evidence – a good deal of which they themselves have gathered – and give the lie to this common and all-too-convenient wisdom.
Tim Bale, Professor of Politics, Queen Mary University of London, UK

This book represents a key development in the study of European populism, showing through rigorous research that populism in power is not what many expect it to be. As populism grows and develops in Europe, this book advances our knowledge in ways that challenge conventional understanding and allows us to make sense of the growing realities of populists in power.
Paul Taggart, Professor of Politics, University of Sussex, UK

Albertazzi and McDonnell do an excellent job in presenting the ideologies, organizational models and recent experiences in power of the most important Italian and Swiss populist parties. The findings of this timely analysis of populists in power make an important contribution to the study of West European party systems.
Hanspeter Kriesi, Stein Rokkan Chair of Comparative Politics, European University Institute, Florence, Italy

Populists in Power

The main area of sustained populist growth in recent decades has been Western Europe, where populist parties have not only endured longer than expected, but have increasingly begun to enter government. Focusing on three high-profile cases in Italy and Switzerland – the Popolo della Libertà (PDL), Lega Nord (LN) and Schweizerische Volkspartei (SVP) – *Populists in Power* is the first in-depth comparative study to examine whether these parties are indeed doomed to failure in office as many commentators have claimed.

Albertazzi and McDonnell's findings run contrary to much of the received wisdom. Based on extensive original research and fieldwork, they show that populist parties can be built to last, can achieve key policy victories and can survive the experience of government, without losing the support of either the voters or those within their parties.

Contributing a new perspective to studies in populist politics, *Populists in Power* is essential reading for undergraduate and postgraduate students, as well as scholars interested in modern government, parties and politics.

Daniele Albertazzi is a Senior Lecturer in European Politics at the University of Birmingham, UK.

Duncan McDonnell is a Senior Lecturer in Politics at the School of Government and International Relations in Griffith University, Brisbane, Australia.

Routledge Studies in Extremism and Democracy

Series Editors: Roger Eatwell, *University of Bath*, and Matthew Goodwin, *University of Nottingham*.

Founding Series Editors: Roger Eatwell, *University of Bath*, and Cas Mudde, *University of Georgia*.

This new series encompasses academic studies within the broad fields of 'extremism' and 'democracy'. These topics have traditionally been considered largely in isolation by academics. A key focus of the series, therefore, is the (inter-)*relation* between extremism and democracy. Works will seek to answer questions such as to what extent 'extremist' groups pose a major threat to democratic parties, or how democracy can respond to extremism without undermining its own democratic credentials.

The books encompass two strands:

Routledge Studies in Extremism and Democracy includes books with an introductory and broad focus which are aimed at students and teachers. These books will be available in hardback and paperback. Titles include:

Right-Wing Radicalism Today
Perspectives from Europe and the US
Edited by Sabine von Mering and
Timothy Wyman McCarty

Revolt on the Right
Explaining support for the radical
right in Britain
Robert Ford and Matthew Goodwin

Routledge Research in Extremism and Democracy offers a forum for innovative
new research intended for a more specialist readership. These books will be in
hardback only. Titles include:

Populists in Power

**Daniele Albertazzi and
Duncan McDonnell**

LONDON AND NEW YORK

First published 2015 by Routledge

2 Park Square, Milton Park, Abingdon, Oxon OX14 4RN
711 Third Avenue, New York, NY 10017, USA

Routledge is an imprint of the Taylor & Francis Group, an informa business

First issued in paperback 2016

British Library Cataloguing in Publication Data
A catalogue record for this book is available from the British Library

Library of Congress Cataloguing in Publication data
Albertazzi, Daniele
  Populists in power / by Daniele Albertazzi and Duncan McDonnell.
    pages cm. – (Routledge studies in extremism and democracy)
  Includes index.
  1. Populism–Europe, Western. 2. Political parties–Europe,
  Western. I. McDonnell, Duncan, 1972– II. Title.
  JN94.A979A38 2015
  324.2′13094–dc23
  2014034239

ISBN 978-1-138-67044-0 (pbk)
ISBN 978-0-415-60097-2 (hbk)
ISBN 978-1-315-72578-9 (ebk)

Typeset in Times New Roman
by Out of House Publishing

Contents

Figures

Tables

Acknowledgements

Many people and organizations supported us while we conducted the research on which this book is based and during the writing-up phase. First and foremost, we would like to thank the Leverhulme Trust for sponsoring the original project (Funder ref: F/00,094/AZ). Second, we would like to thank the three parties which we studied: the Popolo della Libertà (PDL – People of Freedom), the Lega Nord (LN – Northern League), and the Schweizerische Volkspartei (SVP – Swiss People's Party). In particular, we must thank a number of individuals from these parties.

In the Lega Nord party central office, Roberto Marraccini, Gianfranco Salmoiraghi, Giuliana Bortolozzo and Anna Viragh all helped enormously with gathering data; Nicoletta Maggi, head of the press office in Rome, was of great assistance in setting up interviews; so too were Laura Caldan of the party's youth movement and Roberto Zenga in Turin.

In the PDL, the MP for Genoa, Roberto Cassinelli, facilitated the process of securing access for interviews with grassroots members in the city; the municipal councillor, Loris Marchisio, the regional councillor, Piero Camber, and the district councillor Antonio Quaratino did likewise in Cuneo, Trieste and Turin, respectively.

In the SVP, the MP for Zurich, Hans Fehr, helped both with securing interviews with parliamentarians in Berne and with organizing a survey at a national party event. In Zurich, the municipal party leader, Roger Liebi, assisted with contacting subnational representatives, while in Vaud, the Cantonal Assembly member, Fabienne Despot, did likewise with local grassroots members.

We would like to formally express our deep gratitude to the LN, PDL and SVP representatives interviewed for this book, as well as all the grassroots members who must remain anonymous here, but were extremely generous with their time – often at the end of long days at work. We truly appreciated this.

We are very thankful to the following colleagues who helped us directly with the fieldwork: Sean Müller conducted six interviews with SVP representatives and members in Glarus and Graubünden. He also helped compile the appendix on events in Switzerland; Andrej Zaslove did three interviews with SVP national representatives; Davide Pellegrino interviewed five PDL representatives in Puglia; Marian Bohl helped organize the distribution of our questionnaires to those attending the SVP's Festival of the Family, while Simona Feusi and Roman Zwicky distributed the questionnaires and collected responses on the day.

Again regarding data collection, we should thank Fabiano Gambacorta for assisting Duncan McDonnell with a group interview of SVP members in the canton of Thurgau. We are grateful too to Carmela Romano, who produced most of the interview transcripts in Italian, and Alessandra Meregaglia, who did several of those in French. Thanks are also due to Hans Hirter, who gave us access to the electronic version of 'Année politique suisse 1966 to 2006', and to the Organisation for Economic Co-operation and Development (OECD) for allowing us to reproduce Figure 6.1.

Many colleagues helped at key points during the project. Paul Furlong and James Newell commented on the original Leverhulme proposal; Peter Mair gave feedback on our book proposal draft; Mauro Barisione offered expert advice on the surveys at LN and SVP events; Giuliano Bobba helped gather the data and produce two of the figures in Chapter 5. Finally, Duncan McDonnell would like to say a special word of thanks to Alfio Mastropaolo for being a constant source of support.

Numerous friends and family members also came to our assistance. Jean-Claude Trovato offered advice on the SVP survey translation; Stefano Ondelli provided accommodation in Trieste twice; Phyllis McDonnell helped on many occasions with various technical issues; Peter Maguire dug us out of a hole by restoring several interview recordings that had been damaged.

Finally, for putting up with us over the last few years as we worked on this project, Daniele thanks his partner, Liz, and children, Elena and Francesca; and Duncan thanks his wife, Elena, and children May, Alice, and Dylan. It is to all of them that we dedicate the book.

1 From periphery to power

Populists in Western Europe

On 31 January 2000, 14 of the 15 European Union (EU) member states issued an ultimatum to the remaining member, Austria. If the centre-right Österreichische Volkspartei (ÖVP – Austrian People's Party) pressed ahead with plans to form a government containing the right-wing populist Freiheitliche Partei Österreichs (FPÖ – Austrian Freedom Party) – whose values were deemed to be in conflict with those of the EU – bilateral sanctions would be imposed.[1] According to subsequent accounts, the threat of sanctions was intended to make the ÖVP reconsider its plans – the 14 did not, apparently, think they would have to match their words with action (Larsson and Lundgren, 2005). As it turned out, the ÖVP did not back down, the FPÖ duly took its place in the new coalition government, and Austria found itself 'a pariah within the EU' (Merlingen *et al.*, 2001: 60). Its time as an outcast lasted until September 2000, when a report by the three 'wise men' mandated by the European Court of Human Rights said there were no problems with Austria's human rights record and that 'the overall performance of the Ministers of the FPÖ in Government since February 2000 cannot be generally criticized' (Ahtisaari *et al.*, 2000: 30). Keen to avoid a repeat of what had been an embarrassing impasse, the member states agreed to adopt a 'wait and see' approach to any similar situations in the future.

The Austrian case and the international controversy it aroused serves to remind us of how much has changed in the past 15 years as regards populists and government participation. Although populist parties had been growing electorally in Western Europe since the early 1970s, the only two cases of populists in power in the ensuing 30 years were the left-wing Panellinio Sosialistiko Kinima (PASOK – Panhellenic Socialist Movement) governments in Greece after 1981 and the short-lived right-wing government in Italy led by Silvio Berlusconi in 1994, which contained both Forza Italia (FI) and the Lega Nord (LN – Northern League).[2] By contrast, since the turn of the new century, populists have either served in – or provided consistent parliamentary support as part of formal pacts for – governments in Austria, Italy, the Netherlands, Switzerland, Norway, Denmark, and Greece.[3] As Figure 1.1 (overleaf) shows, while many Western European countries have not yet had populist parties in or

Figure 1.1 Western European governments containing populists (or having established formal pacts with them to ensure a parliamentary majority) since 2000.

even close to power (although only a few now lack electorally successful ones), populists are certainly not on the periphery of power in all.

The move of populists from periphery to power in Western Europe raises questions not only for domestic elites and supranational institutions, but also for political scientists. As Cas Mudde (2013: 15) notes, citing the title of an important article on the topic by Reinhard Heinisch (2003), there has been a 'dominant strain in the populism literature that argues that populist parties are destined for success in opposition and failure in government'. This was certainly the case towards the end of the 1990s and in the early 2000s. To take just two prominent examples: in perhaps her most famous article on populism, Margaret Canovan (1999: 12) claimed that if a populist party 'actually gets into power, its own inability to live up to its promises will be revealed' and it will consequently lose support. Adopting a similarly negative view, Yves Mény and Yves Surel (2002: 18) argued in the introduction to their landmark volume *Democracies and the Populist Challenge* that 'populist parties are by nature neither durable nor sustainable parties of government. Their fate is to be integrated into the mainstream, to disappear, or to remain permanently in opposition'. These views in turn echo another which has often been expressed in the literature by key scholars: that populism tends to be episodic (Taggart, 2004: 270).

The research project on which this book is based set out to examine whether, after more than a decade in which populists have not only grown electorally, but increasingly participated in (or supported) governments, the claims about them being doomed to failure hold true. In the ensuing chapters, we therefore look in detail at the cases of three populist parties which have served in government in Italy and Switzerland – the Popolo della Libertà (PDL – People of Freedom) and the Lega Nord in Italy, and the Schweizerische Volkspartei (SVP – Swiss People's Party). Having extensively discussed their organizations and ideologies in Chapters 2–4, we then assess how they fared in elections (Chapter 5), whether they indeed lived up to their promises when in office (Chapter 6), and how elected representatives and grassroots members saw their participation in government (Chapter 7). We do so not only by closely scrutinizing party manifestos, key texts, and policies, but also through intensive fieldwork conducted in Italy and Switzerland. This comprises individual and group interviews with over 100 representatives and members, along with surveys at party events. Given its analytical and methodological scope, we believe this book therefore provides the most comprehensive study to date of populists in power.

Our findings run contrary to much of the received wisdom. Populist parties are neither inevitably episodic nor are they destined to failure in government. As regards their being episodic, while some populist parties may be flash parties or personal parties (McDonnell, 2013a), others have established structures and grassroots organizations that have remained in place for decades and are built to last beyond the current leadership. Moreover, when in government, populists have shown that they can introduce key policies in line with their core ideologies and election promises. Crucially, they have also shown that they can survive the experience of government, despite the inevitable compromises and disappointments this brings, without losing the support of either the voters or those within their parties. In other words, while the Austrian case may have been a defining moment in the history of Western European populism, the traumatic subsequent experience of the FPÖ in government (Heinisch, 2003; Luther, 2011) is not necessarily that of all Western European populists.[4]

Populism

As Benjamin Moffitt and Simon Tormey (2014: 382) have noted, not only is it 'an axiomatic feature of literature on the topic to acknowledge the contested nature of populism', but recent work on populism 'has reached a whole new level of meta-reflexivity, where it is posited that it has become common to acknowledge the acknowledgement of this fact'. We see no need to dwell on these terminological disputes other than to say that, like many political science concepts, populism has suffered at the hands of journalists, politicians, and scholars. The myriad and contradictory ways in which the media uses the term have been well documented (Bale *et al.*, 2011), while Peter Wiles's comment that 'to each his own definition of populism, according to the academic axe he grinds' continues to have a certain validity over 40 years after he wrote it (Wiles, 1969: 166). Hence, we find that among both media commentators and academics, 'populism' is often employed in inconsistent and undefined ways to denote any kind of appeal to the people, mild rebukes of elites, crowd-pleasing measures, and 'catch-all' politics.[5] Adding to the confusion surrounding the term within academia, scholars from different parts of the world tend to view *their* populists as the archetypal ones and to define populism accordingly. For example, Kurt Weyland (2001: 14) asserts that 'populism is best defined as a political strategy through which a personalistic leader seeks or exercises government power based on direct, unmediated, uninstitutionalized support from large numbers of mostly unorganized followers'. However, while this may fit cases of Latin American populism (on which Weyland is an expert), it does not apply to many well-organized populist parties in Western Europe.

Despite the disagreements over definitions, there are some core elements which most scholars would agree are ever-present among populists. First and foremost: the juxtaposition between 'people' and 'elites'. As Canovan (1981: 294) observes, 'all forms of populism without exception involve some kind of exaltation of and appeal to "the people" and all are in one sense or another anti-elitist'. Moreover, there is a moral dimension to this which is expressed in Manichean terms: whether of Left or Right, what unites populists is the fundamental proposition that a 'good' people is suffering due to the deliberate actions of a 'bad' set of elites. This is the basis for what has surely been the most widely used definition of populism in recent years: that by Cas Mudde, which he first presented in his 2004 article 'The Populist Zeitgeist'. In it, Mudde defines populism as 'an ideology that considers society to be ultimately separated into two homogeneous and antagonistic groups, "the pure people" versus "the corrupt elite", and which argues that politics should be an expression of the *volonté générale* (general will) of the people' (2004: 544). Although, as we discuss below, we have reservations about Mudde's description of 'the elite' as a single homogeneous group, we feel the rest of his definition can serve as a useful minimal definition of populism.

Nonetheless, while we agree that all forms of populism – whether Left or Right – are characterized by an antagonistic relationship between a 'good people' and a 'bad elite', we believe there is another element that must be included when defining right-wing populism: 'others'. This is because, for right-wing populists, 'the people' are said not only to be oppressed by the elites, but also to be under threat from the presence of 'others' within society who do not share the identity and/or values of 'the people' (and are alleged to be favoured by the elites against the people). Since the cases we examine in this book are all broadly right-wing parties (albeit different kinds of right-wing, as we explain in Chapters 2–4), it is important to make clear from the start exactly how we define right-wing populism.[6] We understand this as:

> A thin-centred ideology which pits a virtuous and homogeneous people against a set of elites and dangerous 'others' who are together depicted as depriving (or attempting to deprive) the sovereign people of their rights, values, prosperity, identity and voice.[7]

It is worth devoting some attention to the main components of this definition. First of all, we consider populism to be an ideology, in line with an increasing trend in the literature. As Mudde and Cristóbal Rovira Kaltwasser (2013: 498) note, over the past decade 'a growing group of social scientists has defined populism predominantly by making use of an "ideational approach", conceiving it as discourse, ideology, or world-view'. To be clear as regards what we mean by 'ideology', we follow Martin Seliger's conception of ideologies as 'sets of ideas by which men [sic] posit, explain, and justify ends and means of organized social action with the aim to preserve, amend, uproot, or rebuild a given reality' (Seliger, 1970: 325). We also agree with those who view populism as a 'thin-centred ideology' (Mudde, 2007; Stanley, 2008) that is found alongside 'thick' ideologies of Left and Right or with other thin ones (like nationalism, for example). Hence, a party may be 'right-wing populist', 'radical right populist', 'regionalist populist', 'left-wing populist', and so on. But, ideologically, it is never simply 'populist'.

As mentioned above, a key component for all populist ideologies is the notion of a 'good people'. For populists, the people constitutes a homogeneous and inherently virtuous community – with 'community' being a place where, as Zygmunt Bauman (2001: 12) explains, there is mutual trust and 'it is crystal-clear who is one of us and who is not'. Although there is little confusion for individual populist parties about who *their* 'people' is, the term can have different meanings for different types of populists. Mény and Surel (2004: 173–196) identify three separate populist understandings of 'the people': as a class, as a nation, and as a sovereign. Of these three, it is 'the people as sovereign' in our view which is the always-present key feature of populism in democracies. 'The people as nation' and 'the people as class' may also both be present (this is the case for the left-wing nationalist populist Sinn Féin in Ireland), but they are not always so (for example, Berlusconi's parties have had no conception of 'the people as class'). While 'the people' is said to be the rightful sovereign, populists claim that this sovereignty has been taken away from the people by the elites. That brings us to another important aspect of populist ideology: the people is cast as a victim, inevitably of the elites and, for right-wing populists, also of 'the others'. This has two main implications: first, the people is not responsible for the country's many ills (in this sense, populists offer a form of exculpation – their message is: 'the situation is terrible, but it is not your fault'); second, the primary solution to those ills is to make 'the blameless people' sovereign once more (by putting the populist party into power).

By contrast, the enemies of the people – the elites (for all populists) and 'the others' (for right-wing populists) – are neither homogeneous nor virtuous. The former usually consist of a mixture of political, financial, economic, media, bureaucratic, judicial, cultural, and intellectual elites who are charged with being, at best, distant from the people and incompetent (and, at worst, downright corrupt). As we have said, we disagree with Mudde's representation of the elites as a homogeneous block for populists. First of all, as Mudde himself and Kaltwasser (2013: 503) have acknowledged, populists make exceptions for those parts of the elites that are sympathetic to them (for example, in the media). Second, it is also the case that, for populist parties that have been around for several decades – and especially those that have served in national or subnational governments – the relationship with elites (whom they have to deal with far more regularly than when in opposition) becomes increasingly complex, and populists are often therefore forced to distinguish between 'bad' and 'not-so-bad' elites. For example, both Berlusconi and Christoph Blocher of the SVP do not treat all economic elites with the same disdain as they do political or media ones. As for 'the others' – a central element of right-wing populist ideology – their identity differs from case to case, but they too are not a homogeneous group. Rather, they are made up of those whose identity, behaviour, or beliefs preclude them from being considered part of the natural community formed by the people. For right-wing populists in Western Europe, the 'others' include immigrants first and foremost (and, in particular since 9/11, Muslims), but can also comprise 'welfare scroungers', regional minorities, those with 'non-traditional' lifestyles, communists, and so on. All of these are said to want to impose their values and traditions on the people and, in this endeavour, they alledgedly receive the support of liberal elites such as politicians, the judiciary, the media, and those within EU institutions.

Populists of both Right and Left in Western democracies therefore claim they are on a mission to restore sovereignty to the people and set themselves up as the 'true democrats' in contrast to the 'false democrats' of the elites. While not anti-democratic per se (quite the opposite, in fact), populists do, however, criticize the checks, balances, structures, and complexities of liberal democracy (Albertazzi and Mueller, 2013: 348–349). These are said to limit the expression of the will of the people and to consolidate ever-greater power in the hands of elites. As Mény and Surel (2002: 9) observe, 'populist movements speak and behave as if democracy meant the power of the people and only the power of the people'. In this way, they exploit the gap between what the ideal of democracy promises ('government of the people, by the people, for the people') and how liberal democracies actually function ('limited and restrained majority rule in the name of the people').[8] Unlike in liberal democracy, legitimacy to wield power in the populist vision of democracy can only come directly from the people. We can see this principle clearly, for example, when a leader like Berlusconi objects to judges having the power to sanction him, i.e. someone who, unlike the judges, has received the support of millions of Italians. Or in the Italian Five-Star Movement's conception of its elected representatives as mere delegates who must act in accordance with the results of online votes.[9] Or when populists seek to rip up and rewrite constitutions which constrain their powers – a tactic used by leaders as ideologically different as Viktor Orbán in Hungary and Hugo Chávez in Venezuela.[10] Put simply, as far as its relationship to democracy and liberal democracy is concerned, populism is as Takis Pappas (2014: 2–3) has defined it: democratic illiberalism.

Populism and power

The sustained rise of populist parties in Western Europe is a relatively recent historical phenomenon. For example, if we look through Ghiṭa Ionescu and Ernest Gellner's famous 1969 volume *Populism: Its Meaning and National Characteristics*, we find chapters on North America, Latin America, Russia, Eastern Europe and Africa, but nothing on that part of the world in which most of the contributors lived and worked: Western Europe. There had of course been isolated cases in post-war Western Europe of populist parties, but these were flash parties that emerged and enjoyed sudden success before disappearing relatively quickly. Examples include Guglielmo Giannini's Fronte dell'Uomo Qualunque (Common Man's Front) in late 1940s Italy, Clann na Talmhan (Family of the Land) in 1940s and 1950s Ireland, and, most notably, Pierre Poujade's Union de Défense des Commerçants et Artisans (Union for the Defence of Tradesmen and Artisans) in 1950s France. Nonetheless, until the beginning of the 1970s – as the Ionescu and Gellner volume highlights – populism was generally something that was considered to occur elsewhere.

Things began to change in the 1970s: first with anti-tax populist parties in Scandinavia like Anders Lange's Party in Norway and Mogens Glistrup's Progress Party in Denmark (the forerunners of today's Norwegian Progress Party and Danish People's Party), and then with the creation of extreme right movements which would also come to be considered populist like the Front National (FN) in France and the Flemish Vlaams Blok (VB – now the Vlaams Belang). This was followed in the 1980s both by the founding of new parties like the regionalist populist Lega Lombarda in Italy (which would later merge with similar northern Italian movements to form the Lega Nord) and by the transformation of traditional right-wing parties like the SVP in Switzerland and the FPÖ in Austria into more radical populist parties. While this wave of populism in Western Europe obviously attracted a lot of interest from scholars, the prevailing wisdom for many years was that, as in previous decades, populist parties would continue to be episodic. For example, Paul Taggart (2004: 270) observed that 'populist politicians, movements or parties emerge and grow quickly and gain attention but find it difficult to sustain that momentum and therefore will usually fade fast', while Canovan (2005: 89) asserted that 'populist movements tend to be spasmodic, flaring up briefly and dying away almost as fast'.

However, while some Western European populist parties like New Democracy in 1990s Sweden and the Dutch Lijst Pim Fortuyn (LPF – Pim Fortuyn List) in the last decade have indeed conformed to the 'episodic' thesis, many others have not. To take just a few examples: The French FN celebrated its fortieth anniversary in 2012 – the same year that it achieved its best result to date in a presidential election; the Lega Nord is still going strong over 20 years after its creation and registered some of its best ever electoral performances in the 2008–2010 period (see Chapters 3 and 5); The FPÖ recovered from both a party split and a very unhappy experience in government at the beginning of the last decade to bounce back in subsequent elections (see Chapter 5). Moreover, all three of these parties have survived the passage of their 'historic' leaders – Jean-Marie Le Pen, Umberto Bossi and Jörg Haider. The same is true of the Danish People's Party and the Norwegian Progress Party, both of which have been in existence under their current names for several decades and have seen their respective founder-leaders Pia Kjærsgaard and Carl I. Hagen resign and be replaced. Hence, while parties such as Geert Wilders' Partij voor de Vrijheid (PVV – Party for Freedom) in the Netherlands and those led by Berlusconi (see Chapter 2) may be personal parties whose lifespan seems likely to be tied to their leader's political career and others have been flash parties, there are also many populist parties in Western Europe that have institutionalized, establishing deep roots and lasting structures which can survive moments of crisis.

Not only have populist parties continued to grow in recent decades and new successful ones emerged (e.g. the UK Independence Party, the Finns Party and the Five-Star Movement), but they have increasingly also become acceptable partners for mainstream parties in government (see Figure 1.1). This move from the periphery to power, of course, can be fraught with difficulties. First of all, for most populists, the decision itself poses a dilemma that may be summed up as follows: do they run more risk (a) by maintaining their position of 'exit', remaining in 'pure' and outright opposition (but perhaps eventually appearing irrelevant in the eyes of the electorate) or (b) by opting for 'voice' through participation in government alongside other parties, but possibly losing credibility among their core supporters and activists? (McDonnell and Newell, 2011: 444).[11] Second, once the decision for 'voice' has been made, going into government for the first time poses a range of organizational challenges just as it does for all parties entering government for the first time (Bolleyer, 2008: 35–38). In particular, it requires (a) the leadership finding sufficiently competent people to take up ministerial roles and (b) the party in office learning quickly how to communicate and justify its actions to the party on the ground – especially when faced with the inevitable compromises of coalition government.

Given such challenges, and the supposedly unstable, irresponsible, and 'protest' nature of populist parties, much of the key literature in the 1990s and early 2000s questioned whether they could sustain the pressures of power. For example, in their 1995 book *The Radical Right in Western Europe*, Herbert Kitschelt and Anthony J. McGann argued that:

> simple political dichotomies dividing the world into friend and foe may help populist parties to rally support as long as they are in opposition to the partocratic establishment and as long as they are therefore able to confine their actions to negative campaigns in which they express more what they dislike than what they like. It is questionable, however, whether the negative electoral coalition brought together by populist parties will stick together once these parties have to act on policy problems as governing parties.
>
> Kitschelt and McGann (1995: 201)

This view of populists in power is in line with the previously mentioned comment by Mény and Surel (2002: 18) regarding them as 'by nature neither durable nor sustainable parties of government' and that by Canovan (1999: 12) about how, if a populist party comes into power, it will suffer the consequences since 'its own inability to live up to its promises will be revealed'. Likewise, Heinisch (2003: 101) argued that populist parties faced very serious problems caused by their 'inexperience in policy-making', 'lack of qualified personnel', and the pressure 'to tone down the radicalness of their agenda and political presentation'. Although referring to all populists in this comment, Heinisch's view was largely based on the experience of the FPÖ in power after 2000, which certainly supported the thesis that populists are unsuited to government. So too did the brief and acrimonious 1994 Berlusconi government in Italy (see Chapter 2) and the shambolic 87 days which the LPF spent in cabinet in the Netherlands in 2002 (van Holsteyn and Irwin, 2003; Lucardie, 2008).

In all of these cases, the parties concerned were clearly not ready for the demands of power. Berlusconi's Forza Italia was a new party which had been created just months before the general election, while the Lega Nord was also relatively new and – like all parties in the Berlusconi government – was in power for the first time. As for the LPF, not only had it been in existence for a mere five months before entering government, but its leader and founder Pim Fortuyn had been assassinated during the election campaign. As Joop van Holsteyn and Galen Irwin (2003: 63) therefore observe, when it went into government, 'the LPF had not yet become a true political party'. Admittedly, the case of the FPÖ is different. First, because it had been in national government in the 1980s before Haider took over and transformed it into a right-wing populist party. Second, and more importantly, it had been preparing to return to office for many years under Haider (Luther, 2011: 456–459).[12] Nonetheless, it too turned out to be utterly unable to meet the challenges it faced. Its failure was largely one of leadership. In part due to the international sanctions, but also because he wanted to keep his distance from the necessary compromises of coalition, Haider did not take a cabinet seat and instead remained as governor of Carinthia. Moreover, he used this distance to regularly criticize the government from afar (Luther, 2011). As Heinisch (2003: 110) comments, Haider's behaviour 'increasingly created a public image of a cantankerous organisation', especially since the leader sided on some occasions with the beleaguered party in office and, on others, with the discontented party on the ground. In addition, most of those selected as the party's ministers proved to be out of their depth, with over half either resigning or being replaced within two years (Heinisch, 2003: 115). Kurt Richard Luther (2011: 468) therefore concludes that the Austrian case strongly suggests:

> erstwhile outsider parties' likelihood of prospering once in government will owe much to their leadership's capacity to identify and implement strategies and behaviours consonant with the parties' new goal and to deal effectively with the inescapable tensions caused by the transition to incumbency.

Luther (2011: 468) adds that he does not believe such parties are 'necessarily doomed to failure once they change their primary goal to office'. This depends on the abilities of individual leaders – agency is thus extremely important. So too, however, is prior experience. After all, at least some of the problems populist parties face when they go into power for the first time are the same as those encountered by any new party in power for the first time (McDonnell and Newell, 2011: 450). Hence, although Heinisch (2003: 123) argues that 'it is the populism of these parties that accounts for their success while in opposition but which creates nearly insurmountable difficulties once such groups reach public office', it may be the case that populist parties which are not new to power fare better. The obvious way therefore to test whether it really is their populism that makes populist parties fail when in office is to look at subsequent governing experiences. As we explain in the next section, that is precisely what we will do in this book.

Italian and Swiss populists in power

This book focuses on three Italian and Swiss populist parties – the LN, PDL and SVP – during periods when they were in power, but not for the first time: 2003–2007 for the SVP and 2008–2011 for the LN and PDL.[13] As we discuss in Chapter 4, 2003 in some senses did represent a very important first for the SVP since it was only then that Blocher – the man who had led the transformation of the SVP into a populist party and had overseen its electoral rise from fourth to first party in the country – became a member of government and the party secured a second Federal Council seat (as explained in note 13, this makes the 2003–2007 period by far the SVP's most significant *as a populist party* in power). However, those in (or supporting) the party were well used to one of its representatives serving in cabinet. Likewise, although the PDL was technically a new party in 2008 (see Chapter 2), it was the product of a merger between parties that had been in coalitions led by Berlusconi, both when in and out of power, for well over a decade. These alliances had constantly included the LN since 2000, and so it too had accumulated considerable time in office between 2001 and 2006, in addition to the short-lived and unhappy Berlusconi-led 1994 government mentioned earlier (Albertazzi *et al.*, 2011).

All three of our parties therefore, unlike the FPÖ in 2000, the LPF in 2002, or FI and the LN in 1994, had prior experience of being populist parties in power. Moreover, all three – again unlike the FPÖ in 2000, the LPF in 2002, and Forza Italia and the LN in 1994 – were able to propose representatives for ministerial office who had led their parties for many years and/or had served in government on previous occasions. This also means that – once again unlike the FPÖ under Haider – the LN, PDL and SVP during the time frames we examine all had their leaders sitting at the cabinet table rather than pointing the finger at inexperienced party ministers from a distance. In sum, given that populist parties are becoming more acceptable as governing parties in Western Europe (see Figure 1.1) and that we are likely to see them in the coming decades doing so for the second or third times, our case selection of the LN, PDL and SVP should be more revealing about the long-term prospects for populists in power than earlier analyses.

While there are therefore key factors in common regarding the three cases, we are also, of course, presented with a range of very different contextual factors and structural conditions for government participation. In Switzerland's consensus democracy, the number of seats held by each of the four governing parties (including the SVP) had been set in stone since 1959 according to what was known as the 'magic formula' (see Chapter 4). Although this changed in 2003, the SVP still only occupied two of the seven seats in government between 2003 and 2007 – despite being the largest party in the country with 26.7 per cent of the vote. By contrast, in Italy's adversarial democracy, the LN and the PDL in 2008 held a majority in both houses of parliament and had been firm allies both in government and opposition since 2000 (although the LN was very much the junior partner). Given the structural similarities, but also the differences between the three cases, we believe that if we can find commonalities among these governing experiences (whether in terms of policy achievements, electoral performances, the reactions of elected representatives and grassroots members, etc.), then this may tell us something about populists in power that has wider validity. Furthermore, if the claims made about populists in power discussed earlier are proved wrong across some or all of these cases, then those claims will need to be revised and our understanding of the relationship between populists and government participation reassessed.

As mentioned above, our study has involved considerable in-depth investigation and fieldwork for all three cases. In addition to analysis of policies, legislation, economic data, party statutes, campaign manifestos, statements of ideologies, and results at national and second-order elections, this has included surveys of those attending large party events and semi-structured individual and group interviews with 116 elected representatives and grass-roots members in Italy and Switzerland. Interviews focused on a range of topics, from how party organization at grassroots level functioned, to how respondents considered the leader, to how they viewed specific party actions in government, to how they regarded the other governing parties, to whether they believed that the price of power (e.g. concessions, disappointments, possible loss of ideological purity) was worth it. Finally, the surveys at LN and SVP party events focused mainly on how respondents viewed the party's time in power.[14]

Although it would require a far larger number of interviews (along with much greater resources and extensive party central office logistic support) to construct a statistically significant sample, it is worth noting that interviews were conducted in different areas of each country and included elected representatives at several institutional levels (national, regional/cantonal and municipal), along with active grassroots members. Given the sample size and the associated dangers of relying on a random sample, a purposive sampling strategy was used. LN interviews with subnational representatives and grassroots members were conducted between 2009 and 2010 in regions of the north-west and north-east of Italy (since the LN is a regionalist party, this was sufficient).[15] Interviews with national-level LN representatives took place in Rome. PDL interviews were conducted between 2009 and 2011 in regions of the north-west, north-east, south-west and south-east.[16] National PDL representatives were interviewed in Milan and Rome. SVP interviews were conducted between 2010 and 2011 in urban and provincial areas of German- and French-speaking cantons in Switzerland.[17] The party's national representatives were interviewed in Berne. With the exception of the PDL interviews in the south-west of Italy, which were conducted by telephone, all other interviews in Italy and Switzerland were face-to-face. Interviews with LN and PDL representatives and members were conducted in Italian. Those with SVP representatives and members were conducted in French, English, German, Swiss German and Italian. When quoted in the chapters of this book, the names of elected representatives are given along with their roles at the time of interview. Since grassroots members spoke on condition of anonymity, their names are not provided.[18]

Ours of course remains a small-N study which, as we have said, cannot claim statistical significance. Nonetheless, it is the first study of its type in terms of both scope and depth. There is no comparative research that looks at the full set of issues we do. And no comparative work has been produced examining how representatives and members of Western European populist parties assess their experiences in government. As Mudde (2007: 295) observes with regard to populist radical right parties (but the same holds for all populist parties in Western Europe):

One of the key problems in the field of populist radical right studies is the lack of original research. Despite the plethora of publications that have appeared over the past twenty-five years, the field is still full of 'received wisdom' that (so far) has not been tested scientifically. The reason is quite simple: only very few researchers actually study populist radical right parties themselves.

In this book, we put three populist parties in power at the centre of our research. As the ensuing chapters will show, some key points of the 'received wisdom' on populists which Mudde refers to need to be re-thought: as regards their party organizations; as regards their endurance; as regards the views and expectations of their party members; as regards their electoral fortunes once they are in office; as regards their capacity to achieve policy goals; as regards their ability to survive, and even thrive, in power.

Notes

1 These sanctions would mean that 'there would be no bilateral official contacts at the political level with the new government, Austrian ambassadors would be received only at a technical level and there would be no support for Austrian candidates for positions in international organizations' (Merlingen *et al.*, 2001: 60).
2 PASOK, particularly when under the leadership of Andreas Papandreou, has been defined by many scholars as a 'populist party' (e.g. Lyrintzis, 1987; Mudde, 2007: 48; Pappas, 2014). It is interesting to recall that, in the case of the 1994 right-wing government in Italy, the main source of international concern was the presence of the post-Fascist Alleanza Nationale (AN – National Alliance). Little was known about Forza Italia, which had only been in existence for a few months, while the Lega Nord at that time was – in our view – seen outside Italy more as a rather eccentric regionalist movement. Indeed, the Lega was expelled from the regionalist European Free Alliance group in the European Parliament due to its participation in government with AN.
3 In addition to the left-wing populists of PASOK, Greece has also seen the right-wing populist party Laikós Orthódoxos Synagermós (LAOS – Popular Orthodox Rally) serve briefly in a government of national unity from November 2011 to February 2012.
4 As we note later in the chapter, the FPÖ saw half of its ministers either resign or be replaced within the first two years, lost heavily at the subsequent general election and eventually suffered a very serious split in which the party's key figures (including its leader, Jörg Haider) left to form a new party – the Bündnis Zukunft Österreich (BZÖ – Alliance for the Future of Austria) – that took the FPÖ's place in government. Despite this experience, as we discuss in Chapter 5, the FPÖ would bounce back under new leadership to perform very well at the 2008 general election.
5 The ridiculous labelling of the UK Labour Party leader Ed Miliband as 'populist' by numerous commentators in late 2013 following his criticisms of energy companies is a case in point. So too is the description of the Mayor of New York, Bill de Blasio, as 'populist' for his campaign promises to reduce wealth disparity in the city. See McDonnell (2013b).
6 This definition applies only to democratic cases of right-wing populism and not to cases of non-democratic/authoritarian right-wing populism.

7 Other than the replacement of 'ideology' with the more precise 'thin-centred ideology', this definition is identical to the one of populism in our 2008 volume *Twenty-First Century Populism: The Spectre of Western European Democracy* (Albertazzi and McDonnell, 2008: 3). In recent years, however, we have come to agree with two colleagues who pointed out that our original definition had a right-wing bias. These were, first of all, Thomas Poguntke at a seminar presentation on the *Twenty-First Century Populism volume* which Duncan McDonnell gave at the European University Institute in December 2008 and, second, Matthijs Rooduijn in several publications (e.g. Rooduijn, 2013: 2–3). Having reflected at length on this question, we believe that our definition functions very well for cases of right-wing populism, but not necessarily for left-wing ones.

8 See Giovanni Sartori's discussion of limited and restrained majority rule as the working principle of democracy (Sartori, 1987: 32).

9 This also goes against Article 67 of the Italian Constitution which says 'Each Member of Parliament represents the Nation and carries out his duties without a binding mandate'. See: https://www.senato.it/documenti/repository/istituzione/costituzione_inglese.pdf (accessed 30 July 2014).

10 On this point, see the comments by Orbán in July 2014 that he would like to build an 'illiberal state' in Hungary. Available at: http://euobserver.com/political/125128 (accessed 29 July 2014).

11 We say that the decision to enter government poses a dilemma for 'most populists' since this is not universally the case. For example, Forza Italia was created specifically to be a governing party (inevitably alongside others, given Italy's electoral system). While, in the Swiss case, the SVP was automatically a governing party thanks to the 'magic formula' in that country (see Chapter 4).

12 Luther (2011: 459) notes that many important figures in the party's national executive 'judged the party still unprepared for government, but Haider won the day, arguing that, although incumbency might well cost the FPÖ up to a third of its votes, when the "door of history opens" the party had to accept responsibility'.

13 We decided to focus on the 2003–2007 period for the SVP since they were in government for the full legislature and with their key figure, Blocher, as a member of the Federal Council. This is not true of the 2007–2011 period when, following the refusal by the other parties to support Blocher's reappointment, the SVP went into opposition for a year before returning with just one federal councillor (Ueli Maurer), who was given the least significant of the seven ministries – Defence. The 2003–2007 period is thus by far the SVP's most analytically useful period in government since its transformation (under Blocher) into a populist party.

14 We were unable to do an equivalent survey for the PDL due to the fact that no suitable event was held during the period of our fieldwork. We did, however, conduct individual and group interviews with grassroots members of the party.

15 The regions were Piedmont, Veneto, and Friuli-Venezia Giulia.

16 The regions were Piedmont, Liguria, Veneto, Friuli-Venezia Giulia, Campania, and Puglia.

17 The cantons were Zurich, Thurgau, Glarus, Graubünden, Geneva, and Vaud.

18 Members were approached through snowballing with the help of the party: after first contact by phone or email, emails were sent out and snowball chains developed with those who agreed to be interviewed.

Bibliography

Ahtisaari, M., Frowein, J., and Oreja, M. (2000) 'Report', Paris, 8 September. Available at: http://www.eu-oplysningen.dk/upload/application/pdf/78abace8/report.pdf%3Fdownload%3D1 (accessed July 2014).

Albertazzi, D. and McDonnell, D. (2008) 'Introduction: The Sceptre and the Spectre', in Albertazzi, D. and McDonnell, D. (eds), *Twenty-First Century Populism: The Spectre of Western European Democracy*, Basingstoke: Palgrave Macmillan.

Albertazzi, D. and Mueller, S. (2013) 'Populism and Liberal Democracy: Populists in Government in Austria, Italy, Poland and Switzerland', *Government and Opposition*, 48 (3), 343–371.

Albertazzi, D., McDonnell, D., and Newell, J. (2011) '*Di lotta e di governo*: The Lega Nord and Rifondazione Comunista in Office', *Party Politics*, 17 (4), 471–487.

Art, D. (2011) *Inside the Radical Right: The Development of Anti-Immigrant Parties in Western Europe*, New York: Cambridge University Press.

Bale, T., van Kessel, S., and Taggart, P. (2011) 'Thrown Around with Abandon? Popular Understandings of Populism as Conveyed by the Print Media: A UK Case Study', *Acta Politica*, 46 (2), 111–131.

Bauman, Z. (2001) *Community. Seeking Safety in an Insecure World*, Cambridge: Polity Press.

Bolleyer, N. (2008) 'The Organizational Costs of Public Office', in Deschouwer, K. (ed.), *New Parties in Government for the First Time*, London: Routledge.

Canovan, M. (1981) *Populism*, New York: Harcourt Brace Jovanovich.

Canovan, M. (1999) 'Trust the People! Populism and the Two Faces of Democracy', *Political Studies*, 47 (1), 2–16.

Canovan, M. (2005) *The People*, Cambridge: Polity Press.

Heinisch, R. (2003) 'Success in Opposition – Failure in Government: Explaining the Performance of Right-Wing Populist Parties in Public Office', *West European Politics*, 26 (3), 91–130.

Ignazi, P. (2006) *Extreme Right Parties in Western Europe*, Oxford: Oxford University Press.

Ionescu, G. and Gellner, E. (1969) (eds), *Populism: Its Meanings and National Characteristics*, London: Weidenfeld & Nicolson.

Kitschelt, H. with McGann, A.J. (1995) *The Radical Right in Western Europe: A Comparative Analysis*, Ann Arbor, MI: University of Michigan Press.

Larsson, S. and Lundgren, J.(2005) 'The Sanctions Against Austria', in Larsson, S., Olsson, E.-K. and Ramberg, B. (eds), *Crisis Decision Making in the European Union*, Stockholm: CRISMART.

Lucardie, P. (2008) 'The Netherlands: Populism versus Pillarization', in Albertazzi, D. and McDonnell, D. (eds), *Twenty-First Century Populism: The Spectre of Western Democracy*, 151–165.

Luther, K.R. (2011) 'Of Goals and Own Goals: A Case Study of Right-wing Populist Party Strategy for and during Incumbency', *Party Politics*, 17 (4), 453–470.

Lyrintzis, C. (1987) 'The Power of Populism: The Greek Case', *European Journal of Political Research*, 15 (6), 667–686.

McDonnell, D. (2013a) 'Silvio Berlusconi's Personal Parties: From Forza Italia to the Popolo Della Libertà', *Political Studies*, 61 (S1), 217–233.

McDonnell, D. (2013b) 'Abbott, Rudd and de Blasio: Many Things, But Not Populists', *The Conversation*, 19 September. Available at: https://theconversation.com/abbott-rudd-and-de-blasio-many-things-but-not-populists-18390 (accessed 31 July 2014).

McDonnell, D. and Newell, J.L. (2011) 'Outsider Parties in Government in Western Europe', *Party Politics*, 17 (4), 443–452.

Mény, Y. and Surel, Y. (2002) 'The Constitutive Ambiguity of Populism', in Mény, Y. and Surel, Y. (eds), *Democracies and The Populist Challenge*, Basingstoke: Palgrave Macmillan.

Mény, Y. and Surel, Y. (2004) *Populismo e democrazia*, Bologna: Il Mulino. Originally published in French as Mény, Y. and Surel, Y. (2000) *Par le peuple, pour le peuple*, Paris: Librarie Arthème Fayard.

Merlingen, M., Mudde, C., and Sedelmeier, U. (2001) 'The Right and the Righteous? European Norms, Domestic Politics and the Sanctions against Austria', *Journal of Common Market Studies*, 39 (1), 59–77.

Moffitt, B. and Tormey, S. (2014) 'Rethinking Populism: Politics, Mediatisation and Political Style', *Political Studies*, 62 (2), 381–397.

Mudde, C. (2004) 'The Populist Zeitgeist', *Government and Opposition*, 39 (4), 541–563.

Mudde, C. (2007) *Populist Radical Right Parties in Europe*, Cambridge: Cambridge University Press.

Mudde, C. (2013) 'Three Decades of Populist Radical Right Parties in Western Europe: So What?', *European Journal of Political Research*, 52 (1), 1–19.

Mudde, C. and Kaltwasser, C. (2013) 'Populism', in Freeden, M., Sargent, L.T., and Stears, M. (eds), *The Oxford Handbook of Political Ideologies*, Oxford: Oxford University Press.

Pappas, T.S. (2014) 'Populist Democracies: Post-Authoritarian Greece and Post-Communist Hungary', *Government and Opposition*, 49 (1), 1–23.

Rooduijn, M. (2013) 'The Mesmerising Message: The Diffusion of Populism in Public Debates in Western European Media', *Political Studies*. Published online in 'early view' 13 September 2013. DOI: 10.1111/1467–9248.12074.

Sartori, G. (1987) *The Theory of Democracy Revisited*, Chatham, NJ: Chatham House.

Seliger, M. (1970) 'Fundamental and Operative Ideology: The Two Principal Dimensions of Political Argumentation', *Policy Sciences*, 1 (3), 325–338.

Stanley, B. (2008) 'The Thin Ideology of Populism', *Journal of Political Ideologies*, 13 (1), 95–110.

Taggart, P. (2004) 'Populism and Representative Politics in Contemporary Europe', *Journal of Political Ideologies*, 9 (3), 269–288.

Van Holsteyn, J. and Irwin, G. (2003) 'Never a Dull Moment: Pim Fortuyn and the Dutch Parliamentary Election of 2002', *West European Politics*, 26 (2), 41–66.

Weyland, K. (2001) 'Clarifying a Contested Concept: Populism in the Study of Latin American Politics', *Comparative Politics*, 34 (1), 1–22.

Wiles, P. (1969) 'A Syndrome, Not a Doctrine: Some Elementary Theses on Populism', in Ionescu, G. and Gellner, E. (eds), *Populism: Its Meaning and National Characteristics*, London: Weidenfeld & Nicolson.

2 Forza Italia and the Popolo della Libertà

There are few contemporary leaders in established democracies comparable to Silvio Berlusconi, the founder of Forza Italia (FI) and the Popolo della Libertà (PDL – People of Freedom). Not only has he remained at the forefront of Italian politics for two decades and led centre-right coalitions to three general election victories, but he has done so having held no party or representative roles prior to the televised announcement of his entry into politics as leader of the newly founded FI in January 1994. To put it in context: Berlusconi's first election on 27 March 1994 saw him become prime minister and, for the next 17½ years until the fall of his government on 12 November 2011, he was constantly either prime minister or leader of the opposition. Throughout this period, he has been able to call on a stock of financial and media power which would be unimaginable (and perhaps unconstitutional) for politicians in any other Western democracy.

There is certainly not the space here to go into all the details of what has been a long and extraordinary career, so we will focus on those aspects which are most relevant to the aims of this book. We therefore provide below a brief overview of FI and the PDL's history in terms of alliances and electoral results. The rest of the chapter is divided into two main sections. In the first ('The party') we discuss FI and the PDL in organizational terms. Using material from one-to-one and group interviews conducted in the period from 2009 to 2011, we then examine how elected representatives and grassroots members viewed both the party organization and its leader. In the second section ('The ideology') we will discuss the classification of FI and the PDL as populist and consider their ideologies as laid out in official party documents – something which has often been overlooked amidst the attention on the leader.

Forza Italia and its successor, the Popolo della Libertà, have been the leading parties on the Italian centre-right since the collapse of the so-called First Republic in the early 1990s. Not only has Berlusconi proven adept at creating successful parties, but he has also been by far the most competent leader over the past two decades in Italy at creating and leading coalitions which are capable of both winning elections and offering more stable government than their main rivals. This latter achievement has been due in large part, first, to

Berlusconi's undisputed position as coalition leader – in contrast to the centre-left bloc, whose leadership has been almost continuously contested and has changed hands on numerous occasions since 1994 – and, second, the degree of ideological compatibility between his parties and the others present on the centre-right (Albertazzi *et al.*, 2011: 484). Having claimed to be entering politics 'temporarily' in 1994 in order to 'save Italy' from the supposed prospect of communist rule, Berlusconi was swiftly able to put together a coalition bringing two outsider parties in from the cold: the former Fascists of the Movimento Sociale Italiano (MSI – Italian Social Movement), soon to become Alleanza Nazionale (AN – National Alliance), and the northern regionalists of the Lega Nord (LN – Northern League). The new coalition easily won the general election against a divided opposition with 46.1 per cent of the vote.

Although Berlusconi's first government's time in office was short-lived, lasting less than a year due to the LN withdrawing its support, he did not disappear from the political scene either then or following a general election defeat to Romano Prodi's centre-left alliance in 1996 (brought about primarily due to the fact that the LN did not participate in the centre-right coalition). Instead, he remained in politics and, in 2001, led a new centre-right coalition to victory: the Casa della Libertà (CDL – House of Freedom), consisting of Forza Italia, the former Christian Democrats of the Unione di Centro (UDC – Union of the Centre), AN and the Lega Nord which, faced with the offer of devolution reform and seats in an eventual cabinet, abandoned its ultimately unproductive isolationist stance (see Chapter 3) and re-joined the centre-right alliance in 2000 (Albertazzi *et al.*, 2011: 475–477). The election delivered almost half of all votes and a clear parliamentary majority to the CDL, with FI receiving 29.4 per cent of the vote. Although his government was marked by infighting – particularly between the LN on one side and AN and the UDC on the other (Albertazzi and McDonnell, 2005) – Berlusconi remained in power until 2006, thus becoming the first Italian prime minister to serve a full five-year term since the Christian Democrat Alcide De Gasperi did so between 1948 and 1953.

While polls prior to the 2006 general election gave the CDL alliance little chance of returning to government after having clearly failed to deliver the economic miracle it had promised, Berlusconi once again ran a strong, personalized campaign and the final result was the closest in Italian history, with Prodi's extremely broad centre-left Unione (Union) coalition receiving 49.8 per cent of the vote and the CDL 49.7 (it is worth noting, however, that FI's vote declined by almost six points compared to 2001). The ensuing two years were characterized both by governmental instability due to the extremely small majority and heterogeneous nature of the Unione, but also by disputes within the centre-right opposition (Albertazzi and McDonnell, 2009). Berlusconi's position came under its most sustained attack to date, principally from the UDC (which eventually left the alliance), but also from AN, whose leader, Gianfranco Fini, regularly questioned Berlusconi's actions and leadership. However, just when it seemed in November 2007 that his grip on the centre-right was at its weakest ever, Berlusconi surprised everyone – including leading figures in his own party – by announcing the creation of a new party, the PDL, which would incorporate FI and any other members of the centre-right willing to join. This move was initially ridiculed by both Fini and the leader of the UDC, Pierferdinando Casini. However, circumstances quickly worked heavily in Berlusconi's favour. With the fall of the Prodi government just two months later opening up the prospect of an election featuring a fragmented centre-left and an electoral law which rewarded the winning coalition with a majority bonus, Fini and Casini were forced to rethink their positions. Now in a position of great strength, Berlusconi was able to dictate the conditions for a new alliance, telling both the UDC and the AN that they could either merge their parties with FI in the PDL or else stand alone outside his coalition. Only the Lega Nord, by now Berlusconi's most faithful ally, was given the option of running *alongside* – rather than merging *into* – the PDL. While Casini chose not to enter the PDL, Fini decided to take Berlusconi's offer (as also did a couple of very minor parties on the centre-right). The subsequent election delivered a comfortable victory for the PDL-LN coalition with 46.8 per cent of the vote compared to the (slimmed-down) centre-left alliance's 37.6 per cent. The PDL received 37.4 per cent, in line with the respective strengths of its component parts in 2006, although this apparent continuity masked gains in the South and losses in the North to the LN (see Chapter 5).

The prospects for the new government seemed excellent, given that it enjoyed a comfortable majority in parliament and consisted of two main parties – the PDL and the LN – which by now had a long-standing good relationship and were willing to accommodate each other's key policies (Albertazzi and McDonnell, 2010). Moreover, as we show in Chapter 5, although not as spectacular as those of the LN, the results of the PDL in European Parliament (EP) and regional elections in 2009 and 2010 were not at all bad for an incumbent party. Over the course of those two years, however, it became clear that the main threat to government stability came from within the PDL itself. Following a long-running series of criticisms by Fini both of Berlusconi personally and of the lack of internal party democracy, he and his closest supporters were effectively expelled from the PDL in the summer of 2010 (see Appendix 1, years 2009, 2010). Although they initially continued to support the government, Fini and his small band of MPs switched sides towards the end of 2010. With its numbers reduced, Berlusconi's administration was able to do little more than hang on to power for the first half of 2011. Once the financial crisis struck Italy in the summer of that year and the government lost the support of a handful of other deputies, the combination of its parliamentary weakness – along with external pressures from Europe and the markets – led to Berlusconi's resignation in November and his government's replacement by Mario Monti's technocratic executive (Bosco and McDonnell, 2012). Although the PDL, along with the centre-left Partito Democratico (PD – Democratic Party) and the UDC, provided parliamentary support for Monti, it did so reluctantly. The PDL's decision to support Monti's government provoked a suspension of the PDL-LN alliance at national level, which was only resumed at the beginning of 2013 in the run-up to the February general election. As we discuss in Chapter 5, that election saw the PDL perform very poorly indeed, taking just 21.6 per cent of the vote. Nonetheless, due to the inability of either centre-left or centre-right to form a majority, the PDL found itself back in government, alongside the PD – and with the PD's Enrico Letta as prime minister – in April 2013. Finally, while outside the time frame considered in this book, it is worth noting that a split in the PDL in November 2013 saw Berlusconi re-create Forza Italia and lead it into opposition, with the rump of the PDL remaining in government under the name of Nuovo Centrodestra (NCD – New Centre-Right). However, whether this split would hold in the case of a general election, or whether the NCD would join a coalition with the new FI, remained very much an open question.

The party

> Italy's revival is called Forza Italia. Actually, that's an exaggeration. It's called Silvio Berlusconi.
>
> Silvio Berlusconi, 23 November 1994 (Travaglio, 1995: 98)

Most classifications of FI have emphasized the pre-eminent role of the founder-leader in the party's creation and subsequent history. For example, Richard Gunther and Larry Diamond (2003: 187) conceive of it as a 'personalistic party' – the purest type within their wider category of 'electoralist parties'. The sole rationale of personalistic parties, they say, 'is to provide a vehicle for the leader to win an election and exercise power' (ibid.). The conviction that Forza Italia is a product of Berlusconi (and at his service) rather than the leader being a product of it is the cornerstone of most definitions of FI, from Piero Ignazi's 'non-partisan party' (1996) to Jonathan Hopkin and Caterina Paolucci's 'business-firm party' (1999). Where such approaches are problematic, however, in our view, is in their tendency to underplay the importance of FI's programme and ideology in the party's appeal. Berlusconi may have always stood alone in the spotlight at the centre of the stage, but he has never stood empty-handed: FI's vision of a society in which traditional families would be protected and prosper thanks to lower taxes, a programme of public works, and reform of the inefficient public administration – combined with the party's anti-intellectual and anti-communist stances (the latter still appealing to many former Christian Democrats and ex-voters of the First Republic's other governing parties) – were always central planks of the message in campaigns and other communications. Hence, while in this section we focus on Berlusconi's position as leader, in the next we will devote considerable attention to the often marginalized question of party ideology.

What the above-mentioned definitions all correctly emphasize is that FI was both entirely identifiable with its founder-leader and dominated by him. Put simply, we can say that FI, and the PDL after it, were whatever Berlusconi wanted them to be, whenever he wanted them to be so. They have been, as many Italian scholars have labelled them, Berlusconi's 'personal parties'. Although this term has been commonly used in Italy to classify both FI and the PDL (Calise, 2000; Ceccarini *et al.*, 2012), it is rarely found in English-language accounts of Italian politics (although see McDonnell, 2013). However, we consider it particularly useful since, unlike the 'personalistic' or 'non-partisan' labels, 'personal' conveys a lasting proprietorial vision of the party on the part of the leader which goes well beyond its initial creation, electoral success, and communications (McDonnell, 2013: 221–222). This is crucial to understanding why Berlusconi was not only able to dominate FI in the manner he did, but, especially, why he was able to announce on 18 November 2007 – without first engaging in any formal internal party discussion or encountering any subsequent dissent – that FI would be replaced by the PDL. FI was thus not merely a 'personalized' party which focused its communications and campaigns on the leader of the day and/or gave him or her firm control over decisions regarding policies, alliances, and strategies. Rather, as both the interviewees for this book and the demise of the party confirmed, its very existence depended on that leader and this was clearly understood within it. Thus, if Berlusconi decided that FI would change its name and merge with one or more other parties into the new PDL – which he would also of course lead – then so it would be.

While FI was thus a personal party with no internal democracy, it nonetheless regularly claimed to have mass-party characteristics and a territorial presence. The extent to which this was ever really the case is something on which scholars hold different views, with some (e.g. Poli, 2001) contending that the party did achieve success in this regard in the late 1990s, but others (e.g. Paolucci, 2008) vehemently disagreeing. Irrespective of the relative merits of these arguments, what we can say is that – at least according to official party figures – FI membership declined during the party's five years in government at the beginning of the last decade from about 313,000 in 2001 to 190,000 in 2005 (see Table 2.1). Although the meaningfulness of such data should be taken with a pinch of salt (especially given the accounts of PDL members reported later in this section about the lack of grassroots activities), we can at least say that being able to claim a large membership (however inactive it may have been) appears to have become less important to FI after it returned to power in 2001.

As was the case with FI, so too did the PDL seek to portray itself as a party with a genuine territorial presence and grassroots activism. Indeed, after not having released any membership figures for the new party until the end of 2011, the national membership office of the PDL told us in February 2012 that it had *c.*1,122,000 members (more than FI and AN combined in 2003, the last year in which both parties released official figures – see Table 2.1 overleaf). Like those of FI, it seems wise also to treat the significance of these figures with great caution. In fact, based on the interviews done for this book, there is scant evidence that the PDL was interested in cultivating its membership

Table 2.1 Membership figures for Forza Italia and Alleanza Nazionale, 1997–2005

	Forza Italia	*Alleanza Nazionale*
1997	139,546	479,300
1998	161,319	485,657
1999	190,398	532,014
2000	312,863	536,018
2001	271,751	549,236
2002	222,631	560,861
2003	249,824	573,312
2004	None listed	593,951
2005	190,000	None listed

Note: For comparative purposes, the official figures for AN are included.
Source: cited in Ignazi, Bardi and Massari (2010: 201).

and there seemed to be very little going on at grassroots level. Rather, we found a party in which (a) it was the direct relationship between the leader and the voter – played out through the media and party communications – that counted most and (b) little attention was paid either to building up the party on the ground or to fostering permanent horizontal and vertical linkages within the party.

This lack of a continuous and lasting relationship with the grassroots was reflected, for example, in the comments by Michele Coppola (Turin city councillor), who told us that contact with members was not so frequent because the PDL 'is an extremely lean and extremely flexible party that can inflate when there are elections, but then inevitably deflates during the year because it delegates its most important activities to its institutional representatives'. Within this organizational model, the main opportunities for members to interact formally with the party were by means of events open to the wider public, held intermittently every three or four months in a hotel or convention centre, and headlined by a national 'big name speaker'. This image of a party which, beyond election campaigns, was restricted to its institutional representatives and party officials (although most of these were also institutional representatives), was echoed by Carlo Alberto Tesserin (regional councillor from Veneto), who acknowledged that an ordinary member not interested in standing for election 'has very few opportunities for involvement in the party'. Likewise, Alessia Rosolen (Friuli Venezia Giulia regional government member) told us that 'someone who has not been elected and is simply a supporter probably receives a letter of membership and an invitation to the Christmas dinner'.

In interviews, members who had also been in FI not only generally confirmed this picture of a largely absent party at grassroots level, but suggested that opportunities for activism had in fact diminished since the creation of the PDL. Member 1 from Liguria said in July 2010 that, while in FI there had at least been occasional dinners and big events in their city, in the PDL

'there has not been a single meeting for members in the last year' (a claim confirmed by other members in the same city). Indeed, member 4 from the same
city admitted: 'to be honest, I really miss Forza Italia'. Members in other
cities and towns told us the same story as representatives had of meetings
taking place at best every two to three months outside election campaigns.
These were usually held in hotels or other rented venues and were open to the
general public, not just party members. Indeed, as we discovered, the party
lacked the physical structures to provide a more sustained level of contact for
members, given that, even in many of Italy's major cities, the PDL had only
one branch (usually located in the city centre). At the party's office in Milan,
the Lombardy MP Antonio Palmieri (who was also responsible for the party's
Internet communications) told us: 'we don't have branches in the traditional
sense of the term. We have offices like this, where volunteers, mostly pension-
ers, come to lend a hand'. In some other towns, the party did not even have
that. When asked whether the party had a location in his city where members
could meet, Walter Liaci (Lecce city councillor) said that no such structure
existed. This lack of a 'party on the ground' was a source of frustration to
several of the members we spoke to. For example, member 13 in Piedmont
told us 'I've constantly complained that we need branches on the ground. But
instead, we're shut up in that castle, that palace' (referring to the party's lux-
urious, but sole, office in the city). It thus seems clear that, unlike its coalition
partner, the Lega Nord (see Chapter 3), the PDL did not invest in maintaining a strong and constant line of contact with its grassroots members.

Some observers (e.g. Paolucci, 2008) had believed that the creation of the
PDL, incorporating the more orthodox party organization of AN, might
have resulted in a different organizational structure and a greater diffusion of
power than had been the case in FI. That this was never likely to be the case
even on a formal level is clear if one looks at the first PDL statute, approved
by the party's first national congress on 29 March 2009, and the revised statute, approved by the national congress on 1 July 2011. As in FI, so too in the
PDL, we find extensive powers over internal party organs and candidatures
concentrated in the hands of Berlusconi, who was elected (by acclamation)
as president at the inaugural PDL congress. According to the party's statute (Popolo della Libertà, 2011), the President was responsible for convening
and nominating the majority of party bodies. He was also responsible for all
candidatures down to regional level. Most importantly, as regards the party
organization hierarchy, until mid-2011 he nominated the coordinating committee: this was a three-member body (with two members from FI and one
from AN) whose task was to oversee 'the national and periphery organization of the party and all activities of the national party structure and territorial bodies' (Popolo della Libertà, 2009a, Art. 17). In July 2011, however,
this committee was subordinated to the newly created figure of the National
Political Secretary, who, as the 2011 revised party statute says, would be nominated by the president of the party for a three-year term (Art. 16 bis, 2011).
To understand the extent to which rules and offices in the PDL reflected the

whims of the President, it is important to note that this new role was created unilaterally by Berlusconi (there was no mention of it in the 2009 statute or any discussion of it prior to its announcement).

When asked about the role of Berlusconi within the party, Enrico Musso (senator from Liguria) explained to us that:

> The PDL is Berlusconi's party. Berlusconi says what has to be done. He nominates the regional coordinators … and they, having been appointed from on high and not elected by the membership, do likewise with the positions beneath them. It's all top-down.

However, perhaps the most enlightening account of how Berlusconi viewed the PDL party organization was that provided by Guido Possa, a PDL Senator from Lombardy who had worked alongside him in his business empire and then joined him in politics. Possa had been responsible in the mid-1990s for the Forza Italia 'Clubs' (the first attempt by the party to lay claim to some kind of local presence and grassroots membership). As such, he was particularly well placed to comment on Berlusconi's political party organizations. In June 2010, he told us that:

> Berlusconi cannot get his head around the concept of a pyramid-type party … he believes that in the United States parties are only electoral committees, which is not the case, but that is what he thinks. And his ideal is a party which does not give him too much cause for concern, which basically exists to provide him with power and then it is up to him to use that power.

Overall, the strong impression from our interviews is that it was widely accepted by elected PDL representatives that Berlusconi commanded the party and that there was little room for other voices. As Maurizio Bucci (regional councillor from Friuli Venezia Giulia) put it, Berlusconi 'decides the party stances whether you like it or not. If you like it, you stay. If you don't, you leave. That is really clear. Really clear'. Many others similarly referred to Berlusconi's leadership as 'unquestionable'. Indeed, not only did interviewees tend to accept the founder-leader's authority entirely, but over half of both the representatives and members we spoke to said that the PDL would not have a future after Berlusconi or at least expressed strong doubts that it would (McDonnell, 2013).

Another feature to emerge from our interviews with representatives and members was a strong degree of agreement about Berlusconi's qualities. These can be summed up in three broad (interrelated) headings: (1) he is not a life-long politician but someone who was a very successful businessman prior to entering politics; (2) he is a warm person who is in tune with ordinary people; (3) he is a leader who is able to make decisions. The fact that Berlusconi was not a 'real' politician (despite having been in politics since 1994) but a businessman who had sacrificed himself for his country was frequently mentioned. For example, Roberto Cassinelli (member of the Chamber of Deputies from Liguria) described Berlusconi as 'the man who created Forza Italia, he is the man who decided to enter politics even though he could have lived a quieter life as a businessman'. Numerous members also praised the fact that Berlusconi was 'a self-made man' (member 23 from Campania) who came 'from the world of business and not from a party school' (member 16 from Piedmont). As a result of this background, we were told, 'if tomorrow he gave up politics, he would have other things to do' (member 24 from Campania). Not only, therefore, was it a positive quality that Berlusconi did not have to rely on politics for his economic well-being, but his not having been a career politician meant that, as member 2 from Liguria said: 'he therefore has a better understanding of the country's needs and what people really want'. Similarly, a member of the Chamber of Deputies from Campania, Nunzia De Girolamo, told us that Berlusconi 'is the only one in the end who understands the people'. While his empathic nature and motivational abilities were held to be part of what made Berlusconi a great leader, another attribute was that he was 'a man who has always shown that what he decides to do, he achieves successfully' (member 17 from Piedmont). Such accounts tally, of course, with the fact that a key part of the FI and PDL message has been based around the founder-leader's persona and his supposedly extraordinary qualities which can deliver prosperity to Italy. However, as we noted earlier, while important, they are not all there has been to the FI/PDL message. In the next section, therefore, we will consider the ideology of Berlusconi's two personal parties.

The ideology

If we had to define our party as students of politics do, we would call it a programmatic party of values. If we wanted to locate it 'geographically', we would say that it is absolutely a party of the centre, the centre of the Italian political system. It is a liberal party, but not an elite one. Rather, it is a liberal democratic popular party. It is a Catholic party, but not a confessional one. It is a secular party, but not intolerant or excessively secular. It is a national party, but not centralist. It is a party which wants to give itself a very simple name: the party of the people, of sensible people, a party which does good, the party of those Italians who bear in their heart a great love for others and for their country, the party of those Italians who love freedom. Forza Italia, a force for freedom.

> Silvio Berlusconi, 18 April 1998, speech to first national
> FI congress in Milan (Berlusconi, 2000: 41)

The FI manifesto for the 2004 EP election began with the line: 'Forza Italia is a non-ideological political movement founded on leadership, a programme and alliances'. While 'non-ideological' is little more than a slogan, it is true that the ideology of FI and the PDL has at times been difficult to pin down due to the combination of, first, the claims – often in quick succession – both to a wide variety of ideologies and to no ideologies; and second, the shifting of party positions on issues (such as the economy and Europe) according to the strategic needs of the time. Moreover, FI's professions of being 'moderate', 'Liberal' and 'centrist' – aligned with the fact that many of its representatives came from the old ruling parties of the Italian First Republic – have at times led scholars not to group FI among Western European populist parties. FI's 'populism' has thus sometimes been seen as related mainly to the style and content of the leader's communications. For example, Marco Tarchi (2008: 86) claims that Forza Italia's populism 'is entirely delegated to the leader, who has made it a trademark of his political style, but not a source of ideological inspiration'. Tarchi adds that another key reason why the party is not populist is because it 'has conservative connotations and includes amongst its middle ranks many who came from old centrist parties' of the First Republic (Tarchi, 2008: 92).

We disagree with such views on a number of grounds. First, as explained in the introduction, we conceive of populism as a thin ideology which presents itself alongside other ideologies. Although populism in Europe in recent decades has tended to be of the radical right, there is no reason why it cannot be found among more moderate parties. The claim that the sovereignty, rights and values of a homogeneous and virtuous people are under threat from a set of corrupt and incapable elites is by no means a priori exclusive to the radical right or left. And it is precisely this claim that has been the core message of Berlusconi and his parties right from the start. Second, the contention that the presence of former First Republic Christian Democrats, Liberals and Republicans precludes FI (or the PDL) from being defined as populist simply does not stand up to scrutiny. It makes no sense to adopt a leadership/party separation of this type in the case of a personal party, i.e. one which is totally dominated by the founder/leader and whose lifespan appears tied to his political career (McDonnell, 2013: 222–223). In other words, if we accept that (a) 'Berlusconi is a populist', and (b) 'FI is a personal party utterly dominated by its leader and centred on him', then the syllogism cannot be: 'the populist Berlusconi's personal party is not populist'. Moreover, viewpoints like that of Tarchi overlook the likely political opportunism on the part of those old elites who found themselves with nowhere to go when the First Republic collapsed. For many of these politicians, the simple fact is that the best way to maintain their careers, privilege and local influence was by joining Berlusconi's populist party (and accepting its populism).

Other scholars, of course, do consider Forza Italia populist. For example, Cas Mudde (2007: 47) classifies the party as 'neoliberal populist'. What distinguishes these populists from those of the 'populist radical right' is, he says, the fact that neo-Liberalism rather than nativism is central to their ideology (2007: 30). In other words, FI is not considered by Mudde to be strongly nationalistic and consistently anti-immigrant, but rather to have neo-Liberalism as its core message. Similarly, Pierre-André Taguieff (2003: 104) refers to Berlusconi's 'liberal-populism' as being akin to that of Ross Perot, Carlos Menem and Alberto Fujimori. As we shall see below, the 'neo-Liberal' and 'Liberal' labels are problematic, however, in the case of both FI and the PDL, given that Berlusconi's parties moved steadily away from the neo-Liberal positions of the 1990s towards professions of support for a 'social market economy'. In this sense, we might say that – at least in terms of their stated economic policies – FI and the PDL are best classified as 'centre-right' (like many of their counterparts in the European People's Party). However, if this is the 'thick' ideology of FI and the PDL, it is very heavily coloured (as we will show below) by its 'thin' ideology: populism.

To examine the ideology of FI and the PDL, we have decided to consider the 'Charter of Values' produced by each of the two parties. These very clearly set out party ideology and, as documents with identical intentions, are perfectly comparable. They thus help us overcome the fact that we are dealing here with a party and its successor. Moreover, membership is specifically stated in the party statute to be dependent on 'freely subscribing to the Charter of Values' (Popolo della Libertà, 2011, Art. 2). It seems legitimate therefore to take these documents as best representing the party's official vision of politics, society, and itself.

FI Charter of Values

The FI Charter of Values (published in January 2004) begins by immediately emphasizing Berlusconi's threefold role as (1) the sole founder of the party; (2) the provider of representation to 'moderates' in Italian society; and (3) the saviour of the nation at a time of crisis when democracy in Italy was under threat from the Left. It says that FI:

> was born from the appeal by one man, Silvio Berlusconi, to an electorate in which an enormous historical-political vacuum of representation risked opening up. Forza Italia was created as a response to the crisis of the parties of the First Republic, as a reaction to a possible illiberal turn of the political system, as an offer of representation to moderates within a new democracy of alternation, as a proposal for government which would bring about a second period of Italian modernization.
>
> Forza Italia (2004: 4)

We are told that Italian democracy in 1994 was under threat (the supposed dangers posed by the Left to democracy both then and since have been fixed points in FI and PDL discourse) thanks to a conspiracy between the judges, the media, and the Left, who were set to plunge the country 'into an institutional crisis' (Forza Italia, 2004: 6). Berlusconi therefore did not just found a party: he reclaimed democracy (ibid.). This discussion leads to the presentation of FI's view of democracy which is 'based first and foremost on the direct relationship between the electorate and the prime minister' (ibid.: 7) – in keeping with the claims throughout Berlusconi's periods in office that he was chosen as leader by the people (despite Italy being a parliamentary democracy, of course). Since the relationship between leader and people is the cornerstone of democracy, it is therefore essential 'to refer constantly to the true sovereign: the people' (ibid.: 8).

The enemies of the people (and democracy) seek to obstruct this direct bond, however. These include the Left, the judges, the media, and public administration bureaucrats. While bureaucrats are frequently criticized in the Charter, far stronger condemnation is reserved for the judiciary, which is 'self-referential' and unaccountable (Forza Italia, 2004: 9). Indeed, until this problem is tackled, it is claimed that 'Italy will not be a full liberal democracy' (ibid.: 10). This links to another key theme for Berlusconi over the past two decades: his battles with magistrates regarding trials he has been involved in and his efforts to reduce the power of the judiciary. Of particular damage to Italy's democratic health, the Charter continues, is the Left's 'demonization and moral delegitimation of adversaries', which is the 'product of totalitarian and fundamentalist mentalities' (ibid.). On this point, we are told that 'for too long, the word "anticommunism" has struggled to enter fully into the shared national vocabulary and still today is not accepted by everyone' (ibid.: 13).

Unlike the Left and cultural elites which have created 'hatred professionals' (Forza Italia, 2004: 44), Berlusconi and his parties portray themselves as optimistic, positive, and full of love. Recalling the 'love will triumph over hate and envy' slogan which Berlusconi and the PDL would often use after 2008, we are told in the Charter that Forza Italia 'believes in a civilization based on love and creativity, not in one founded on envy and hate' (ibid.: 44). In fact, the party has an 'interclass nature' and embraces both employers and workers – categories which the Left has instead sought to set against one another (ibid.: 16). FI rejects such divisions and believes that all citizens are part of a 'single cultural universe: that of a society which seeks to extend, at all levels, the free choice of the individual and, at the same time, removes as many citizens as possible from poverty' (ibid.). For FI, 'freedom is a truth in itself' (ibid.:12), which it says is based on Christian ethical principles and political Liberalism. The party locates itself therefore 'within the large area of Christian and lay humanism, which inspired the most important political and cultural traditions of our country' (ibid.: 23). Indeed, Forza Italia not only encompasses secular Liberalism and Christianity, but represents the union of 'liberal and popular Catholicism; lay, liberal and Republican humanism, and liberal-socialism' (ibid.: 24). Consequently, we are told that 'the definition of Forza Italia as a centre-right party is not correct' since FI embraces all the above ideologies within a new party of the centre (ibid.: 25).

One of the most frequently repeated words in the document is 'freedom'. We are told that the freedom in which FI believes 'is not just freedom within the state, but freedom from the state' (Forza Italia, 2004: 14). Consequently, they reject a 'welfarist conception of the state' as this leads to elephantine bureaucracy and 'ends up suffocating individual liberty' (ibid.: 16). The Italian welfare state is said to have become 'bureaucratized' over time and fostered situations of 'social and trade union privilege which are in contradiction with the reasons for its creation' (ibid.: 17). We are told that FI therefore seeks to bring about 'the realization of a great new social model in Italy and in Europe: the change from the Welfare State to the Welfare Society. This can be defined as a free choice society ... a single public system in which there is the fullest and freest possible choice for citizens and families' (ibid.: 18). This 'full freedom of choice' would include, for example, financial bonuses for citizens choosing private schools and private health care (ibid.).

The vision of society presented is thus one in which people are 'free to exploit their own talent, free to risk and to exploit the market without bureaucratic shackles' (Forza Italia, 2004: 15). This is said to represent a society created by the 'social market economy' (ibid.). The many references in the Charter to 'social market economy' are especially interesting as this represents a significant shift from the claims by Berlusconi and FI in the 1990s that they were pursuing a neo-Liberal, Thatcherite transformation of society and the economy. Far from recalling the policies of the UK Conservative Party in the 1980s, the term 'social market economy' is normally used to describe the economy introduced by Ludwig Erhard (whom the FI Charter cites), Minister of Economics in Konrad Adenauer's government in West Germany from 1949 to 1963 and Chancellor from 1963 to 1966. Erhard's 'social market economy' envisaged a strong role for the state as a regulator, a welfare state with unemployment benefit and universal health care, and national collective bargaining between employers' associations and trade unions (Peacock and Willgerodt, 1989). As Ulrich Witt (2002: 367) puts it, the aim of a social market economy is 'to allow free competition in the markets (subject to legal regulations that exclude, for example, cartelization in the markets for goods and services), but not to accept the result of the competitive market process unless it results in a "social balance"'.

There do, of course, appear to be contradictions between FI's vision of the state and that originally proposed by Erhard. Likewise, FI's promotion of the social market economy sits uneasily with the party's references in the Charter to the United States as an economic, political, and societal model. It says that the US example proves that 'today the best way to defend the weak and fight against poverty is by encouraging business, overcoming union inflexibility and reforming pension systems' (Forza Italia, 2004: 17). The Charter also warns against viewing globalization as a destructive force, but rather says it is essential for the developing world and that solidarity goes hand-in-hand with interdependence (ibid.: 38). Finally, it is worth noting here – given our purposes in this book – that the main themes of its closest coalition partner since 2001, the LN, are mentioned only briefly. Federalism is quickly and only vaguely discussed (ibid.: 20) while, on the topic of what it terms 'mass immigration', the Charter affirms that 'hospitality to those who arrive in our land with hopes for the future is an obligation. But it is also essential that we demand respect for our culture, our religion, our traditions and our laws' (ibid.: 36). This lack of discussion of what, as we will see, are the two key themes for the Lega and its supporters, fits with the division of tasks and issues which FI/PDL and the Lega practised both in government and opposition after 2001.

PDL Charter of Values

The PDL Charter of Values (published in April 2009) is much shorter at 18 pages than the 46-page FI Charter. While most of the themes covered are the same, there are a number of noteworthy shifts in emphasis and several additions – some of which may reflect the merger with AN. For example, given that entrance to the European People's Party (EPP) represented a final step of legitimacy for AN on its long journey from the neo-Fascist MSI, it seems significant that the document begins by stressing the new party's adherence to the values of the EPP, termed 'the great family of democracy and freedom in Europe' (Popolo della Libertà, 2009b: 1). We are told that the Popolo della Libertà 'is born of freedom, in freedom, and for freedom, so that Italy will be ever more modern, free, just, prosperous and genuinely solidaristic' (ibid.: 5). It then explains that the basis of the party's vision of society lies in 'the Judeo-Christian roots of Europe and its common classical and humanistic cultural heritage, along with the best elements of the Enlightenment' (ibid.: 7). The PDL's adherence to the values of the 'social market economy' is repeated and also cited as a core value of the EPP (ibid.: 7).

The main 'enemy of the people' is once again the Left. On this point, it is worth quoting the following passage in full as it provides a very clear example of the PDL's populist Manichean 'good' vs 'evil' view of political competition. We are told that:

> the Left has only ever given Italy uncertainty, divisions, social hatred and poverty. The Left makes policies that destroy the family and do not respect the moral values of the Italian people, the values of our tradition. Given what it has been and still is deep-down, the Left wants to divide workers and employers, men and women, fathers and sons, young and old, northern and southern Italians.
>
> Popolo della Libertà (2009b: 15)

While the Left apparently 'sees enemies everywhere', the PDL 'everywhere sees those like us' (Popolo della Libertà, 2009b: 15). The PDL – like FI before it – thus offers a view of the people as homogeneous and virtuous. As in the FI Charter, here too the interclass and all-embracing character of the party is affirmed as we are told that 'secular people and Catholics, workers and employers, young and old identify with the PDL. And so do women and men from the North, Centre and South' (ibid.: 14). The party says that it is proud of its 'popular character', which reflects its desire to 'unite Italian society and lead it, all together, towards a better future' (ibid.). Again, this is in line with the populist view that cleavages among the people are simply artificial creations of the political and cultural elites, designed to make it easier to divide and rule.

The above-mentioned 'better future' which the PDL wishes to construct is one in which individuals are 'free and responsible', where they can shape their destinies and 'raise their children according to their own values and ideas' (Popolo della Libertà, 2009b: 16). While individual freedoms are again given importance, it is noticeable that there are far more references to community and the family than was the case in the FI Charter. In particular, the pre-eminence of the family (understood as the traditional Catholic family) is strongly emphasized and linked to the requirement for the state not to interfere in family affairs. We should perhaps read this not just as an appeal to Catholic voters, but also as reflecting the PDL's desire for Vatican approval (during the centre-left's time in office between 2006 and 2008, ethical issues such as civil unions and euthanasia were prominent in Italian public debate, with Church representatives frequently speaking out about them in the media). This can also be easily seen in the statement that the PDL 'clearly recognizes the active role of the family' and that the family 'cannot be replaced by other social figures' (ibid.: 11). Moving noticeably away from the attempt to balance secular and Christian values in the 2004 FI Charter, the 2009 document promotes a 'society based on liberal and Christian values', but which is firmly based 'on the natural family created by marriage, formed by a man and a woman' (ibid.: 15). Finally, immigration is again mentioned only once, as was the case in the FI Charter, although in slightly harsher tones since the necessity of 'reinforcing our traditions, identity and freedom' (rather than simply requiring that they be respected) is stressed (ibid.: 14).

In conclusion, what emerges from these two charters is that for FI and the PDL – and in line with what we have said about populist ideology in the introductory chapter – 'the people' constitute a homogeneous, united, and virtuous community of family- and freedom-loving, anti-Communist, 'moderate' Italians. The people are forced, during what is first portrayed as a moment of crisis in the 1990s, but then becomes a permanent battle, to make a choice between 'good' (Berlusconi and his parties) and 'evil' (the Left, the judiciary, the bureaucracy, cultural and media elites), with the latter group eagerly conspiring to take away the people's freedom, attack their values and usurp democracy. As Mudde (2007: 154) notes, 'in the populist ideology, the will of the people cannot be limited by anything, not even the law' and for FI and the PDL, popular consensus is clearly the only true source of democratic legitimacy (Albertazzi and Mueller, 2013). Checks and balances are delegitimized, in some cases very strongly (the judiciary, the opposition parties, and unfriendly media). As regards the type of society proposed, this changes to some extent between the two documents, with the traditional Catholic family occupying a more prominent role for the PDL than was the case in the FI Charter. Nonetheless, the stand-out commonality between the two is the vision of a community in which divisions have been put aside and both individuals and families are able to pursue their dreams and live according to their values, free from state interference and within an economically prosperous society. In conclusion, therefore, we believe we can definitively say that it is not just the communication style of Berlusconi that is infused with populism, but the charters which have set out the ideologies of his two political parties. To deny the populist character of Forza Italia and the Popolo della Libertà or to distinguish between the 'populist' leader and his personal, yet somehow 'non-populist', party thus seems extremely misguided and based more on pre-conceived ideas that populist parties must be of the radical right (or left) than on the reality of both Forza Italia and the PDL.

Bibliography

Albertazzi, D. and McDonnell, D. (2005) 'The Lega Nord in the Second Berlusconi Government: In a League of Its Own', *West European Politics*, 28 (5), 952–972.

Albertazzi, D. and McDonnell, D. (2009) 'The Parties of the Centre Right: Many Oppositions, One Leader', in Newell, J. (ed.), *The Italian General Election of 2008: Berlusconi Strikes Back*, Basingstoke: Palgrave Macmillan.

Albertazzi, D. and McDonnell, D. (2010) 'The Lega Nord Back in Government', *West European Politics*, 33 (6), 1318–1340.

Albertazzi, D. and Mueller, S. (2013) 'Populism and Liberal Democracy: Populists in Government in Austria, Italy, Poland and Switzerland', *Government and Opposition*, 48 (3), 343–371.

Albertazzi, D., McDonnell, D., and Newell, J. (2011) '*Di lotta e di governo*: The Lega Nord and Rifondazione Comunista in Office', *Party Politics*, 17 (4), 471–487.

Berlusconi, S. (2000) *L'Italia che ho in mente*, Milan: Mondadori.

Bosco, A. and McDonnell, D. (2012) 'Introduction: the Monti Government and the Downgrade of Italian Parties', in Bosco, A. and McDonnell, D. (eds), *Italian Politics: From Berlusconi to Monti*, New York: Berghahn.

Calise, M. (2000) *Il partito personale*, Bari: Laterza.

Ceccarini, L., Diamanti, I., and Lazar, M. (2012) 'The End of an Era: The Crumbling of the Italian Party System', in Bosco, A. and McDonnell, D. (eds), *Italian Politics: From Berlusconi to Monti*, New York: Berghahn.

Forza Italia (2004) 'Carta dei Valori'. Available at: http://forzaitalia.it/speciali/cartadeivalori.pdf (accessed December 2013).

Gunther, R. and Diamond, L. (2003) 'Species of Political Parties: A New Typology', *Party Politics*, 9 (2), 167–199.

Hopkin, J. and Paolucci, C. (1999) 'The Business Firm Model of Party Organisation: Cases from Spain and Italy', *European Journal of Political Research*, 35 (3), 307–339.

Ignazi, P. (1996) 'The Crisis of Parties and the Rise of New Political Parties', *Party Politics*, 2 (4), 549–566.

Ignazi, P., Bardi, L., and Massari, O. (2010) 'Party Organisational Change in Italy (1991–2006)', *Modern Italy*, 15 (2), 197–216.

McDonnell, D. (2013) 'Silvio Berlusconi's Personal Parties: From Forza Italia to the Popolo Della Libertà', *Political Studies*, 61 (S1), 217–233.

Mudde, C. (2007) *Populist Radical Right Parties in Europe*, Cambridge: Cambridge University Press.

Paolucci, C. (2008) 'From Democrazia Cristiana to Forza Italia and the Popolo della Libertà: Partisan Change in Italy', *Modern Italy*, 13 (4), 465–480.

Peacock, A. and Willgerodt, H. (eds) (1989) *Germany's Social Market Economy: Origins and Evolution*, London: Macmillan.

Poli, E. (2001) *Forza Italia. Strutture, leadership e radicamento territoriale*, Bologna: Il Mulino.

Popolo della Libertà (2009a) 'Statuto del Popolo della Libertà'. Available at: http://www.astrid-online.it/--il-siste/Documenti/statuto-del-pdl.pdf (accessed December 2013).

Popolo della Libertà (2009b) 'Carta dei Valori'. Available at: http://www.pdl.it/notizie/15346/carta-dei-valori (accessed December 2013).

Popolo della Libertà (2011) 'Statuto del Popolo della Libertà'. Available at: http://www.pdl.it/notizie/15377/statuto-del-popolo-della-liberta (accessed December 2013).

Taguieff, P.-A. (2003) *L'illusione populista*, Milan: Mondadori.

Tarchi, M. (2008) 'Italy: A Country of Many Populisms', in Albertazzi, D. and McDonnell, D. (eds), *Twenty-First Century Populism: The Spectre of Western Democracy*, Basingstoke: Palgrave Macmillan.

Travaglio, M. (1995) *Il pollaio delle libertà*, Florence: Vallecchi.

Witt, U. (2002) 'Germany's "Social Market Economy" Between Social Ethos and Rent Seeking', *The Independent Review*, 6 (3), 365–375.

3   The Lega Nord

In 2008, the Lega Nord (LN – Northern League) became the oldest party group in the Italian parliament. While this statistic reflects the unstable nature of Italian parties since the early 1990s, it also underlines the durability of a movement which originated in the northern regionalist leagues of the 1980s, was united by Umberto Bossi in 1991, and led by him until April 2012. Proving to be far from a 'flash-in-the-pan' protest movement, the Lega was instrumental in the demise of the First Republic party system in the early 1990s, was a member of the first government of the new so-called Second Republic in 1994, and, despite an ill-fated flirtation with secessionism later that decade, went on to serve in government for eight of the ten years between 2001 and 2011. In terms of electoral results and institutional roles occupied at national and subnational levels, the Lega has been one of Europe's most successful regionalist parties to date. It has also, as we have argued elsewhere (Albertazzi and McDonnell, 2005, 2010), been one of the few populist parties in Western Europe to serve in government without suffering splits, toning down its rhetoric or losing votes.

This chapter follows the same structure and logic as the previous one on Forza Italia/Popolo della Libertà (FI/PDL). Below we provide a brief overview of the LN's history until 2008, particularly as regards alliances and election results. The period after 2008 will be examined in detail later in the book and so is not treated in this chapter. It should also be noted that, since Bossi's resignation and replacement as party leader by Roberto Maroni in 2012 occurred after the party's time in government and was unrelated to it, we will not analyse it in depth here. The rest of the chapter consists of two sections. In the first, 'The party', we focus on the Lega in organizational terms. This is based in part on material from one-to-one and group interviews which we conducted in northern Italy in 2009–2010 with elected representatives and grassroots members (see Chapter 1). In the second section of the chapter, 'The ideology', we consider how scholars have defined the party and assess the ideology of the Lega as it is set out in official party documents.

Formally created in 1991 by the union of six regionalist 'leagues' which had emerged in the 1980s across the north of Italy (Biorcio, 1997: 39–53), the Lega was led from its inception by Umberto Bossi – founder of the most electorally successful of these leagues, the Lega Lombarda (LL – Lombard League). In a country where vote shifts of just a few percentage points were regarded as highly significant and territorial parties with elected representatives had only existed in a few peripheral regions such as Sardinia and the Aosta Valley, the rise of the leagues and then the LN in the 1980s and early 1990s in Italy's most productive regions provided an enormous jolt to the Italian political system. After the small initial breakthroughs of the Liga Veneta (LV – Veneto League) in 1983 and the LL in 1987 – resulting in a single seat in both the Chamber of Deputies and the Senate for the LV in 1983 and the LL in 1987 – in 1992 the LN received 8.7 per cent of the national vote and 80 seats in parliament. Moreover, the combination of the support it received along with the issues it raised was one of the key contributing factors to the collapse of the First Republic party system.

As mentioned in the previous chapter, the LN entered government for the first time in 1994 as part of a new centre-right coalition led by Silvio Berlusconi. Although an advantageous seat pact at the 1994 election with FI in the North gave the LN its largest parliamentary presence to date with 180 MPs (despite its vote share falling slightly to 8.4 per cent), it was clear from the beginning that the alliance between FI and Alleanza Nazionale (AN – National Alliance) was the cornerstone of the coalition. There were evident tensions between FI and the LN on policies such as pension reform and on a personal level between the prime minister and Bossi. More importantly, perhaps, the European Parliament (EP) elections in June 1994 showed that FI was swiftly eroding LN support in the North, with Berlusconi's party taking 30.6 per cent (up from 21 per cent at the general election less than three months previously) and the Lega seeing its share decline further to 6.6 per cent. With the LN increasingly (and publicly) estranged from its coalition partners, it was no surprise when the party brought down the government in December 1994. Over the following 18 months, the LN – along with the centre-left – supported a technocratic, non-party cabinet led by Lamberto Dini. While this period saw the LN move much closer to the centre-left and provoked rumours of a possible alliance, the party ultimately decided to stand alone at the 1996 general election. Initially, this seemed to pay off when it achieved its highest vote share to date with 10.1 per cent. However, as quickly became apparent, this result meant little in practical terms since the party subsequently had no influence in determining the composition of the new government and was left stuck in the no-man's land of bipolar politics, irrelevant to both the governing parties of the centre-left and the centre-right opposition coalition.

The Lega's isolation from the mid-1990s onwards was reinforced by its switch from a federalist position to advocating independence for the North (or 'Padania' as it termed the new nation). However, this found little support among the party's key constituencies in the North. The late 1990s were thus very difficult years for the LN, marked by poor election results and bitter splits among the party elites. Moreover, in addition to its secessionist stance, the Lega's self-imposed isolation and damning criticisms of all other parties

meant that, with very few exceptions, it had no prospect of entering governing coalitions at local and regional levels in key areas such as Lombardy and
Veneto. However, while the bipolar logic of Second Republic political competition certainly penalized the Lega during this period, it also made victory
for centre-right alliances without the Lega at national and subnational levels
less likely due to the need to create the widest possible pre-electoral coalitions.
For example, although we obviously cannot say for sure that the LN would
have achieved the same vote share in 1996 as it did by standing alone, it is
almost certain that a centre-right coalition containing the Lega would have
won that election and many others in the ensuing years at regional and local
levels (Diamanti, 2007: 756). As a result, and despite the vitriol which Bossi
had directed at Berlusconi since 1994, the main parties of the centre-right and
the Lega had little alternative other than to seek a reconciliation. This rap-
prochement duly occurred in time for the 2000 regional elections, when the
LN gave up its secessionist stance and re-joined the Berlusconi-led alliance in
return for the guarantee that, should the coalition win the 2001 general election, it would introduce greater regional autonomy in the form of what the
LN termed 'devolution' (Albertazzi *et al.*, 2011: 475–477).

Both in terms of percentages and numbers of members elected to parliament, the 2001 election was the Lega's worst since its foundation, as it only
received 3.9 per cent of the vote and returned just 43 representatives to parliament – a far cry from its previous time in power. However, unlike 1994,
although the party was weak numerically, it rapidly became apparent that
Bossi now enjoyed an excellent relationship with the two key FI politicians
in government – Berlusconi and the Finance Minister Giulio Tremonti, who
had been instrumental in bringing the LN back into the centre-right fold. By
singling out these non-traditional northern politicians as his allies in contrast to the pro-South, more traditional politicians of AN and the former
Christian Democrats of the Unione di Centro (UDC – Union of the Centre),
Bossi thus struck on a combination of friends and enemies within the governing coalition which allowed him to respect the LN's regionalist populist 'outsider' identity while also appearing to be in an inner circle containing the two
most important members of the cabinet (Albertazzi and McDonnell, 2005:
959–960). This in turn enabled the LN to paint a picture of its government
participation providing major influence on policy. Furthermore, its return to
office also saw a small rise in the party's vote at the 2006 general election when
it received 4.6 per cent. The party's achievements in this period were made all
the more impressive given that Bossi suffered a stroke which sidelined him
for over a year in 2004–2005. Following the centre-right alliance's return to
opposition in 2006, the LN maintained its position as FI's most faithful ally
and, as discussed in the previous chapter, it was the only one of those from
the centre-right to which Berlusconi gave the option of running alongside
the new PDL at the 2008 general election rather than merging with it. This
election would be the most successful for the LN since 1996, with the party
gaining 8.3 per cent of the vote – a result which not only almost doubled its

2006 performance, but was the harbinger of a new period of success at the ballot box (see Chapter 5).

After its first year back in government, the Lega achieved its highest ever share of the national vote, 10.2 per cent, in the 2009 EP elections. The following year, the 2010 regional elections delivered the party's best subnational performance to date across the North, with LN candidates for regional presidencies securing victory in two key regions (Piedmont and Veneto). The party's time in office came to an end, however, with the fall of the government in November, under the pressure of the financial crisis (see Appendix 1, year 2011). The subsequent decision by the PDL to support Mario Monti's technocratic government also provoked the end of the LN–PDL alliance, with the LN going into opposition. Although the LN's support remained high in opinion polls throughout this period (see Chapter 5), it dropped quickly after April 2012 with the allegation of serious financial irregularities, including the misappropriation of party funds for personal use, in particular by Bossi, some of his associates, and members of his family. This led to calls for the leader to step down and strong tensions emerged between those supporting Bossi and those favouring the other leading figure in the party, Maroni. In the end, Bossi resigned in April 2012 (becoming 'Life President' of the Lega) and Maroni was elected as Federal Secretary at the party congress in July 2012. As we explain in Chapter 5, it was this set of events – rather than the LN's actions in the 2008–2011 government – which seem to have been the main cause of the party's poor subsequent performance at the February 2013 general election, when it received just 4.1 per cent. Finally, although it does not concern the time period analysed in this book, we should note that Maroni decided to step down as leader after having been elected president of the Lombardy region in February 2013, thus triggering primaries held in December at which Bossi attempted a comeback. This ended ignominiously for the party's founder as he took just 18 per cent of the vote, over 60 percentage points behind Matteo Salvini, who won easily with 82 per cent. It thus seems evident that the scandal which emerged in 2012 has stripped Bossi of the charismatic relationship he previously enjoyed with those in the party (see the material from interviews in the section below).

The party

In his study of populist radical right parties (a category in which he includes the LN), Cas Mudde (2007: 268) claims: 'it seems safe to assume that, on average, populist radical right parties have relatively few members and at best a moderately elaborated party organization, compared to the older, established parties'. Having cited the French Front National (FN – National Front) as a partial exception, he says that the LN 'tried to create a mass party, but failed' (ibid.: fn. 5). We disagree with Mudde's generalizations on this point. First, he seems to be overlooking the fact that many of those 'established parties' he refers to have been downsizing their party organizations and haemorrhaging members for decades (Katz and Mair, 2009; van Biezen *et al.*, 2012). Second, his evaluation of the LN does not correspond to what we or other scholars who have conducted fieldwork on the party have found (see Biorcio, 1997; Passarelli and Tuorto, 2012). Contrary to Mudde, we contend that the Lega has in fact quite closely resembled a mass party. As we show below, it has cultivated – and taken great pride in – a strong territorial presence and a degree of contact with grassroots activists and local citizens which is in stark contrast to what we found in the case of FI/PDL (see Chapter 2). Moreover, unlike many mainstream parties, in the Lega, we do not find any 'erosion of the boundary between formal members and supporters' (Katz and Mair, 2009: 761). Rather, full membership of the LN is something which must be earned and is prized. We can see this, for example, if we look at the 2002 party statute and regulations (we will use these here rather than the almost identical 2012 ones given that the 2002 editions were those in force when the fieldwork for this book took place). Articles 29 and 30 explain that members are divided into two hierarchical categories: the 'Soci Ordinari-Militanti' ('ordinary members-activists') and 'Soci Sostenitori' ('supporting members'). Supporting members can only progress to the 'ordinary member-activist' level after having satisfactorily completed 'a period of voluntary activism of at least six months' (Lega Nord, 2002b: art. 4.9). After they have done so, and once their promotion to 'ordinary member-activist' has been approved by the local party hierarchy, they are 'obliged to actively participate in the life and activities of the movement' (Lega Nord, 2002a: art. 30). Hence, while Knut Heidar (2006: 301) notes that the trend in Europe in recent decades is for parties to 'lower the threshold for party membership by limiting obligations', this is certainly not the case for the Lega (although, as we saw in the previous chapter, it is very much so for the PDL).

Notwithstanding the demands of activism (or, perhaps, partly because of the consequent opportunities for activism), the number of LN members increased over the two decades between 1991 and 2011, thus bucking the general trend of membership decline affecting parties across Western Europe during the same period (van Biezen *et al.*, 2012). According to the LN central office in Milan, by the end of 2011 (and the party's time in government), it had 173,044 members (see Table 3.1). Although down on the 2010 total of 182,502 – LN's highest ever number of members – the 2011 figure still constituted almost a 40 per cent increase on the membership total ten years previously. It also was almost 25,000 more than the total at the end of 2007 – i.e. the last year before the party entered government. There is, of course, a possibility that these figures are inflated – as was clearly true of FI/PDL.[1] However, in contrast to the picture of scarce grassroots activity which emerged from our interviews with PDL representatives and ordinary members, in our fieldwork on the Lega in 2009–2010, we found a party which was constantly present at grassroots level, providing numerous activities for members.

Table 3.1 Membership of the Lega Nord, 1992–2011

Year	Members	Year	Members
1992	112,400	2002	119,753
1993	147,297	2003	131,423
1994	167,650	2004	122,576
1995	123,031	2005	148,321
1996	112,970	2006	147,982
1997	136,503	2007	148,383
1998	121,777	2008	155,478
1999	123,352	2009	155,969
2000	120,897	2010	182,502
2001	124,310	2011	173,044

Source: Segreteria Organizzativa Federale della Lega
Nord (Federal Organizational Secretariat of the
Lega Nord).

In the interviews we conducted, many representatives and members – irrespective of the regions they came from – in fact stressed that one of the main ways in which the party was distinct from others was as regards its traditional mass-party characteristics. For example, Franco Manzato (vice-president of the Veneto regional government) told us that the party organization is 'typically communist ... with a strong national leadership, deeply rooted at local level and with very active branches'. Similarly, Mario Carossa (Turin city councillor) claimed that 'we are a real party, perhaps the last one left organizationally speaking'. Ordinary party members, like numerous representatives, also pointed out the parallels with former mass parties (particularly of the Left). For example, member 13 from Veneto commented that 'if we take the Lega as a party, as a movement, we can compare it to a party of the Left with a particular type of structure'. Likewise, member 5 from Piedmont said that the Lega 'has a structure which no other party has any more'. In contrast to the PDL interviewee accounts of party organization which we saw in the previous chapter – with the organization 'inflating' for election campaigns and 'deflating' thereafter – LN interviewees almost unanimously emphasized the continuity of their party's local activities and pointed to how this distinguished them from the PDL. For example, the president of the LN group in the Senate, Federico Bricolo, commented that the PDL 'is not rooted at ground level like us', while Lorenzo Fontana (Verona city councillor) asserted that the Lega was very different from those 'plastic parties which do not exist at local level' (Berlusconi's parties have often been termed 'plastic' in Italian political commentary).

This grassroots presence of the LN is described by members as functioning on two main levels: first, they draw attention to the fact that elected LN representatives regularly come to meet party members and discuss current issues with them. Second, members stress the extent and frequency of their own activism, both as regards branch meetings amongst themselves and their efforts to promote the party to the wider public. In relation to the first point, members in a large city in the north-west explained that one of the party's MPs would regularly attend their weekly meetings for members every Thursday evening – indeed, the MP often came straight from the airport having just flown back from Rome. We attended several of these meetings and were able to confirm that this was indeed the case. Member 3 from the city explained that the MP 'comes to tell us what is going on in Rome, so we don't have to find out about it in the newspaper or on television. We can hear it directly'. Even in small towns, LN representatives made the effort to be present at party meetings – something which local members clearly appreciated. While not necessarily an MP (although these too would come occasionally), at least some elected representative would visit regularly to speak to members and, if necessary, would pass on information both to and from the highest levels of the party. As member 10 from a small town in the Veneto told us:

> there is always this direct line of communication from the MP to the member of regional or provincial government to the lowest part of the pyramid, the grassroots. And that helps the party to explain lots of things which otherwise could be interpreted badly.

As for their own activism, LN members explained that they would usually meet one another on party business at least once a week and sometimes more often. In addition to weekly meetings for members of the type mentioned above, another regular activity was manning stands in public places at which they would hand out leaflets and explain party policy. This was something which members were particularly proud of. For example, member 14 from Veneto observed, 'how many other parties do this? They only do it during election campaigns'. Likewise, member 3 said that 'every Saturday morning I go with my friends, with other activists to these stands that the Lega organizes at the markets'. He added that they would often be joined at these by elected representatives of the party.

Of course, it is likely that those members who were willing to take the time to talk to us were also particularly active. However, even in a survey of a random sample of 327 Lega Nord members in 2011, Gianluca Passarelli and Dario Tuorto (2012: 269–270) found that 54.1 per cent participated 'often' in campaign events and 51.4 per cent often attended meetings in the local party branch. Indeed, when they added together the numbers of members who said they participated in campaign events and party meetings 'every so often' or 'often', they found that over 94 per cent of members did so (ibid.: 270). In other words, there were hardly any 'virtual' or 'on-paper' members as appeared overwhelmingly the case with the PDL. In our research, we found that LN members were very eager to emphasize the real commitment which being an activist implied. As member 1 in Piedmont put it: 'being a leghista is not about sticking a badge on your jacket. It means certain things: it means participating in Pontida, it means working at party events, it means going to Venice'.[2] In fact, as Passarelli and Tuorto (ibid.) find, 75.8 per cent of their sample had been at least once between 2005 and 2011 to the annual Pontida rally.

According to many members, the strong bonds of loyalty and collective sense of commitment fostered by the party also helped to preclude internal dissent. As member 7 from Veneto said: 'the good thing is that when a decision is taken by the leadership ... that is that, the grassroots members accept it, whether it is right or wrong'. Likewise, member 1 commented that 'if the leadership decides something, the true leghista in the end accepts it'.

This brings us to the question of the role of the leader within the party. Scholars have often pointed to the strongly hierarchical and centralized structure of the Lega as granting Bossi 'an exceptional level of internal control' (Bolleyer *et al.*, 2012: 187). However, while true, as Piero Ignazi (2006: 58) put it, that the LN was 'totally dominated by its leader', it is interesting to note that the party statute in force while Bossi was leader (Lega Nord, 2002a) did not grant anything like the same degree of power to the Federal Secretary (the leader's official title) as the FI and PDL statutes did to Berlusconi (see Chapter 2). Rather, what is indicative of Bossi's domination of the party is not what was written in the statute, but the fact that he was able to entirely ignore it. To take just one pertinent example: article 10 stated that the Federal Congress (which, according to article 9, had to be held every three years) should elect the Federal Secretary and that his/her mandate was set at three years (Art. 14). Nonetheless, despite these very clear rules, the party did not hold a single Federal Congress (and therefore no leadership election) for ten years from 2002 until July 2012, when Maroni was elected the new Federal Secretary.

Bossi's dominant position was therefore not reflected in specific rules but rather through practices and communications. It was also apparent, as we discuss below, from accounts of Bossi's role by those in the Lega Nord. Pierre-André Taguieff (2003: 63) described the Lega as a 'mass nationalist movement which was founded, led and incarnated by Umberto Bossi' and we can see this idea of Bossi as the 'incarnation' of the Lega in how those in the party viewed him. In his research on the Lega in the mid-1990s, Roberto Biorcio (1997: 237–248) noted that representatives and members would often say 'Bossi is the Lega' and we encountered the same sentiment (and often the same phrase) repeated by many interviewees – from local grassroots members right up to those at the top of the party. Biorcio (1997: 243) also noted that Bossi's 'most cited quality by members is his political vision'. As one member told him: 'I see Bossi as an extremely sharp person politically ... I see him like someone who is ten years ahead of the rest' (ibid.). In our interviews, we too found Bossi's political intelligence and visionary powers to be the most frequently cited of his qualities by both representatives and members alike. For example, Danilo Narduzzi (Friuli Venezia Giulia regional councillor) told us that 'Bossi is a charismatic leader, the one who shows the way ... he is a prophet, not just a politician'. The leader's far-sightedness and political ability were also said by interviewees to reinforce the weight within the party of Bossi's decisions. Member 1 told us: 'history has shown that our leader – Umberto, as we call him – can see further than others. That's why we have blind faith in him. Whatever he decides is fine with us'. This being the case, even major shifts on key issues of policy or strategy (such as the return to the centre-right coalition in 2000) or the removal of high-profile challengers within the party (as happened on several occasions in the 1990s) could thus be attributed to the 'vision' of the leader and presented as articles of faith rather than matters for debate.

While Bossi's qualities (in the eyes of interviewees) and formal statutory powers differed from those we saw in the previous chapter regarding Berlusconi, what the two men have in common is the clear acknowledgement by representatives and members that, at least at the time of interview, they were the undisputable leaders of their parties. In the case of Bossi, a significant number of those we spoke to seemed keen to point out that this remained the situation despite his stroke in 2004. For example, the head of the party's press office in Rome, Nicoletta Maggi, claimed that Bossi still took all decisions regarding the party's communications and even designed the posters (right down to the choice of colours). The same account was repeated to us both by interviewees and informally by several party functionaries at the LN's headquarters in Milan. Like many interviewees, Narduzzi stated that Bossi 'continues to be the undisputed leader of the movement'. Grassroots members expressed similar sentiments about Bossi's position in the party. Emphasizing that Bossi's leadership was accepted 'by the lowliest member, right up to the government minister', member 7 from Veneto stated that Bossi 'is the only reference point. There are no other leaders'. Although this was the dominant view expressed, it is interesting to note, however, that we also found a strong, widespread conviction that the LN would outlive its leader. For example, member 13 from Veneto commented that although 'Bossi's charisma is irreplaceable today ... certainly there will be other people who will lead the movement', while several other interviewees pointed to the possibility that Maroni could be the next leader. This, of course, as we saw in the previous chapter, stands in contrast to what we found among PDL interviewees, many of whom believed the party could not survive the end of Berlusconi's political career.

The ideology

Unlike the more controversial case of FI in the previous chapter, there is little need for us to justify here the classification of the Lega Nord as 'populist' since numerous scholars from both Italy and abroad over the past two decades have defined the party in this way (Betz, 1994; Biorcio, 1997; Taggart, 2000; Mény and Surel, 2001; Spektorowski, 2003; Tarchi, 2003; Mudde, 2007). Rather, where there has been less definitional agreement regards the issue of whether the LN should also be defined as 'radical right'. We do not feel the need to attach too much importance to this question since our main concern in this book is that the parties we study are populist and, on this point, there is very broad consensus. It is worth noting briefly, however, that among those scholars who do classify the Lega as radical right, doubts are often expressed. For example, in her 2005 comparative study, Pippa Norris (2005: 65) comments that the party 'may not be strictly part of the radical right' and that its designation as such is 'more ambiguous than other parties'. Nonetheless, she decides to include the LN on the basis of an expert survey which classifies the party as strongly anti-immigrant (ibid.). Mudde (2007: 56) also says that the classification of the LN as 'populist radical right' is 'contested and problematic'. This is so, he explains, because although 'populism has always been a core feature of the LN', the party's qualification as 'radical right' is more complicated (ibid.). He concludes, however, that 'the LN might not (always) be a perfect example of the populist radical right, but it is too similar to be excluded from the party family' (ibid.). This uncertainty aside, we can certainly say that the LN is firmly placed within the broader sphere of the populist Right in Europe.

Irrespective of the above debate, when classifying the Lega ideologically, we believe it is more useful to emphasize its populism and regionalism rather than its left–right collocation. Put simply, it is impossible to understand the Lega from its foundation to the present day without highlighting its territorial politics. Whatever policy or strategy U-turns the party has made (for example, its position on European integration or its alliances), the *raison d'être* professed by the Lega has always been linked to the attainment of some form of northern autonomy, whether federalism, independence, or devolution. As Ilvo Diamanti (1994: 672) wrote, Bossi 'redefined the concept of territory' within Italian politics in the late 1980s and early 1990s. The LN reshaped the economic, political, historical, and cultural reference points of the North into a community of 'interests' and 'values' and juxtaposed them with those of the Italian state and the South. It constructed a framework of interpretation in which a virtuous and homogeneous 'us' – honest, hard-working and simple-living northern Italians attached to their local traditions – was posited as under siege from above by the financial and political elites and from below by a series of others, in particular southern Italians and immigrants. In this sense, the Lega provided 'a new source of self-respect' for northerners (Tambini, 2001: 105). It told them that not only were they not to blame for the problems of Italy, but that they were the principal victims: they were the ones who were constantly neglected and forced to pay for the misdeeds of others. After decades in which territorial politics had been restricted to peripheral regions of Italy, this reinterpretation of the issues facing the North quickly found favour at the ballot box, making the Lega not only one of the newest, but also one of the most successful regionalist parties in Western Europe.

If we adopt the categorizations of new parties developed by Thomas Rochon (1985) and Paul Lucardie (2000), we can therefore consider the LN as a 'prophetic' or a 'mobilizing' party. In its focus on northern autonomy and identity, the LN has developed a new ideology around a new issue (Lucardie, 2000: 177) and 'looks at old issues from a new ideological vantage point' (Rochon, 1985: 421). In line with this, we find it most useful to classify the Lega ideologically as 'regionalist populist' (Biorcio, 1991; McDonnell, 2006) or, if we want to be more precise, 'ethnoregionalist populist' (Spektorowski, 2003). Following the definition by Huri Türsan (1998: 5) of ethnoregionalist parties based 'on the two common denominators that unite them: (1) a subnational territorial border; (2) an exclusive group identity', we can say that the LN fulfils both of these. Whether advocating independence for Padania or federalism/devolution for the regions of the North, it has always appealed to a specific territorial area and ethnically defined people, proposing itself as the defenders of their identity, values, prosperity, rights, traditions, and voice. In other words, it has appealed to a distinct northern people which, as Marco Tarchi (2003: 151) writes, is conceived of as 'a single entity, ethnos and demos together, an idealized community'.

LN 'proposals and objectives' and 'political school' manual

We can see the Lega's ethnoregionalist populism clearly if we look at the key documents outlining the ideology of the party. Given that the LN has no equivalent to the FI/PDL Charter of Values, we instead chose the following two documents as the fullest representations of the party's ideology during the time period (2008–2011) which was of most interest to us: (1) 'Proposte e Obiettivi' (Proposals and Objectives) from April 2009, a 63-page-long publication produced both for party candidates and the general public. In the preface, it says that the document provides 'explanation and discussion of the principles and values which have constantly been the force of the Lega Nord' (Lega Nord, 2009: 2); (2) The manual for its 'political schools', i.e. the courses it runs for members to teach them about the party's ideology. We decided to use the 2011 edition of this, which is a 263-page document covering broadly the same themes as the 'Proposals and Objectives' publication, but in far greater detail. For the sake of brevity, we will refer to this as the 'party manual' in the remainder of the chapter.

What is immediately apparent from both documents is the importance attached first and foremost to federalism and, second, to immigration. In 'Proposals and Objectives', the first section is dedicated to federalism and the second to immigration and security. All the subsequent sections – whether on Europe, the family, agriculture, the economy, or infrastructure – are to greater and lesser extents related back to these two central issues. In the preface to the party manual, we are told that 'there are objectives which the Lega Nord has always pursued such as federalism and the fight against illegal immigration.

These objectives can be synthesized in the phrase: "masters in our own homes'" (Lega Nord, 2011: 3). This message is also present at the beginning of the first section in 'Proposals and Objectives' where, alongside the text, we find a poster with the slogan 'Federalism = Masters in our own homes' (Lega Nord, 2009: 5). The opening lines of this section explain:

> the objective which has always inspired the political actions of the Lega Nord has been that of transforming our country – which is highly centralized – into a modern federal state, i.e. by introducing federalism.
>
> Lega Nord (2009: 5)

Changing the relationship between the northern regions and the state is posited here and elsewhere as the core goal of the LN. It is interesting to note, however, that at no point is the possibility of secession (or the Lega's previous support for it) mentioned in any of the 320 pages that make up the two documents. This is slightly surprising, not only given the party's history, but also because the party's official name (at the time of both publications) was still 'Lega Nord per l'indipendenza della Padania' (Lega Nord for Padanian Independence). Indeed, the first article of the party's 2002 statute said that the Lega 'has the ultimate objective of achieving independence for Padania by democratic means and its international recognition as an independent sovereign Federal Republic' (Lega Nord, 2002a: Art.1). It seems fair to assume that the official party name and opening statute article, at least at the time, were nostalgic anachronisms given the complete absence of this goal in the two ideological documents. Instead, both 'Proposals and Objectives' and the party manual repeatedly stress the importance of federalism in the Lega's history and the transformative effect it would have on northern communities and the Italian nation-state.

Amongst the many benefits of federalism listed in the two documents are: increased subsidiarity, a heightened civic spirit, greater democracy and a resolution to what we learn in 'Proposals and Objectives' is 'the real national question in the country: the northern question' (Lega Nord, 2009: 5–6). The party manual explores this in more depth, explaining that the Lega Nord and the northern question emerged together as a reaction to the long-standing southern question (Lega Nord, 2011: 248). We are told that not only did 'huge sums of public money used for the development of the South' fail to have the desired effect, but that the neglected northern regions have long suffered 'genuine injustices' by the state (ibid.). Northerners are thus cast as the victims of the state and the inefficient South. Moreover, while other parties are said to have since jumped on the bandwagon, claiming to favour federal reform too, 'in reality only the Lega Nord really wants it' (Lega Nord, 2011: 11). This is because federalism is not just a policy goal for the Lega, but is said to be the fundamental principle underpinning its view of politics. The party manual explains that:

According to our political vision, federalism represents – nothing more and nothing less – than a *new way of understanding Politics* [emphasis and capitalization in original]. A Politics which, thanks precisely to federalism, will be better able to resolve the daily problems of citizens. A Politics with a capital 'P', as the Lega Nord has always understood it. A Politics which works for the good of citizens and our own Community [capitalization in original].

Lega Nord (2011: 6)

If federalism is one key way of defending the people of the North, another is by opposing immigration and promoting security. Although the section 'immigration and security' in 'Proposals and Objectives' begins with the statement 'the Lega Nord strongly opposes the phenomenon of illegal immigration' (Lega Nord, 2009: 9), the impression from the two documents is that the party has problems generally with the presence of outsiders in northern communities (whether these outsiders are legal or not). This is particularly the case for Muslims – an 'enemy of the people' which has gained in prominence, especially since 9/11. The Lega's position on Muslim immigration tallies with what Hans-Georg Betz and Carol Johnson (2004: 318) describe as 'selective exclusion', according to which, 'certain groups cannot be integrated into society and therefore represent a fundamental threat to the values, way of life and cultural integrity of the "indigenous" people'. Islam is thus presented in the LN party manual as not only being incompatible with Western values, but as a force that actively seeks to destroy local cultures and traditions. Take, for example, the following passage in which we are told that:

Today the Islamic communities present on Padanian territory are increasingly trying to impose measures in our schools which are unacceptable for our students such as the removal of the crucifix from classrooms, the disappearance of the traditional Christmas crib, the placing of boys and girls in separate classes, the banning of the use of food such as ham in canteens, and the introduction of the chador (and even the Burqa). They are thus mapping out a dangerous path towards the progressive abolition of the most basic civil rights.

Lega Nord (2011: 177)

This type of claim is accompanied by many others highlighting the imminence of the threat to 'the people' posed by Islam, such as the allegation that 'there are thousands of cases in which Koranic law is prevailing over that of the host country' (Lega Nord, 2009: 38) and the warning that we are facing 'a loss of Christian and Western identity due to the aggressiveness of the Islamic community' (Lega Nord, 2011: 177). Although the party reiterates it is 'traditionally secular', it claims that, since nobody else is doing so, it is forced to defend Christian symbols in order to 'save the identities and traditions of the Padanian peoples in the face of the cultural uprooting provoked by the influx of millions of immigrants from outside the EU' (ibid.). Amongst those complicit in the attacks on the people's identity are the courts, which are said to favour minority rights over those of the indigenous majority, and the European Union (EU), which not only fails to do enough to prevent the arrival of immigrants, but also does not defend the common Christian roots of the people from the threats posed by the religion of many of the migrants already in Europe (Lega Nord, 2009: 61). This is also one of the reasons why the Lega claims to be against the entry of Turkey into the EU, since the party is 'against the Islamization of Europe and of our country' (Lega Nord, 2011: 34).

On the issue of Europe, the 'Proposals and Objectives' document says that, although the party has been described as Eurosceptic, it is not 'against Europe *per se*' (Lega Nord, 2009: 60). Rather, it is against the creation of 'a genuine continental super-state in which democracy is, in practice, non-existent' (ibid.). In the party manual, we are told that the LN wants a 'Europe of the peoples' which is not 'run by politically irresponsible technocrats' and in which 'the people can freely express their views on their destiny' and not simply 'suffer decisions, made on high, such as the institution of the Euro' (Lega Nord, 2011: 30). The Europe which the Lega says it 'dreams of' is a Europe 'in which local areas are appreciated as essential reserves of identities, cultures, values and traditions' (ibid.). As things stand, however, the EU not only fails to defend northern Italian communities and their values, but is also guilty of not protecting local small and medium enterprises from unfair non-EU competition. The EU is also said to be a key promoter of globalization, a process which is cited on numerous occasions in the two documents as representing a particular danger for the people since it seeks to 'create a single world – the global world – in which differences are evened out and slowly eliminated' (ibid.: 8). Globalization, moreover, is responsible for the post-2008 Great Crisis,[3] which the party claims was provoked in particular by high finance 'abandoning the real economy' (Lega Nord, 2009: 53). Nonetheless, the party believes that in the Great Crisis there also lies an opportunity:

> to return to the real values of man (the family, work, respect for people, genuine solidarity between peoples, religion), thus returning to prominence the spiritual and ethical values which, unfortunately, have been trampled on by this valueless globalization.
>
> Lega Nord (2009: 64).

These sentiments are reflected in the party manual's section on education, in which we are told that: 'to regain competitiveness in Europe, we need to have teachers who know about local history, culture, values and economy' (Lega Nord, 2011: 167). For the Lega, this means that teachers from the region should be favoured over those from outside – again reflecting the fundamental principle that the people of the North should be 'masters in their own homes' (ibid.). The same logic also implies that people should be supported with state vouchers if they wish to send their children to private schools – something the 'centralist' and '1968-inspired' Left opposes (ibid.: 171). Although here and elsewhere, the centralist and allegedly elitist values of the Left are criticized, it is worth noting that there is nothing like the same degree of venom towards the party's political opponents that we found in the FI and PDL Charters of Values. For example, in the two LN documents, there is an almost complete lack of association of the current Italian Left with the history and principles of Communism (an accusation which Berlusconi has always been fond of using). Likewise, we do not find the kind of criticism of cultural elites that was present in the FI and PDL documents. Nor, despite the LN's agreement with the FI/PDL proposals to reform the judiciary, is there the same attempt to depict magistrates as anti-democratic agents.

In conclusion, it is worth noting that a big missing element in both 'Proposals and Objectives' and the 'Political School' manual is the leader, Umberto Bossi. Although occasionally quoted at the beginning of sections, there are almost no references to Bossi's role as founder-leader of the party. This is obviously in stark contrast to Berlusconi's prominence in the FI Charter and seems to reinforce what we said earlier about the differences between the two leaders and their relationships to their parties. In fact, as we have seen in this chapter, and as LN representatives and members were eager to point out in interviews, the party also had a strong grassroots organization, a clear *raison d'être* and a well-defined set of goals. Bossi may well have been 'the Lega' in the sense that he 'incarnated' the movement, as we were so often told, but the LN was about much more than just the personal appeal and domination of Bossi. Put simply, although Bossi's authority and unique talents were widely accepted by interviewees, the LN was a party that was built to last, while the PDL clearly was not.

In this section, we have also seen how the ideology of the party was firmly constructed around a number of fixed pillars. These were informed by the fundamental ethnoregionalist principle of making an exclusively conceived northern people 'masters in their own homes'. Northerners were thus cast as virtuous, hard-working people whose communities are under siege from above by centralizing and undemocratic elites and from below by immigrants (and also, in areas like education, by southerners). From these basic notions spring the key themes – federalism and immigration – which colour all other aspects of the LN's ideology. As we will see in later chapters, these two issues have been the cornerstones of the party's policy offers to voters (Chapter 6) and its members' satisfaction with the Lega's actions in government (Chapter 7).

Notes

1 We should note on this point that the Federal Organizational Secretariat of the Lega Nord (which provided us with the membership figures for the 1991–2011 period) also told us in June 2013 that, by the end of December 2012, the party's membership had plummeted to 56,074. It is hard not to view this drop as directly related to the scandal concerning Bossi and his family which emerged in April 2012. In any case,

the fact that the party was willing to share data showing such a dramatic fall gives us greater confidence about the reliability of the figures previously provided.

2 The main annual rallies of the Lega since the 1990s have been the Pontida rally in Lombardy, usually held at the beginning of the summer, and the Venice rally held in September.

3 Here and throughout the book, we use the term 'Great Crisis' (following several commentators and scholars) to denote the crisis which struck Europe (and elsewhere) after September 2008.

Bibliography

Albertazzi, D. and McDonnell, D. (2005) 'The Lega Nord in the Second Berlusconi Government: In a League of Its Own', *West European Politics*, 28 (5), 952–972.

Albertazzi, D. and McDonnell, D. (2010) 'The Lega Nord Back in Government', *West European Politics*, 33 (6), 1318–1340.

Albertazzi, D., McDonnell, D., and Newell, J. (2011) '*Di lotta e di governo*: The Lega Nord and Rifondazione Comunista in Office', *Party Politics*, 17 (4), 471–487.

Betz, H.-G. (1994) *Radical Right-Wing Populism in Western Europe*, New York: St. Martin's Press.

Betz, H.-G. and Johnson, C. (2004) 'Against the Current – Stemming the Tide: The Nostalgic Ideology of the Contemporary Radical Populist Right', *Journal of Political Ideologies*, 9 (3), 311–327.

van Biezen, I., Mair, P., and Poguntke, T. (2012) 'Going, Going, … Gone? The Decline of Party Membership in Contemporary Europe', *European Journal of Political Research*, 51 (1), 24–56.

Biorcio, R. (1991) 'La Lega come attore politico: dal federalismo al populismo regionalista', in Mannheimer, R. (ed.), *La Lega Lombarda*, Milan: Feltrinelli.

Biorcio, R. (1997) *La Padania promessa*, Milan: Il Saggiatore.

Bolleyer, N., van Spanje, J., and Wilson, A. (2012) 'New Parties in Government: Party Organisation and the Costs of Public Office', *West European Politics*, 35 (5), 971–998.

Diamanti, I. (1994) 'Lega Nord: un partito per le periferie', in Ginsborg, P. (ed.), *Stato dell'Italia*, Milan: Il Saggiatore.

Diamanti, I. (2007) 'The Italian Centre-Right and Centre-Left: Between Parties and "the Party"', *West European Politics*, 30 (4), 733–762.

Heidar, K. (2006) 'Party Membership and Participation', in Katz, R.S. and Crotty, W. (eds), *Handbook of Party Politics*, London: Sage.

Ignazi, P. (2006) *Extreme Right Parties in Western Europe*, Oxford: Oxford University Press.

Katz, R. S. and Mair, P. (2009) 'The Cartel Party Thesis: A Restatement', *Perspectives on Politics*, 7 (4): 753–766.

Lega Nord (2002a) 'Statuto della Lega Nord per l'indipendenza della Padania'.

Lega Nord (2002b) 'Regolamento della Lega Nord per l'indipendenza della Padania'.

Lega Nord (2009) 'Proposte e Obiettivi'. Available at: http://www.leganordtrentino.org/allegati/200904119080824_97proposte%20e%20obiettivi001.pdf (accessed August 2012).

Lega Nord (2011) 'Scuola Quadri Politici'. Available at: http://www.padaniaoffice.org/pdf/scuola_politica_federale/firenze_29_01_2011/Volume_Toscana_Firenze.pdf (accessed August 2012).

Lucardie, P. (2000) 'Prophets, Purifiers and Prolocutors: Towards a Theory on the Emergence of New Parties', *Party Politics*, 6 (2), 175–185.

McDonnell, D. (2006) 'A Weekend in Padania: Regionalist Populism and the Lega Nord', *Politics*, 26 (2), 126–132.

McDonnell, D. (2013) 'Silvio Berlusconi's Personal Parties: From Forza Italia to the Popolo Della Libertà', *Political Studies*, 61 (S1), 217–233.

Mény, Y. and Surel, Y. (2001) *Populismo e Democrazia*, Bologna: Il Mulino.

Mudde, C. (2007) *Populist Radical Right Parties in Europe*, Cambridge: Cambridge University Press.

Norris, P. (2005) *Radical Right: Voters and Parties in the Electoral Market*, Cambridge: Cambridge University Press.

Passarelli, G. and Tuorto, D. (2012) 'Attivisti di partito nella Lega Nord: Un caso anomalo?', *Polis*, 26 (2), 255–284.

Rochon, T.R. (1985) 'Mobilizers and Challengers: Toward a Theory of New Party Success', *International Political Science Review*, 6 (4), 419–39.

Spektorowski, A. (2003) 'Ethnoregionalism: The Intellectual New Right and the Lega Nord', *The Global Review of Ethnopolitics*, 2 (3), 55–70.

Taggart, P. (2000) *Populism*, Buckingham: Open University Press.

Taguieff, P.-A. (2003) *L'illusione populista*, Milan: Mondadori.

Tambini, D. (2001) *Nationalism in Italian Politics – The Stories of the Northern League, 1980–2000*, London: Routledge.

Tarchi, M. (2003) *L'Italia Populista: Dal Qualunquismo ai Girotondi*, Bologna: Il Mulino.

Türsan H. (1998) 'Introduction: Ethnoregionalist Parties as Ethnic Entrepreneurs', in De Winter, L. and Türsan, H. (eds), *Regionalist Parties in Western Europe*, London: Routledge/ECPR.

4   The Schweizerische Volkspartei

The Schweizerische Volkspartei (SVP – Swiss People's Party) presents us with quite a different populist party in terms of its genesis and evolution from the two discussed so far. Unlike the Popolo della Libertà (PDL) and the Lega Nord (LN), the SVP is more similar to the Freiheitliche Partei Österreichs (FPÖ – Austrian Freedom Party) in that we are faced with a long-standing Conservative party which has become populist since the 1980s. And, like the FPÖ under Jörg Haider, the SVP's transformation was thanks largely to the actions of a new leader: Christoph Blocher. It is thus a party which has 'converted' to populism rather than one which was born 'populist'. It is also, like the FPÖ, a party that has generated what Damir Skenderovic (2009: 160) calls 'a process of realignment', reflected in the fact that many voters have abandoned other parties in favour of the SVP and its strong stances on the European Union (EU), immigration, and the role of the state. This has occurred to an extent which would have once been unthinkable in Swiss politics, with the SVP rising over just three general elections from under 12 per cent and fourth position among the main Swiss parties in 1991 to almost 27 per cent of the vote and first position in 2003.

As in the previous two chapters, in this introductory section we will provide a brief overview of the SVP's history, particularly since the early 1990s. Although we will note the key events of the last decade, we will not discuss in detail the period from 2003–2007 since this will be dealt with later in the book. Nor will we say much about the years since 2007, given that, for the reasons mentioned in Chapter 1 (see n. 13), this is not the focus of our study. The remainder of the chapter will proceed like those on the LN and FI–PDL. We will therefore first discuss the SVP in organizational terms, paying particular attention to the changes introduced by Blocher and his allies. Thereafter, we will examine how elected representatives and ordinary members of the SVP conceived of the relationship between the party and its members and how they viewed the leader. This will be based primarily on material collected in interviews conducted between 2010 and 2011 across Switzerland. In the second part of the chapter, we will consider the ideology of the SVP since its 'populist shift', using mostly official party documents and key speeches by Blocher.

It is not possible (or necessary) here to discuss the entire history of the SVP and its predecessor parties. Its origins stretch back to the first half of the twentieth century when several canton-based parties defending the interests of farmers and small business owners grouped together in 1936 to form the Bauern-, Gewerbe- und Bürgerpartei (BGB – Party of Peasants, Craftsmen and Burghers). This party, which had its strongholds in Protestant, German-speaking areas of Switzerland, received between 10 and 12 per cent of the vote in National Council elections, retaining fourth position among the main Swiss parties and occupying one seat out of the seven in the governing Federal Council for decades (Skenderovic, 2009: 127–129). This stability continued both before and after the BGB's merger with two minor parties from the cantons of Glarus and Graubünden to create the SVP in 1971 (ibid.: 128).

Although the groundwork in terms of party organizational change began with Blocher and the Zurich branch of the SVP in the 1980s, it is generally recognized that the key moment for the SVP's rise in support was its campaign against Swiss membership of the European Economic Area (EEA) – the subject of a referendum in December 1992 (Kriesi and Trechsel, 2008: 94). This campaign, in which the SVP was the only major party opposing EEA membership, not only saw Blocher emerge as a national leader, but produced a spectacular (albeit narrow) victory for the SVP, with just over 50 per cent voting against accession. While Euroscepticism was at the root of the party's rise, however, it was accompanied by a tougher stance on immigration, again driven by Blocher and his Zurich wing. Thus, also in 1992, the SVP launched an initiative to make asylum policy far more restrictive (Skenderovic, 2009: 136). As we will see in the 'ideology' section later in this chapter, these two issues have subsequently been key pillars for the SVP.

We examine the electoral performances of the party in detail in the next chapter, but the main point to note here is that, from 11.9 per cent and 25 seats in the National Council in 1991, the SVP increased its share at each of the 1995, 1999, 2003 and 2007 elections. This enabled it to draw level with the centre-left Sozialdemokratische Partei der Schweiz (SPS – Swiss Social Democratic Party) as the most-voted party on 22.5 per cent in 1999 and then to become the largest single party in Swiss politics with 26.7 per cent in 2003. As we discuss in Chapter 5, after Blocher had served for four years in the Federal Council, the party increased its share in 2007 to 28.9 per cent, taking 62 seats in the National Council. Finally, although it is not part of our analysis in this book, we should note that the SVP declined slightly to 26.6 per cent (and 54 seats) in 2011. However, this election also saw the other three main parties lose votes in the face of new challengers both on the centre-right and centre-left (Lutz, 2012). In sum, we can say that the 20 years from 1991 to 2011 witnessed a remarkable electoral ascent of the SVP, not simply in terms of its share, but also geographically, with the party finishing first or second in many Catholic and French-speaking cantons, where it had previously been weak or non-existent (Kriesi and Trechsel, 2008: 94–95). This was accompanied, as we show in the next section, by a territorial expansion of the party organization which, by the end of the 1990s, had established branches in all of Switzerland's 26 cantons, having been present in just over half of them at the beginning of the decade.

As we have already noted in the introductory chapter, 2003 was not only a significant year for the SVP because of the election result, but also because it saw Blocher become a member of the Federal Council. Although the party continued to hold a single seat in government throughout the years of its radicalization, the SVP federal councillor had been selected on each relevant occasion from the ranks of its more traditional and far less radical centre-right wing. Hence, from 1987, Adolf Ogi – a moderate from the Bernese section of the party – was the sole SVP federal councillor for 13 years until 2000 when he stepped down and was succeeded by Samuel Schmid, another moderate from Berne. Given the SVP's increasing share of the vote, however, its allocation of just one seat on the Federal Council became ever less justifiable, especially once it was the largest party in the country. By the same token, it also became less justifiable within the SVP itself that the now-dominant wing of the party, led by Blocher and his Zurich branch, was not represented in government.

These twin pressures came to a head on election night in 2003 when the SVP President, Ueli Maurer (a close ally of Blocher), announced on television that the party would present Blocher as a candidate for the Federal Council and, were he not elected (in addition to Schmid), then they would go into opposition (Burgos *et al.*, 2011: 83; Hardmeier, 2004: 1151). This was a radical proposal for several reasons: first, the number of seats held by each party had been set in stone since 1959 according to what was known as the 'magic formula'; second, Blocher's election would require not re-electing a sitting federal councillor (who was seeking re-election) for the first time in 130 years (Hardmeier, 2004: 1154); third, the idea of the largest party in a long-standing consociational democracy like Switzerland being in opposition is ground-breaking in itself. The upshot of Maurer's ultimatum was that, on 10 December 2003, with the support of the centre-right Freisinnig-Demokratische Partei der Schweiz (FDP – The Free Democrats), Blocher was indeed (narrowly) elected as a federal councillor, in place of Ruth Metzler of the Christlichdemokratische Volkspartei der Schweiz (CVP – The Christian Democrats). The magic formula was thus altered since the SVP (like the FDP and SPS) now had two seats and the CVP just one, but the continuing participation of all four major parties in government had been saved.

Having benefited from parliament's willingness in 2003 to set the precedent of not reappointing a sitting federal councillor who wanted to continue, Blocher was instead its victim in 2007. Following four years of difficult cohabitation in the Federal Council and an election campaign in which the SVP had urged voters to support the party in order to keep Blocher in government (see Chapter 5), the SPS, the Grüne Partei der Schweiz (The Greens), most of the CVP and some members of the FDP replaced him (by 125 to 115 votes) with a little-known SVP member of the Graubünden cantonal government,

Eveline Widmer-Schlumpf (Milic, 2008: 1153). The SVP responded by refusing to recognize Widmer-Schlumpf and Schmid (who was re-elected) as its legitimate representatives and announcing that it was going into opposition. It also requested its Graubünden branch to expel Widmer-Schlumpf. When they refused, the entire branch was expelled from the national SVP. This in turn led to the creation in June 2008 of a new centre-right party, the Bürgerlich-Demokratische Partei (BDP – Conservative Democratic Party) formed by moderate parts of the SVP (and including both Widmer-Schlumpf and Schmid). The SVP's time out of government did not last too long, however, as, when Schmid resigned in November 2008, he was replaced by Ueli Maurer, who has remained as the party's sole federal councillor up until the time of writing in 2014.

The party

As Anthony J. McGann and Herbert Kitschelt (2005: 148) observe, if we are to understand cases of 'populist converts' like the SVP and the FPÖ, we need to consider how specific leaders have driven change both within the party and as regards how it relates to competitors. For the SVP, this means looking at the fundamental role played by Blocher and his allies in the party's organizational and ideological evolution. Before doing so, however, it is important to note that when we speak of Blocher's 'leadership', we are talking about something which is formally different from the leadership of Jörg Haider (or Umberto Bossi and Silvio Berlusconi). Indeed, while it is customary for scholars to refer to Blocher as 'the leader of the Swiss People's Party' (Kriesi, 2012: 840), this has never officially been the case. Rather, a more accurate description of Blocher's position is that by Georg Lutz (2012: 684), who refers to Blocher as 'the strong man in the SVP and the informal party leader'. This slight ambiguity is mainly due to the fact that Swiss parties do not usually have powerful national leaders and they certainly do not have ones whose preeminence is officially recognized in ways comparable to the likes of Berlusconi or Bossi (Albertazzi, 2008: 102). In addition, we should note that Blocher had to exercise his leadership within a party that, at least until the creation of the BDP in 2007, contained a significant (and once dominant) minority moderate wing.

Despite these constraints, when we examine the history of the SVP in recent decades, it is clear that we are faced with a case of extremely successful agency by Blocher and his allies (ibid.: 116). However, although Blocher became president of the Zurich branch in 1977, it was only really in the 1990s that the SVP across Switzerland underwent what Skenderovic (2009: 129) terms 'a process of structural transformation and nationalisation which resulted in both organisational centralisation and increased ideological cohesion of the national party'. These two processes – of ideological and organizational change – went hand-in-hand, with each feeding off the success of the other. We discuss the ideology of the 'new' SVP in the next section, so here our focus is on organization. The first point to be made in this regard is that Blocher and his colleagues were not faced with a strong existing party organization. On the contrary, the SVP was like other Swiss parties, which, as Hanspeter Kriesi and Alexander Trechsel (2008: 90) observe: 'are generally rather weak organizations. Compared to parties in other western democracies and to Swiss interest associations they are underfunded, understaffed and generally lacking in resources'. Furthermore, they are weakened at central level by the fact that cantonal branches of parties are used to enjoying a high degree of autonomy.

The organizational strategy of Blocher and his allies was fourfold and complementary: first of all, they were the driving force behind a territorial expansion of the party which saw the SVP increase its cantonal branches from 14 to 26 (i.e. all cantons) between 1990 and 2001. New branches were established especially in Catholic areas of central Switzerland and French-speaking cantons such as Geneva and Valais (Ladner, 2007: 315). Although these were formally independent, Zurich's role in their creation and their adherence to the more radical ideology of the 'new' SVP meant that most of the new branches were loyal to Blocher and Zurich (Skenderovic and Mazzoleni, 2007: 88). They were also, in many cases, quickly electorally successful. This leads us to the second strategic element. As Skenderovic (2009: 133) notes, these new branches 'helped the Zurich section to alter the balance of power within the institutions of the national party'. In particular, by changing the rules of the party statute to give greater weight within the Assembly of Delegates to cantonal branches based on the number of votes gained in elections, the Zurich wing was able to gain control over the party's main ruling body. One of the early payoffs of this was the election of Ueli Maurer as party president in 1995 (the first time that a Blocher ally had held this role). Since the Assembly is also responsible for electing other key party offices, in addition to adopting 'important programmatic documents' (SVP, 2008: Art. 13.5) and deciding the party line in federal voting (ibid.: Art. 5.8), securing a stable majority in the Assembly was obviously a key step for the Zurich wing (Mazzoleni and Rossini, 2013: 9–10).

The third main element of the Blocherite strategy for organizational change was greater centralization and vertical integration after the Zurich wing was in control of the party in central office. This was reflected, as Oscar Mazzoleni and Carolina Rossini (2013: 9–10) note, first by the bolstering of the role of the party's Central Committee (which included Blocher). Amongst its other tasks, this body makes decisions about the organization of referendums (SVP, 2008: Art. 17.3) and determines the party's position on federal voting in those cases where the Assembly of Delegates has not already done so (SVP, 2008: Art. 17. 2); second, the party's national central office was given a more powerful role in planning and strategy. This saw the SVP at national level taking increased responsibility for campaigns, including 'producing campaign documents (electoral platform, programmes, etc.) for the cantonal branches' (Mazzoleni and Rossini, 2013: 10). These changes were in order to make sure, first, that the SVP had a single, national message and, second, that the Blocher faction was in control of that message.

This brings us to the fourth strategic organizational element: the professionalization of campaigning and the provision of considerable financial resources. Blocher and his allies professionalized the SVP's campaigns and communications strategies, for example by hiring the 'Goal' agency in Zurich, which has designed the party's many successful (and notorious) posters and slogans (Kimmelman, 2010). Professionalization of campaigning, of course, costs money – a particular problem in Switzerland, given the almost complete absence of public funding for parties (Ladner, 2001: 135). This was not an obstacle for the SVP, however, primarily thanks to the wealth of its leader. As Skenderovic and Mazzoleni (2007: 91) detail, Blocher contributed enormously financially, for example paying for advertising campaigns, the production of posters and even for brochures to be sent to every home in the country. The SVP has thus constantly outspent its main competitors since the early 1990s. For example, while the party spent 8.8 million Swiss francs between 1996 and 1998, in the same period the FDP spent 5.8 million, the SPS 4.6 and the CVP 2.8 (Burgos *et al.*, 2011: 74). More recently, a study found that the SVP's outlay on campaigns between 2008 and 2011 was as much as those of its three main rivals combined – with the SVP spending 21 million francs compared to the FDP's 11 million, the CVP's 6 and the SPS's 4 (Geiser, 2012).

These four pillars of organizational change helped to produce sustained electoral success and a more efficient party under the control of the Blocher wing. Unsurprisingly, especially since the SVP's territorial presence increased enormously, the same period also saw party membership rise. Traditionally, it has been difficult to assess membership levels in Swiss parties given that the difference between members and supporters has often been blurred and that some cantonal branches do not even have a formalized membership (Ladner, 2007: 324). There is also the problem (as of course is also the case for Italy) that 'party officials tend to put their membership figures in too favourable a light' (Ladner, 2001: 138). Mathieu Gunzinger (2008: 89–91) uses a method to counteract this, involving limiting the maximum credible membership of a party in a canton at 20 per cent of the absolute number of votes the party receives in that canton. In other words, in those cases where party officials state that the number of members is higher than 20 per cent of its voters at the most recent elections, this is discounted and the total is automatically reduced to the 20 per cent threshold. One could of course object to the arbitrary nature of this; however, since comparative party membership scholars have chosen to use Gunzinger's data (van Biezen *et al.*, 2012: 52), we feel that this is the most reliable source. According to Gunzinger's calculations (see Table 4.1), the SVP had more members in 2007 than any other Swiss party and was the only one of the four main parties to have gained members between 1997 and 2007: as we can see from the table, while the SVP's 67,400 members in 2007 represented an increase of over 7,000, the FDP lost over 20,000 members, the CVP almost 15,000 and the SPS over 3,000.

Table 4.1 Members of the four main Swiss Parties, 1997 and 2007

	1997	2007	*Difference*
SVP	59,900	67,400	+7,500
FDP	87,300	65,900	−21,400
CVP	74,400	59,700	−14,700
SPS	37,800	34,700	−3,100

Source: Gunzinger (2008: 89).

As regards the activism of these members, the picture that emerged from our interviews across Switzerland was a mixed one, with variation between different cities and cantons. Overall, while the model of activism in the SVP seemed closer to the LN than the PDL, it had aspects in common with each of those parties. For example, Roger Liebi (Zurich City Council member and president of the party in the city of Zurich) told us that, like the PDL, the SVP did not have a wide network of branches on the ground and only had one party office in Zurich. However, like the LN, contact both between members and representatives and between members themselves was quite frequent since they tended to meet 'at least once a month' in restaurants and at party stands on the streets. Like the PDL, however, it was clear that these stands were usually only present in the run-up to elections and referendums (of which, however, there are obviously far more in Switzerland than in Italy). In other words, in Zurich, the SVP did not seem to have the same level and quality of constant contact with its members as the Lega did in northern Italy.

In Geneva, party representatives emphasized the fact that most SVP members in the city did not seem to have time to devote to activism. Eric Bertinat (Geneva Cantonal Assembly member) told us that 'you never see the vast majority of members', while Eric Leyvraz (Geneva Cantonal Assembly member) said that, although they held meetings around once a month in the city, 'it's always the same – it's difficult to have a lot of members coming'. In the neighbouring (and also French-speaking) canton, Vaud, the situation appeared slightly more vibrant. Fabrice Moscheni (Lausanne City Council member and cantonal president of the party) told us that members in Lausanne had 'regular meetings, like every month or two months and then they have actions or marketing actions' such as manning stands in markets and distributing leaflets on Saturday mornings. Meanwhile, in the provincial area of Vevey, Fabienne Despot (Vaud Cantonal Assembly member) said that 'at least once a month, and sometimes twice or three times a month, we are in the market with a stand, collecting signatures, because there is always a referendum or initiative and we talk about it with the people'.

Members also focused on the importance for them of being at party stands in public places and campaigning. For example, member 2 from the canton of Thurgau (in north-west Switzerland) told us: 'We fight for our votations! We man party stands, through which we inform people, we give out leaflets, we put up wall posters'. Likewise, when asked what activism entailed, member 4 from Vaud said 'what we are doing all the time is we participate at demonstrations, or with a stand, we distribute leaflets and fliers of all kinds'. Members also drew attention to the fact that, since there were so many campaigns (whether electoral or for referendums) in Switzerland, this type of activity was very frequent. So, while members confirmed that there were few formal meetings (in some small towns, these were only once or twice a year), the 'proselytizing' role of members was important and brought them into regular contact with one another and with party representatives. It is also worth noting that we found the situation for those in the Young SVP youth movement was different again. Member 3 from Vaud, who was in the Young SVP, told us that he went to two meetings a week on average and that party representatives would often come to talk to young members. In sum, the feeling among those active members we spoke to was that, as member 1 from Thurgau said, they 'understand what the local leadership – whether at district or cantonal level – does; as a consequence, usually they accept it'. This, of course, recalls the type of view we heard expressed by LN members.

Before moving on to the views of representatives and members about Blocher (as we did in the two previous chapters for the LN and PDL leaders, Bossi and Berlusconi), there are couple of important contextual provisos worth noting. First, as explained in the introductory chapter, we interviewed SVP representatives and members in 2010/2011. In other words, we spoke to them after Blocher had been in government and at a time when his role had become less prominent than was the case in the 2003–2007 period. Interviewees therefore were aware of how his time in government had ended and what had occurred afterwards (i.e. his non-re-election to the Federal Council in December 2007; the SVP's year in opposition and Maurer's election as the party's sole federal councillor in December 2008). Consequently, it is quite likely that they might have seen his qualities differently had we interviewed them while he was in government or in the run-up to the 2007 election campaign when his image had become almost synonymous with that of the SVP (Kriesi, 2012: 840). Second, as we have already explained, leadership has different formal and informal meanings in Switzerland than it does in Italy. For example, the SVP statutes make no mention of a clear, duly mandated, party leader. Although the official party president (both at the time of interview and of writing), Toni Brunner, is considered very much Blocher's protégé, it would be unusual to find a populist leader elsewhere not occupying this position. As for Blocher's own official role in the party, following his failure to be re-elected as a federal councillor in December 2007, he was able to secure agreement to change the SVP statute and increase the number of vice-presidents from three to five. Hence, since 1 March 2008, Blocher has been vice-president of the party with responsibility for 'research, strategies and campaigns'.

Not surprisingly, especially given that the party pre-dates Blocher, no interviewees expressed fears that the SVP would disappear after he retires from politics (as PDL members had done about Berlusconi). At most, they said that the party might suffer a small drop in its vote share and that it would be difficult to replace such a capable leader. Those interviewed drew attention in particular to Blocher's intelligence, strategic abilities, and leadership qualities. For example, Andreas Aebi (National Council member for Berne) stressed that 'Blocher has good ideas', while Jedidjah Bollag (Zurich City Council member) underlined 'his ideas, his know-how'. Rolf Siegenthaler (Zurich City Council member and former president of the local party) claimed that Blocher was 'very original' and 'whether you like him or not – he is intelligent', more so than other politicians. He added that Blocher 'is a full-flesh politician'. This ability was linked to Blocher's strong leadership skills and determination. Anita Borer (Head of the SVP youth wing in Zurich and Zurich City Council member) attributed Blocher's capacity to achieve political goals to his career as a businessman. As she said: 'Blocher is a strategist and he has a lot of success in his own profession, in his private life. He knows what he is talking about. He can reach his aims.'

Like Berlusconi, however, Blocher's success and wealth have supposedly not served to distance him from the people. Like other interviewees across Switzerland, Jan Koch (Graubünden Cantonal Assembly member) claimed that 'many people can identify with him and follow him, because he has the gift to express very complex matters in a very simple way and get them across'. This was linked, by member 3 from Canton Vaud, to Blocher's background which was 'very humble', yet nonetheless he had become an extremely successful businessman, employing thousands of people. In sum, it was clear from the interviews that Blocher was highly respected within the SVP and was recognized as a determined and uniquely talented leader who was nonetheless 'like a common man'. That determination and vision, as we have seen, helped bring about an organizational transformation of the party that contributed to its stunning electoral rise in the 1990s and 2000s. The other major contributory factor, of course, was the ideological transformation of the party (again shaped by Blocher and his Zurich wing), which we will examine in the next section.

The ideology

Similarly to FI and the PDL, covered in Chapter 2, it is difficult to pin down how the SVP should be defined, due to the shifts in its ideology and core message in recent decades. However, unlike FI/PDL, which has lacked ideological consistency and coherence throughout its history, the process the SVP embarked upon once Blocher's Zurich wing became dominant was unambiguous and unidirectional: it constituted a radicalization of the party's existing conservative ideology, combined with the adoption of populism (Albertazzi, 2008; Mazzoleni, 2003). This evolution began at national level in the late 1980s and, once set in motion, led to the SVP adapting its views on several interconnected topics, in particular as regards its relationships with other parties and its stances on foreign policy, immigration, and law and order.

It is not difficult to identify the key ideas characterizing the SVP since the end of the 1980s, as it has focused relentlessly on these. However, defining the party ideologically is more problematic, since this implies making a decision about the extent to which a definition should reflect not only what the party has become, but also its roots and where it comes from. The ambiguity characterizing some of the definitions put forward with reference to the SVP (see Mazzoleni, 2007: 18–21), and the variety of labels adopted by scholars – with the same authors employing more than one at times, even within the same article (e.g. McGann and Kitschelt, 2005) – fully demonstrate this point. Indeed, even after the watershed federal election in 1999 (which rewarded the party's radicalization in electoral terms and constituted a 'point of no return' ideologically), some still regarded the SVP as 'no further to the right than other right-wing parties, such as the Bavarian CSU' and 'little different from most other West European centre or centre-right parties' (Linder and Lutz, 2002: 128). However, the majority of scholars have been persuaded that its anti-establishment populism and 'tough' discourse on foreign policy (especially concerning Switzerland's relations with the EU), immigration, and law and order have rendered the SVP under Blocher a very different party from what it was some decades ago. Some therefore argue that the SVP now belongs to the 'radical right' family (e.g. Norris, 2005: 62–63), while many others have emphasized its populism (see, for instance, Caramani and Mény, 2005, who call it 'right-wing populist'). There are also those who have combined these labels: Damir Skenderovic (2009) has thus put forward 'radical right populist', Hans-Georg Betz (2005) 'radical right-wing populist' and Cas Mudde (2007) 'populist radical right'.

While we believe the now widely accepted definition of the SVP as a 'populist' party is useful for the reasons explained in Chapter 1, we have reservations about the 'radical right' label. According to Cas Mudde, the 'ultimate core feature' of radical right ideology is nativism (2007: 26) – i.e. the belief that 'states should be inhabited *exclusively* by members of the native group ("the nation")' (ibid.: 19, our emphasis). However, despite its radicalization, the SVP has not argued that Switzerland should be inhabited exclusively by the Swiss, either during the 2003–2007 period under consideration in this volume, or since then. On the contrary, Switzerland's need for legal and regulated migration is acknowledged by the party (which is attentive to the needs of business), as too is the fact that not all foreigners may want to give up their culture and way of life after settling down in their adopted country (SVP, 2003: 40–41; Blocher, 2006a: 2–3). Lastly, and even according to Blocher, who is not known for pulling his punches on immigration, most foreigners are well integrated into Swiss society (e.g. Blocher 2006a, 2006b). Following Mudde's definition, therefore, the SVP should not be included in the radical right family (despite the fact that Mudde himself does so).

As Oscar Mazzoleni (2007: 41) argues: 'classifying a party when conducting research should not be an end in itself, but a means: once they have been theoretically defined as concepts, the terms used should constitute a lens which enables us to understand the object of study in its *complexity and specific history*' (our emphasis). In line with this reasoning, we believe the most fitting definition for the post-1980s SVP is that of 'conservative populist', as this fully accounts not only for what the party has long been and continues to be (i.e. 'conservative', due to its nationalism, advocacy of neo-Liberal economic policies, and conservatism in social matters), but also for what it has become (i.e. 'populist', due to its positing of two opposing and irreconcilable camps: the 'people' and the 'elite').[1] The discussion of the party ideology provided below shows the appropriateness of this definition.

First, a few words about our choice of documentation here. Given that the SVP's positions have evolved in recent years, it was important to analyse a text that could help us get a sense of where the party stood in ideological terms during the period we examine later in this book (i.e. between 2003 and 2007). The most appropriate document therefore is clearly the party's 2003 manifesto, which, since the SVP was not a member of any pre-electoral coalition (unlike FI/PDL and the LN), can rightly be considered indicative of its fundamental ideology in that period. However, since Blocher is widely accredited to have played a crucial role in the transformation of the party, as we have seen in the first part of this chapter, we also decided to consider a selection of the speeches he delivered during the period we are interested in.[2] As we will see, there is complete correspondence between the SVP's official position on all its key themes, and what Blocher was saying just before becoming a minister and during his tenure.

The SVP 2003 manifesto covered a variety of themes, which were listed in alphabetical order (24 in total). While this shows that the party was keen to be seen as active on a variety of fronts, it does not, of course, mean that it cared about each of them to the same extent. In fact, the manifesto's introduction focused on a much smaller selection of topics. Signed by Ueli Maurer – the party president at the time (and, since late 2008, a member of the Federal Council) – it mentioned the following as the party's key objectives: (a) increasing security (with reference made to 'foreign criminals' and 'drug traffickers from across the world'); (b) reducing taxes and putting the public finances in order; (c) encouraging individual responsibility; and (d) defending the country's independence (SVP, 2003: 5–6). These are the principal themes the party has campaigned on since the end of the 1980s. They are also what have attracted party members and sympathizers to the SVP in recent years (see Chapter 7) and what Blocher argued was necessary to focus upon while he served in government (Blocher, 2007a: 6). As Caspar Baader, an SVP member of the National Council for Basel-Landschaft, succinctly put it in an interview for this book: 'We stand for safety [law and order], for independence against entry into the EU, and we are for less taxes; the people understand this.' Moreover, the discussion of these themes in the SVP's discourse has constantly been underpinned by fierce and unrelenting criticism of the ruling political, economic, and media elites. We will therefore start our discussion by considering the party's anti-elitism, before then proceeding to examine its other key ideas.

In the SVP's literature, members of the elite are depicted as self-serving, if not outright corrupt, and keen to profit from their positions. They are charged with spreading untruths and conspiring behind the backs of 'the people'. As Mazzoleni explains (2003: 70), while the SVP depicts the people as 'virtuous', the elites are, instead, invariably 'evil'. The importance of this criticism is apparent right from the beginning of the 2003 manifesto. The party argues that: 'The Federal Council and the other parties [i.e. CVP, FDP, and SPS] are progressively sacrificing Switzerland and its independence in favour of a servile foreign policy stance. Instead of defending the interests of the Swiss, our well-paid functionaries saunter around the world at the tax-payer's expense' (SVP, 2003: 7). The only party that stands out from this crowd of profiteers, it is explained, is the SVP, which is prepared to 'turn down extremely well-paid positions and lavish benefits and to do so without pretentious celebrations and honours' (ibid.), in order to avoid compromising on its beliefs. Alongside the political elite, Swiss companies are also targeted in the manifesto when they expect support from the state and exploit their connections with politicians, rather than focusing on their ability to compete (see the section: 'C for Complicity' in ibid.: 12–13). Last but not least among the elites, the state media and sectors of the press are also criticized: the former, held to be spreading nothing but propaganda, are said to be controlled by the Left, while the latter are accused of being conformists bent on disseminating their *pensée unique* to their readers (ibid.: 32).

Blocher's criticism of the elites in the same period is perfectly consistent with the party manifesto. He contends that the other governing parties (CVP, FDP, and SPS) 'no longer stand for the values on which the success and strength of our country is based' (Blocher, 2003: 7) and have created a 'centre-left bloc' against the SVP. He variously defines this group of parties as the 'united left' (ibid.: 6 and 7), 'the Centre-Left SP[S], FDP and CVP coalition' (ibid.: 9), and the 'coalition of losers' (ibid.: 6). The only aim of this political elite, we are told just before the 2003 election, is to remain in power, in order to 'contain' the threat posed to them by the SVP: 'in this election year, it is the stated aim of all the political parties, from the SP[S] to the CVP and FDP, to weaken the SVP. Not very substantial in terms of an election programme! But understandable' (ibid.: 7). Blocher also shows contempt for media elites, by accusing them of being a '"bleeding hearts [sic]" Mafia' (ibid.: 6) which keep attacking the party (Blocher, 2004a: 5), and spreading their *'pensée unique'* (ibid.: 6). Besides having failed in their stewardship of the Swiss economy (Blocher, 2004b), the elites also ought to take the blame for their inability (or, perhaps, unwillingness) to defend Switzerland's independence, freedom, and identity – this being a deeply felt concern for the SVP, due to the enduring strength of its nationalism.

The importance of the criticism of the 'elites' to the SVP's discourse also becomes apparent when considering the other themes that the party has focused on since the end of the 1980s (and which were also paramount during the 2003–2007 period). To start with, as we have seen, the SVP wants to preserve the 'Sonderfall Schweiz' (SVP, 2003: 5), i.e. Switzerland's uniqueness, as a country that has chosen a 'solitary' path (ibid.: 42–43). Blocher (2005a, 2005b) sees the country's exceptionalism as being grounded in its original political system, neutrality in international affairs, and tradition of autonomy and independence from European powers. Indeed, 'turning our backs on Swiss exceptionalism has never brought any benefit' (Blocher, 2005a: 1), he claims. Therefore, Swiss exceptionalism should continue to be treasured, since it is the key to the country's success. Interestingly, when extolling the nation's virtues, the SVP does not linger much on a mythologized rural past, as nationalists sometimes do, but rather tends to focus on the role allegedly played by the country's 'uniqueness' in facilitating its economic development: simply put, the party has chosen to concentrate on the financial benefits of independence. According to Blocher, the freedom and autonomy enjoyed by Switzerland have created 'the essential conditions for promoting wealth and security' (Blocher, 2005b: 3).

Not unexpectedly, the party makes frequent negative references to international organizations and foreign powers, such as the EU, The North Atlantic Treaty Organization (NATO), the United Nations (UN), and the United States of America (USA), accusing them of meddling in Switzerland's affairs. According to the 2003 manifesto, the most serious threat to Switzerland's uniqueness, independence, and profoundly democratic system of government originates from the national elites' desire to establish closer relations with the EU – which is said to have 'hypnotized' the Federal Council (SVP, 2003: 18). While in Switzerland the people is 'sovereign', since it has the ability to shape political developments through a variety of direct democratic means, within the EU 'basically the People [original capitalization] are excluded from such decisions – even those that are important' (Blocher, 2005b: 2). The EU has to 'satisfy its need to accumulate the maximum amount of competencies and authority possible' (Blocher, 2005a: 3); therefore, joining it would be detrimental to the quality of Swiss democracy, while doing little to help its economy.

The SVP's unrelenting focus on nationalist themes is also very much apparent when we consider what the party says, and does, concerning immigration – allegedly to defend the country against those who threaten it *from within*. The party's main targets in this respect are illegal migrants, 'bogus' asylum seekers, and criminals (the latter category often being conflated with the first two) (SVP, 2003: 36–37, 40–41, 50–51). The principal criticism voiced by the SVP against illegal migrants and 'bogus' asylum seekers is that they impact negatively on Swiss society and the country's economy, causing overcrowding and taking precious resources 'out' of the system. Some cantonal branches such as the Zurich one have also argued that foreign cultures, especially Islam, pose a fundamental threat to Swiss identity and are incompatible with liberal Western values (Betz, 2005: 160). In line with this position, there have been some high-profile campaigns in recent years focusing on the need to preserve Swiss culture against foreign influences – most notably, the one launched in 2007 which eventually led to a constitutional ban on the construction of minarets (Albertazzi and Mueller, 2013: 362). These (admittedly important) episodes and the position of SVP Zurich notwithstanding, the national party's opposition to certain categories of foreigners during the 2003–2007 period was usually predicated not on a supposed incompatibility between different cultures and ways of life but rather on the alleged need to put Switzerland's economic and social needs first. In fact, no claims concerning the necessity to defend Western/Swiss culture against 'alien' influences can be found in the party's 2003 manifesto, and Blocher himself noted more than once during those years the economic benefits that legal and regulated migration was bringing to Switzerland – a point which Lega Nord politicians, for instance, would never be willing to dwell upon.

In line with this approach, the proposals in the 2003 manifesto concerning migration, asylum, and crime focus entirely on legal, economic, and social (but not cultural) matters. We therefore find material advocating the need to punish criminals, limit the number of foreigners resident in the country (and their alleged cost to the taxpayer), and ensure that the asylum system is not 'abused' (SVP, 2003: 36–37, 40–41, 50–51). As the party says with reference to asylum, once again identifying the political elites as the cause of a serious problem:

> Switzerland is now one of the main destinations for bogus refugees. It is claimed that blame for this lies with the Federal Council and the parliament which, despite the warnings of the SVP, are willing to accept the most outrageous abuses of asylum law. The number of asylum requests is going up and drug trafficking is controlled by asylum seekers and other illegal immigrants.
>
> (Ibid.: 36)

While in charge of the Ministry of Justice and Police between 2003 and 2007, Blocher constantly conflated the issues of illegal immigration/asylum and crime, supporting his claims with references to official data (e.g. Blocher, 2007b, 2007c). The aim was to demonstrate how mistaken 'certain media and political groups [were in] denying, hiding and playing down the issue of violence committed by young foreigners' (Blocher, 2007c: 1). Consistent with this approach, as the minister in charge of law and order, Blocher took several initiatives on foreigners, asylum, and law and order that were clearly inspired by the principles his party had set out during those years (see Chapter 6).

In addition to the nationalist and populist elements just discussed, another key part of the SVP's ideology – and one of great importance to the party's identity in recent decades – has been its promotion of neo-Liberal economic principles. The SVP has usually been consistent in advocating a reduction in government spending, more freedom for businesses and individuals, less interference by the state, the lowering of taxation, and the cutting of red tape.[3] Interestingly, the advocacy of neo-Liberal economic policies, alongside deficit-reduction programmes (SVP, 2003: 13), is linked to the party's efforts to dismantle the country's 'vast political and economic network of fraud' (ibid.: 12) by reducing the amount of money that bureaucrats and state officials can distribute to their clients. So, while for the LN there is little that cannot be resolved by taking power away from 'Rome' and giving it to Italian regions, for the SVP the adoption by the state of truly neo-Liberal economic policies would immediately translate into progress on some of the party's key themes (such as reducing corruption and limiting the power of the elites). We therefore concur with Betz that the SVP's 'heavily producer-oriented programme' (Betz, 2005: 151) has been used by the party as a political weapon 'against the established political institutions and their alleged monopolization of political power which hampers economic progress and suppresses true democracy' (Betz, 1993, cited in Skenderovic, 2009: 170). On this point, the 2003 manifesto states: 'if the economy is suffering now, it is because the state is interfering much more by imposing restrictive norms and redistributing wealth, instead of creating a favourable environment for business ... the SVP demands a reduction in tariffs, taxes and levies and calls for greater freedom for business' (SVP, 2003: 15). For Blocher, a battle needs to be waged against 'a state which is dedicated to direct transfers and wishes to redistribute private property to a well-organized community of benefit recipients' (Blocher, 2004b: 7). The responsibility for this situation rests with left-wing and centrist parties, says the SVP (2003: 52), since these are profiting from the state 'becoming increasingly active and assuming an ever-growing number of roles in the private sector [while] neglecting its basic duties such as guaranteeing security' (ibid.). In line with its conservatism, the SVP has advocated a 'return' to what the country has purportedly always believed: the importance of 'individual responsibility and personal freedom' (ibid.).

In sum, therefore, we can say that *every* key proposal made by the SVP in the 2003–2007 period – from its defence of Switzerland's independence, to its advocacy of the 'small state' and light taxation – was also justified by its wish to contain, and possibly even reduce, the power of national and international elites. This is why we believe that populism – at the core of which is anti-elitism, as we have explained in Chapter 1 – underpins every proposal made by the SVP in recent decades.

The discussion of the key features of the SVP's ideology brings the first part of this book – concerned with the histories, organizations and ideologies of our three parties – to a close. The second part will focus on the populists' experiences in government by considering their electoral performances (Chapter 5), their policies (Chapter 6), and the views of their members and representatives (Chapter 7). This analysis will allow us to assess what populists managed to do while in office and what the reactions were both inside their parties and among the wider public. As far as the SVP is concerned, we will see that its ideological consistency and the perceived correspondence between what it said before Blocher became a minister and what he actually did when in government, were positively evaluated by the party's members and its representatives.

Notes

1 How we understand the term 'populism' has already been discussed in Chapter 1, and with reference to both the LN and FI/PDL. We will not dwell on its definition again in this context.
2 The sample comprises 46 speeches made by Blocher in front of various audiences. It starts with the speech given on 17 January 2003 (i.e. several months before entering government) to the SVP representatives gathered for the 15th Albisgüetli conference of the Canton of Zurich, and ends with the speech made on 18 August 2007 (i.e. not long before losing his place in government) at the SVP Extraordinary National Party Congress in Basel.
3 However, while advocating cuts in government spending across the board, the SVP also continued to claim that farmers – one of its key constituencies – deserved financial support from the state (SVP, 2003: 10–11).

Bibliography

Albertazzi, D. (2008) 'Switzerland: Yet Another Populist Paradise', in Albertazzi, D. and McDonnell, D. (eds), *Twenty-First Century Populism: The Spectre of Western European Democracy*, Basingstoke: Palgrave Macmillan.
Albertazzi, D. and Mueller, S. (2013) 'Populism and Liberal Democracy: Populists in Government in Austria, Italy, Poland and Switzerland', *Government and Opposition*, (48) 3, 345–373.
Betz, H.-G. (2005) 'Mobilizing Resentment in the Alps: the Swiss SVP, the Italian Lega Nord and the Austrian FPÖ', in Caramani, D. and Mény, Y. (eds), *Challenges to Consensual Politics. Democracy, Identity and Populist Protest in the Alpine Region*, Brussels: Peter Lang.
Blocher, C. (2003) 'A Dialogue with Absentees – Albisgüetli Speech 2003'. Available at: http://www.blocher.ch/uploads/media/Albis2003e.pdf, 17 January 2003 (accessed 24 September 2013).
Blocher, C. (2004a) 'Imprimere la svolta borghese'. Available at: http://www.ejpd.admin.ch/content/ejpd/it/home/dokumentation/red/archiv/reden_christoph_blocher/2004/2004-01-16.html, 16 January 2004 (accessed 24 September 2013).
Blocher, C. (2004b) 'I problemi primari della Svizzera e le loro soluzioni'. Available at: http://www.ejpd.admin.ch/content/ejpd/it/home/dokumentation/red/archiv/reden_christoph_blocher/2004/2004-10-25.html, 25 October 2004 (accessed 24 September 2013).
Blocher, C. (2005a) 'L'eccezione Svizzera: soluzione unilaterale come opportunità o intralcio'. Available at: http://www.ejpd.admin.ch/content/ejpd/it/home/dokumentation/red/archiv/reden_christoph_blocher/2005/2005-03-15.html, 15 March 2005 (accessed 24 September 2013).

Blocher, C. (2005b) 'Del valore dell'indipendenza svizzera'. Available at: http://www. bfm.admin.ch/content/ejpd/it/home/dokumentation/red/archiv/reden_christoph_ blocher/2005/2005-12-03.html, 3 December 2005 (accessed 24 September 2013).

Blocher, C. (2006a) 'Gli influssi della legge sull'asilo e della legge sugli stranieri sulla gastronomia svizzera'. Available at: http://www.ejpd.admin.ch/content/ejpd/it/ home/dokumentation/red/archiv/reden_christoph_blocher/2006/2006-05-30.html, 30 May 2006 (accessed 24 September 2013).

Blocher, C. (2006b) 'Nuove leggi sugli stranieri e sull'asilo'. Available at: http://www. ejpd.admin.ch/content/ejpd/it/home/dokumentation/red/archiv/reden_christoph_ blocher/2006/2006-08-15.html, 15 August 2006 (accessed 24 September 2013).

Blocher, C. (2007a) 'Per il bene del Popolo e del Paese'. Available at: http://www. ejpd.admin.ch/content/ejpd/it/home/dokumentation/red/archiv/reden_christoph_ blocher/2007/2007-01-19.html, 19 January 2007 (accessed 23 September 2013).

Blocher, C. (2007b) 'Criminalità, sicurezza, stranieri – il punto della situazione'. Available at: http://www.ejpd.admin.ch/content/ejpd/it/home/dokumentation/red/ archiv/reden_christoph_blocher/2007/2007-03-17.html, 17 March 2007 (accessed 23 September 2013).

Blocher, C. (2007c) 'Violenza e criminalità giovanili'. Available at: http://www.ejpd. admin.ch/content/ejpd/it/home/dokumentation/red/archiv/reden_christoph_ blocher/2007/2007-03-27.html, 27 March 2007 (accessed 23 September 2013).

Burgos, E., Mazzoleni, O., and Rayner, H. (2011) *La formule magique: Conflits et consensus partisans dans l'élection du Conseil fédéral*, Lausanne: Presses Polytechniques Romandes.

Caramani, D. and Mény, Y. (2005) 'The Alpine Challenge to Identity, Consensus, and European Integration', in Caramani, D. and Mény, Y. (eds), *Challenges to Consensual Politics. Democracy, Identity and Populist Protest in the Alpine Region*, Brussels: Peter Lang.

Geiser, U. (2012) 'Party Pockets Lined by Business Interests', *SwissInfo*. Available at: http://www.swissinfo.ch/eng/politics/Party_pockets_lined_by_business_interests. html?cid=32160592, 21 February 2012 (accessed 15 November 2013).

Gunzinger, M. (2008) *Analyse Comparative des ressources financières des partis politiques suisses*, Cahier de l'IDHEAP 240–2008. Available at: http://www.badac.ch/ docs/publications/articles/Financement_partis_1994_2007_Cahier_IDHEAP_240_ Gunzinger.pdf (accessed 20 November 2013).

Hardmeier, S. (2004) 'Switzerland', *European Journal of Political Research*, 43 (7–8), 1151–1159.

Kimmelman, M. (2010) 'When Fear Turns Graphic', *The New York Times*, 14 January.

Kriesi, H. (2012) 'Personalization of National Election Campaigns', *Party Politics*, 18 (6), 825–844.

Kriesi, H. and Trechsel, A. (2008) *The Politics of Switzerland. Continuity and Change in a Consensus Democracy*, Cambridge: Cambridge University Press.

Ladner, A. (2001) 'Swiss Political Parties: Between Persistence and Change', *West European Politics*, 24 (2), 123–144.

Ladner, A. (2007) 'Political Parties', in Kloti, U., Knoepfel, P., and Kriesi, H. (eds), *Handbook of Swiss Politics*, Zurich: NZZ Verlag.

Linder, W. and Lutz, G. (2002) 'The Parliamentary Elections in Switzerland, October 1999', *Electoral Studies*, (21) 1, 128–134.

Lutz, G. (2012) 'The 2011 Swiss Federal Elections: Right-wing Defeat and Increased Fractionalisation', *West European Politics*, 35 (3), 682–693.

McDonnell, D. (2013) 'Silvio Berlusconi's Personal Parties: From Forza Italia to the Popolo Della Libertà', *Political Studies*, 61 (S1), 217–233.

McGann, A.J. and Kitschelt, H. (2005) 'The Radical Right in the Alps: Evolution of Support for the Swiss SVP and Austrian FPÖ', *Party Politics*, 11 (2), 147–171.

Mazzoleni, O. (2003) *Nationalisme et populisme en Suisse. La radicalisation de la 'nouvelle' UDC*. Lausanne: Presses politechniques et universitaires romandes.

Mazzoleni, O. (2007) 'Définir le parti: un enjeu scientifique et politique', in Mazzoleni, O., Gottraux, P., and Péchu, C. (eds), *L'Union démocratique du centre: un parti, son action, ses soutiens*, Lausanne: Antipodes.

Mazzoleni, O. and Rossini, C. (2013) 'The Swiss People's Party: A "Populist" Party Between Leadership and Organisation', Paper presented at the 2013 Council for European Studies Conference, Amsterdam, 25–27 June 2013.

Milic, T. (2008) 'Switzerland', *European Journal of Political Research*, 47 (7–8), 1148–1155.

Mudde, C. (2007) *Populist Radical Right Parties in Europe*, Cambridge: Cambridge University Press.

Norris, P. (2005) *Radical Right. Voters and Parties in the Electoral Market*, Cambridge: Cambridge University Press.

SVP – Schweizerische Volkspartei (2003) *Piattaforma elettorale 2003–2007*. Berne: Segretariato Generale SVP/UDC.

SVP – Schweizerische Volkspartei (2008) 'Statuts'. Available at: http://www.svp.ch/documents/database/dokumente/%24svp/Default%20Folder/partei/Statuten/Statuten%20franz.pdf (accessed 24 September 2013).

Skenderovic, D. (2009) *The Radical Right in Switzerland – Continuity and Change, 1945–2000*, Oxford and New York: Berghahn Books.

Skenderovic, D. and Mazzoleni, O. (2007) 'Contester et utiliser les règles du jeu institutionnel', in Mazzoleni, O., Gottraux, P., and Péchu, C. (eds), *L'Union démocratique du centre: un parti, son action, ses soutiens*, Lausanne: Antipodes.

Van Biezen, I., Mair, P., and Poguntke, T. (2012) 'Going, Going, … Gone? The Decline of Party Membership in Contemporary Europe', *European Journal of Political Research*, 51 (1), 24–56.

5   Elections

How do populists in government fare in elections before, during, and after their terms in office? Do the pressures of office inevitably result in losses? The aim of this chapter is to answer these questions with regard to the Popolo della Libertà (PDL – People of Freedom), the Lega Nord (LN – Northern League) and the Schweizerische Volkspartei (SVP – Swiss People's Party). In the first section ('Negative incumbency effects and populist parties in government'), following a synopsis of the generally negative incumbency effects suffered by Western European parties in coalitions, we show that not only is the evidence about the electoral effects of office on populists in Western Europe sparse due to the small number of cases available, but what little material there is has perhaps presented an overly negative view. Looking at the cases of populists in the Netherlands, Austria and Denmark, we explain why the picture is in fact not quite so clear-cut.

The rest of the chapter is devoted to a close examination of the electoral fortunes of our three parties. In the second section ('Studying the electoral performances of the PDL, LN, and SVP'), we briefly consider the electoral effects of their previous experiences in government and explain which types of elections will subsequently be analysed. In the cases of the PDL and LN, we examine the elections which brought them into power in 2008 (section 3 – 'The pre-incumbency elections'), the two key elections during their time in office (section 4 – 'Second-order elections') and then the 2013 general election (section 5 – 'Post-incumbency general elections'). Given that the latter election took place over a year after the PDL–LN government fell, we also look at opinion polling data on the two parties for the entire period between the two general elections in order to gain a better idea of how the public viewed them while in office. For the SVP, we focus (in sections 3 and 5, respectively) on the National Council elections immediately preceding (2003) and following (2007) the entry of the party's leading figure, Christoph Blocher, into the Federal Council. Although we also present data on the party's performances in subnational elections between 2003 and 2007 (section 4), we do not explore these in depth, for reasons explained in section 2. As the chapter will demonstrate, the evidence – based, of course, on a limited amount of cases – is that populist parties, especially when it is not their first time in office, are by no means condemned to suffer electorally due to their participation in government. Indeed, the experiences of the SVP and the LN show that populists can both serve in office and thrive at the ballot box.

Negative incumbency effects and populist parties in government

It has long been claimed that there is generally a negative incumbency effect on parties in power in established parliamentary democracies. In their landmark work on the topic, Richard Rose and Thomas Mackie (1983) showed that two-thirds of governing parties lose votes in the subsequent general election and that in only one out of twenty coalitions do all component parties gain votes. More recent studies confirm that these negative incumbency effects have persisted. For example, based on the evidence presented in their volume, Wolfgang C. Müller and Kaare Strøm (2006: 120) assert that government participation is electorally 'more a liability than an asset' for parties in Western European coalitions. This is because, as Hanne Marthe Narud and Henry Valen (2008: 398) demonstrate, 'governing parties considered collectively tend to lose votes' in Western Europe and 'their average losses have become progressively larger over the last few decades'. Similarly, although taking a broader geographical perspective, Peter Nannestad and Martin Paldam (1999: 1) find that 'the average government (ruling in a normal election period) in an established democracy loses about 2¼% of the vote'. As a result, they conclude it is an 'an unusually strong fact' that 'the cost of ruling is almost constant in all stable developed democracies' (Nannestad and Paldam, 1999: 21).

So, government tends to cost votes in Western Europe. However, as is clear from the above quotes, the unit of analysis in most research on the cost of governing has tended to be the coalition as a whole, rather than the individual parties. We thus know little about the specific electoral effects of power on parties which may be very different in terms of ideology, lifespan and representative weight within their coalitions. One of the few studies to partially address this problem is that by Jo Buelens and Airo Hino (2008), which looks at the cost of governing from 1945 to 2004 in 11 Western European states. Distinguishing between party families and new/old parties, they find that while all families lose more often than they win, there are significant variations among them (Buelens and Hino, 2008: 159–160). In particular, those parties they classify as 'Liberals' (42.3 per cent of whom gain after incumbency) and 'Christian Democrats' (41.6 per cent) usually do best, while those belonging to 'Communists/Extreme left' (none of whom gain after incumbency) and 'Right-wing populists' (16.7 per cent) fare worst. The authors thus assert that, for these types of radical/non-mainstream parties, 'the effect of governing is quite disastrous' (Buelens and Hino, 2008: 160). While nonetheless interesting for our study, we have two main problems with this analysis: (1) we do not know how all parties were classified and what the criteria was for doing so. Indeed, on this point it is worth noting that the authors use the terms 'right-wing populist' and 'extreme right' interchangeably. Moreover, although they do not provide full lists of parties, it emerges from the text that they classify Alleanza Nazionale (AN – National Alliance) – but not the LN – as 'right-wing populist'; (2) the numbers involved for several of the party families seem too small to allow us to draw the type of conclusions which the authors propose. This is particularly so for 'right-wing populists' in government (of which, we are told, there have only been six cases).

Another attempt to examine the electoral cost of incumbency for non-mainstream parties is that by Joost Van Spanje (2011), who looks at the wider category of 'anti-political-establishment parties' in seven Western European countries from 1945 to 2008 and claims to demonstrate that the cost of ruling is higher for these than for others. Unfortunately, the case selection in his study is rather questionable and casts doubt over the reliability of his conclusions. If we look just at his five Italian cases – which make up nearly a third of the 16 'anti-establishment' parties he says have been in government – we can immediately see a series of problems. For example, the Federazione dei Verdi (Federation of the Greens) are listed in 1993 despite, first, their dubious credentials as 'anti-establishment' and, second, the fact that their sole minister in Carlo Azeglio's Ciampi 1993 government resigned after just one day. Similarly surprising is the presence of the Democratici di Sinistra (DS – Left Democrats) from 1996–2001, given that most Italian politics specialists would classify this without any hesitation as a mainstream centre-left party and not at all 'anti-establishment'. Finally, it is also odd to find that the author includes the LN, Forza Italia (FI) and AN in 1994, but omits all three when they again served in government from 2001 to 2006.

Of more relevance for our purposes is the study by Tjitske Akkerman and Sarah de Lange (2012), which examines the effects of government participation on seven Western European radical right parties – all of whom are also considered 'populist' by most scholars. Their selection comprises parties which have served in government in five different countries since the beginning of the twenty-first century: the Freiheitliche Partei Österreichs (FPÖ – Austrian Freedom Party) and its Jörg Haider-led offshoot, the Bündnis Zukunft Österreich (BZÖ – Alliance for the Future of Austria); the Dutch Lijst Pim Fortuyn (LPF – Pim Fortuyn List) and Geert Wilders' Partij voor de Vrijheid (PVV – Freedom Party) – although the latter did not take any seats in cabinet; the LN in Italy and the SVP in Switzerland. The Dansk Folkeparti (DF – Danish People's Party) is also included on the grounds that it supported a minority centre-right government from 2001 to 2011. The authors show that while 'on average the incumbency effect has been negative' (Akkerman and de Lange, 2012: 575), the majority of radical right populists in their study have in fact gained votes in post-incumbency elections (ibid.: 575–577). In other words, the very considerable losses suffered by the FPÖ and the LPF in 2002 and 2003, respectively, distort what is really a less negative picture. Moreover, if we look closely at their analysis, we can see that the authors themselves unnecessarily skew the results towards a gloomier assessment by calculating the BZÖ's 4.1 per cent share of the vote in 2006 as representing a post-incumbency loss of 5.9 percentage points. This is misleading, however, since they are subtracting that 4.1 per cent not from any previous result of the BZÖ (which would be impossible since it was only created in 2005), but from the 10 per cent of the FPÖ in 2002 – thus ignoring the fact that we are dealing with two separate parties and that the FPÖ also ran in 2006 and secured 11 per cent of the vote (i.e. an improvement on its 2002 performance).

The literature on the effects of incumbency on parties similar to those in our study is thus scarce and not always helpful. Before moving on to our own analysis of the electoral performances of the LN, FI/PDL and SVP, however, it is worth looking in more detail at the other cases of populists in power cited above. First of all, when looking at these results we should bear in mind that the FPÖ in 2000, the LPF in 2002 and the PVV in 2010 were all new to government (see Table 5.1).[1] Hence, at least some of the problems they subsequently faced were inevitably the same as those encountered by *any* party in government (especially coalition government) for the first time (McDonnell and Newell, 2011: 450). In our view, this makes it problematic to use them as evidence for claims (see Chapter 1) that populist parties will necessarily tend to pay a higher price than other types of parties for govern-ment participation. Indeed, the particular circumstances of the LPF – i.e. a very recently created party whose founder-leader was killed before the party entered government – suggest this case is so *sui generis* that it can provide few comparative insights other than to underline the obvious importance of leadership and organization (Lucardie, 2008: 161–163). Albeit under very different circumstances, this was also demonstrated by the FPÖ after 2000. As Richard Luther (2011) shows, despite the external perception of Haider's dominant role, the party's entry into coalition government posed serious problems of internal cohesion which its leader was unable to resolve. Consequently, the FPÖ has been presented as a prototypical case of why incumbency can be so damaging for populist parties (Heinisch, 2008).

As Table 5.1 shows, Austria and the Netherlands provide examples of three populist parties (the FPÖ, LPF, and PVV) whose vote declined sharply follow-ing their first period in coalition government. In addition to the cases already mentioned, the PVV also suffered a significant drop in the 2012 election, after two years of providing support for Mark Rutte's centre-right government. Nonetheless, it is worth noting that – apart from the LPF – the other three populist parties in the two countries all recovered rather quickly after their post-incumbency election setbacks. For Austria, given that the BZÖ did not exist before the FPÖ went into government, we have calculated the combined vote share totals of these two parties after the split in 2005 and compared them to the FPÖ results from the preceding period (see Figure 5.1). From this, we can see that there was already a clear increase in their total vote by 2006. Indeed, by the 2008 general election, the total radical right populist vote in Austria was actually higher (28.2 per cent – comprising 17.5 per cent for the FPÖ and 10.7 per cent for the BZÖ) than it had been at the 1999 election

Table 5.1 Pre- and post-incumbency results for populists in Austria and the Netherlands

Party	Years in office	Pre-incumbency (%)	Post-incumbency (%)	Difference
FPÖ	2000–2002	26.9	10.0	−16.9
FPÖ	2002–2005	10.0	11.0[c]	+1.0
BZÖ	2005–2006	N/A[b]	4.1	N/A
LPF	2002[a]	17.0	5.7	−11.3
PVV	2010–2012	15.5	10.1	−5.4

[a] Although a new general election was not held until January 2003, the government of which the LPF was a member collapsed in October 2002.

[b] The BZÖ was created as a result of a split from the FPÖ and took its place in government without a general election being held.

[c] Although we consider the FPÖ 2006 result as 'post-incumbency', it is important to note that it had been replaced in government by the BZÖ in 2005 and so spent the year before the general election in opposition.

Sources: Inter-Parliamentary Union, PARLINE database on national parliaments: http://www.ipu.org/parline-e/parlinesearch.asp; NSD European election database: http://www.nsd.uib.no/european_election_database/index.html; Austrian government election database: http://www.bmi.gv.at/cms/BMI_wahlen/ergebnisse/start.aspx.

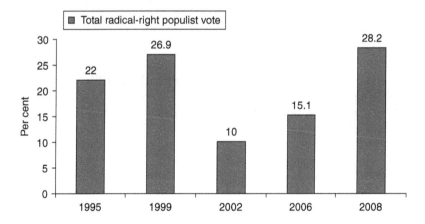

Figure 5.1 Total radical right populist vote in Austrian general elections, 1995–2008.

Sources: Inter-Parliamentary Union, PARLINE database on national parliaments: http://www.ipu.org/parline-e/reports/2017_arc.htm; NSD European election database (Austria): http://www.nsd.uib.no/european_election_database/country/austria/; Austrian government election database: http://www.bmi.gv.at/cms/BMI_wahlen/ergebnisse/start.aspx.

(26.9 per cent for the FPÖ). In other words, although the 2002 FPÖ result – in which it declined from 26.9 per cent to 10 per cent after its first period in government –was obviously very poor, it did not set a new course either for the electoral fortunes of the party or for radical right populism in general in

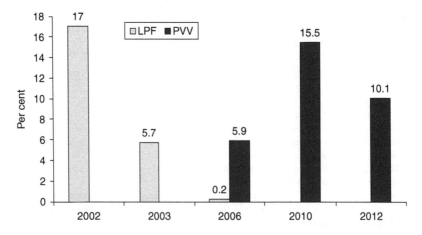

Figure 5.2 Radical right populist general election results in the Netherlands, 2002–2012.

Sources: Inter-Parliamentary Union, PARLINE database on national parliaments: http://www.ipu.org/parline-e/reports/2231_E.htm (2012 election) and http://www.ipu.org/parline-e/reports/2231_arc.htm (elections from 2002 to 2010); NSD European election database (Netherlands): http://www.nsd.uib.no/european_election_database/country/netherlands/.

Austria. Likewise in the Netherlands, although both the LFP and the PVV declined after proximity to government in 2003 and 2012 respectively (see Figure 5.2), it is worth noting that the PVV recovered at the 2014 European Parliament (EP) elections to take 13.3 per cent of the vote. Furthermore, as Figure 5.2 shows, the demise of one radical right populist party, the LPF, following a poor performance in office, clearly did not deter the Dutch electorate from supporting another such party, the PVV, shortly afterwards.

Lastly, the Danish case offers an example of how providing external support for a minority government can be a winning strategy for a populist party, even the first time it is practised. As we can see from Figure 5.3, after beginning its collaboration with the centre-right in 2001, the DF actually increased its vote share slightly in both the 2005 and 2007 general elections, before eventually suffering a drop at the 2011 one. Moreover, the subsequent period has seen the DF rise in voting intentions surveys and score an unprecedented 26.6 per cent at the 2014 EP elections.[2] Hence, as in the cases of the FPÖ and PVV, there is no evidence of co-operation with governing mainstream parties necessarily causing significant long-term damage to populist support levels.

The DF decline in the 2011 election and that of the PVV in 2012 raise a final important issue which is especially relevant to our understanding of the Italian case examined later in this chapter: i.e. the fact that during the Great Crisis (taken as denoting the period since September 2008), incumbent

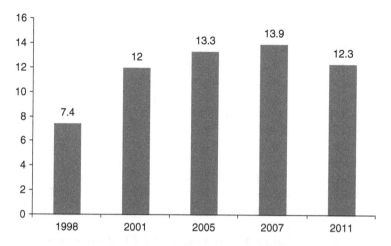

Figure 5.3 Danish People's Party general election results, 1998–2011.

Sources: Inter-Parliamentary Union, PARLINE database on national parliaments: http://www.ipu.org/parline-e/reports/2087_E.htm (2011 election) and http://www.ipu.org/parline-e/reports/2087_arc.htm (elections from 1998 to 2007); NSD European election database (Denmark): http://www.nsd.uib.no/european_election_database/country/denmark/parliamentary_elections.html.

parties in Europe have suffered even more at the ballot box than was the case beforehand. Looking at the electoral results of outgoing governments in 29 European states (the EU-28 plus Iceland) between March 2008 and June 2012, Pedro Maghalhães (2012: 7) discovers that 'European Prime Ministers' parties have lost, on average, about 6.6 percentage points in relation to their previous vote share in legislative elections'. Moreover, he shows that this decline is 'above and beyond what could be expected on the basis of other factors' and that it 'seems to be mostly a phenomenon that has taken place in the countries of the Eurozone' (Maghalhães, 2012: 30). Albeit using slightly different timeframes, these findings are confirmed by both Josep M. Colomer (2012) and Hanspeter Kriesi (2014). So, while there was already a negative incumbency effect on parties in Western European coalitions before the Great Crisis, as we have discussed earlier, this has further increased in the years since 2008. This does not, of course, affect our study of the SVP from 2003 to 2007, but it is highly relevant to the PDL and LN given that they took office in May 2008 and governed one of the Eurozone's worst-hit countries.

Studying the electoral performances of the PDL, LN, and SVP

The rest of this chapter will examine the electoral fortunes of the LN, PDL, and SVP after they entered government in 2008 (LN and PDL) and in 2003 (SVP). Unlike most of the cases elsewhere in Western Europe discussed in the previous section, it is important to note that these were not the first experiences of government participation for any of our three parties (see Chapter 1). Certainly, as explained in Chapter 4, 2003 was a highly significant juncture for the SVP since it not only saw the party secure a second seat in the Federal Council, but also marked Blocher's election as a federal councillor – thus bringing the leader of the dominant, and more radical, Zurich wing into government for the first time. However, as we know, the SVP had maintained a constant (albeit more moderate) presence in the Federal Council for decades. So, while 2003 indeed marked a new departure for the party, it is obviously not classifiable as a 'first time in office' akin to those of parties like the LPF in 2002 or the PVV in 2010. Nor is this the case for the PDL. Although technically a new party in 2008, it was – as discussed in Chapter 2 – the product of the merger between two parties which had been allies both in and out of government for almost fifteen years: Berlusconi's FI and Alleanza Nazionale (AN). Finally, in the case of the LN, as outlined in Chapter 3, by 2008 the party had already served twice with FI and AN in centre-right coalition governments led by Berlusconi: briefly and acrimoniously in 1994, and then from 2001 to 2006 (Albertazzi *et al.*, 2011).

While they are not the focus of our analysis, in Table 5.2 we list the pre- and post-incumbency general election results of the three parties in those prior experiences of government mentioned above. In the case of the SVP, we do not cover all such elections over the decades, but take the 1991 election as our point of departure (in line with the transformation of the party explained in Chapter 4). As we can see in Table 5.2, the party increased its vote in each post-incumbency general election during the period. Of course, as explained in the introductory chapter, we should again note that the idea of incumbency, along with those of 'government' and 'opposition', is different in Switzerland compared to western European democracies in which alternation is a regular occurrence. First of all, the main four parties have been in government together since 1959 (with the brief exception of the SVP in 2008, i.e. after the period we focus on in this book). Second, although it has traditionally been customary for all federal councillors to back government decisions, the parties of those councillors are by no means obliged to support them. Indeed, the SVP has often taken positions against those adopted by the Federal Council. Such provisos notwithstanding, we can see from Table 5.2 that the party improved its share of the vote at both the 1995 and 1999 general elections. So, while talking about the electoral effects of government is problematic in the Swiss case, we can certainly say that these were not negative prior to Blocher's entry into the Federal Council in 2003. The LN share of the vote also rose in both 1996 and 2006 after its first two periods in office. Nonetheless, it is slightly misleading to consider 1996 as representing a true response by voters to the party's preceding time in power given that the government of which it had been a part fell over a year previously in December 1994. This logic also applies to the FI decline in its vote share at the 1996 election. However, such caveats do not apply for either party in 2006 when, as Table 5.2 shows, the LN

Table 5.2 Pre- and post-incumbency general election results for populists in Italy (1994–2006) and Switzerland (1991–1999)

Party	Years in office	Pre-incumbency (%)	Post-incumbency (%)	Difference
SVP	1991–1995	11.9	14.9	+3.0
SVP	1995–1999	14.9	22.5	+7.6
LN	1994[a]	8.4	10.1	+1.7
LN	2001–2006	3.9	4.6	+0.7
FI	1994[a]	21.0	20.6	−0.4
FI	2001–2006	29.4	23.7	−5.7

[a] Although a new general election was not held until April 1996, the first government of which the LN and FI were members collapsed in December 1994 and was replaced by a technocratic executive led by Lamberto Dini.

Sources: Electoral archive of the Italian Interior Ministry: www.elezionistorico.interno.it; Swiss Confederation Federal Statistics Office: http://www.portal-stat.admin.ch/nrw/files/fr/01b2.xml and http://www.politik-stat.ch/nrw2011CH_it.html.

vote rose and FI's decreased after five years together in power. To sum up: we can say that, prior to the periods considered in this chapter, neither the SVP nor the LN had suffered obvious post-incumbency electoral setbacks in the previous 15 years. FI/PDL, on the other hand, had done so, most notably in 2006 when it declined by almost six percentage points.

Before moving on to the presentation and discussion of results for the periods in government we are most interested in, it is important to explain which elections we will look at in each country and why. In the case of Italy, in addition to general elections, we also examine the results of 'second-order' elections during the LN's and PDL's time in office. This is a level of analysis which, to our knowledge, no other comparative study of populist parties in Europe has considered. Following Karlheinz Reif and Hermann Schmitt (1980), we understand 'second-order elections' as those in which (a) turnout is lower than in general elections; (b) voters are less inclined to vote strategically than in general elections, thus benefiting small parties; (c) voters tend to punish the parties in national government, especially after the initial 'honeymoon period' is over. In fact, the closer to the mid-term point in an electoral cycle that a second-order election is held, the greater this punishment is likely to be for the governing parties. While Reif and Schmitt's original study focused on the 1979 EP elections as second-order elections, this category may include others such as regional elections and by-elections for seats in national parliament. It is also worth noting here, given the use we make of them, that Schmitt (2005: 668) reassessed the 'second-orderness' of EP elections based on those held in 2004 and found that in Western Europe 'European Parliament elections are still very much second-order elections: participation is low, first-order government parties lose support in a cyclical manner, and small parties do better than they would do if a first order election was held.'

The other second-order set of elections we examine in the Italian case are the regional elections.[3] Different studies in recent years have shown that it is legitimate to treat these elections as second-order. For example, John Loughlin and Silvia Bolgherini (2006: 154) conclude their study of the topic by affirming that Italian regional elections continue to be 'second-order elections' and 'the big shift of the early 1990s from the First to the Second Republic has not fundamentally altered this assessment'. Likewise, Emanuele Massetti and Giulia Sandri (2013: 161) find that 'a classic pattern of "second-order" electoral behaviour' can be seen in 'ordinary statute' regions over the past two decades, while Filippo Tronconi and Christophe Roux (2009) also demonstrate that regional elections – at least since the mid-1990s – can legitimately be considered 'second-order'. In this chapter, we will therefore consider the 2010 regional elections, when 13 of the 15 'ordinary statute' regions voted. These regions comprise over 80 per cent of the Italian population and so have a strong nationwide character (Loughlin and Bolgherini, 2006: 155).

Finally, as regards the Italian elections considered in this chapter, although we discuss the February 2013 general election results, the extent to which we can consider this a post-incumbency election is complicated by the fact that, in November 2011, the PDL–LN coalition government was replaced by Mario Monti's technocratic executive (Bosco and McDonnell, 2012: 43–45). There was thus a 14-month break between the end of the PDL–LN government and the 2013 general election. During this time, along with the centre-left Partito Democratico (PD – Democratic Party) and the centrist Unione di Centro (UDC – Union of the Centre), the PDL reluctantly provided parliamentary backing for Monti until eventually withdrawing support in December 2012. The Lega, meanwhile, went into opposition, thus temporarily suspending its 12-year alliance with the PDL. More traumatically for the party, in April 2012 the LN founder and leader Umberto Bossi resigned, following an expenses scandal concerning him and members of his family. Given these factors and events, it is problematic to view the levels of support for the PDL and LN in February 2013 as representing an expression of views on the PDL–LN 2008–2011 government in the same way as an election in late 2011 or early 2012 would have done. We will therefore also look at pooled monthly opinion poll data for the period between the 2008 and 2013 general elections. This will allow us to gain a greater sense of how the public reacted to the parties in government over time.

In the case of Switzerland, we are faced with the opposite set of complications compared to those concerning the LN and PDL. In other words, while there are no problems with analysing the SVP's post-incumbency performance in the 2007 National Council elections, we cannot take cantonal elections in Switzerland as being second-order elections like the regional ones in Italy. In his study of the topic, Peter Selb (2006: 70) finds that 'regional election outcomes in Switzerland are to some extent snapshots of national trends in party support in nationally well-integrated cantons, while in more peripheral regions they are more properly conceived of as expressions of regional ebbs and flows in parties' electoral fortunes'. He concludes that, overall, in the Swiss case, 'the conception of regional elections as second-order national elections is clearly dismissed by the data' (ibid.; see also Caramani, 2004). We share this view, particularly since, if we return to the proposition by Reif and Schmitt (1980: 9–10) that government parties are likely to lose and opposition ones to gain in second-order elections, then this is obviously far more complicated in a political system like Switzerland's where all four major parties were in government during the 2003–2007 period. We will therefore provide details about the changes in terms of seat numbers in cantonal and municipal assemblies regarding the SVP and the other main parties between 2003 and 2007, but we will not discuss these elections in any depth. Their outcomes serve as an additional, but weak, indicator of how the SVP fared electorally as a result of its actions in national government.

Nor will we look closely at the results of the Council of States elections in Switzerland, i.e. those for the federal parliament's second chamber which are held alongside elections for the National Council. The main reason is that, due in particular to the two-round majority electoral system and consequent alliances between the centre-right Freisinnig-Demokratische Partei der Schweiz (FDP – The Free Democrats) and centrist Christlichdemokratische Volkspartei der Schweiz (CVP – The Christian Democrats), the number of seats gained by each party cannot be taken as an indication of its relative strength. For example, although the SVP since 2003 has always gained the largest number of seats in the National Council which is elected by a proportional system, it has also been the weakest of the four main parties in the Council of States. The same phenomenon, albeit to a lesser extent, also occurs in the case of the Sozialdemokratische Partei der Schweiz (SPS – Swiss Social Democratic Party), which has held more seats than the FDP and the CVP in the National Council since 1995, but has remained well behind both in the Council of States. As Romain Lachat (2006) shows, there is also a lot of strategic voting in the Council of States elections, with voters seeking to back candidates likely to win under the two-round system rather than necessarily supporting their preferred choice, and this seems to work to the advantage of the two centre/centre-right parties. Furthermore, Lachat (2006: 97) notes that 'the informal alliances reached by parties may be one additional factor explaining the weakness of the SVP' in the Council of States. This refers to the practice in many cantons of the other parties coalescing against the SVP candidate. Consequently, although we will list the Council of States results when discussing the SVP's performance in 2007, we will devote almost all of our attention to the National Council elections.

The pre-incumbency elections

In this section, we look at the pre-incumbency general elections for our three parties: 2008 in the cases of the PDL and the LN; 2003 in that of the SVP. This is not only essential information for evaluating the subsequent electoral performances of the parties, but also provides important context for understanding the policies they pursued (discussed in the next chapter) and the reactions of representatives and members to their party's time in office (the subject of Chapter 7).

Italy 2008

We have already outlined the events prior to the April 2008 general election in Chapters 2 and 3, so there is no need to go through these again. The key points here are that this election was the first for the PDL (created by the merger of FI and AN, along with several very small parties) and that the centre-right coalition consisted of just two main parties, the PDL and the LN. It thus stood in contrast to the larger centre-right coalition of four principal components (FI, AN, LN, and UDC) which had contested and won the 2001 general election. As we can see from Figures 5.4 and 5.5, the 2008 election was a successful one not only for the centre-right alliance as a whole, but for both the PDL and the LN individually. The Lega increased its share from 4.6

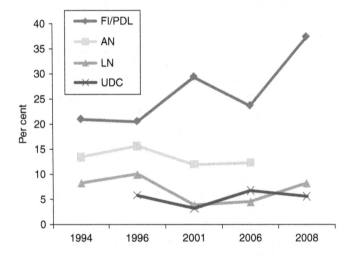

Figure 5.4 Italian centre-right parties (FI/PDL, AN, UDC, and LN) in general elections, 1994–2008.

Note: General election results refer to the proportional part of the elections for the Chamber of Deputies. On two occasions since 1994, one of the centre-right parties listed did not run as part of the coalition: the LN in 1996 and the UDC in 2008. As explained, FI and AN ran together as the PDL in 2008 – hence the apparent sudden rise in the FI line for that year. It is also worth noting that several minor parties (none of whom secured more than 1 per cent in the 2006 general election) also joined the PDL.

Source: Electoral archive of the Italian Interior Ministry, www.elezionistorico. interno.it.

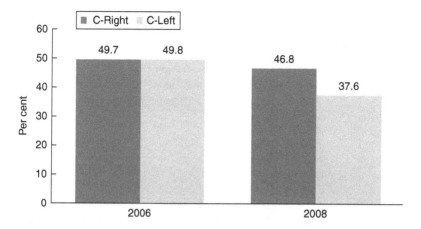

Figure 5.5 Centre-right and centre-left coalition results in Italian general elections, 2006–2008.

Note: General election results refer to those for the Chamber of Deputies. As mentioned, both coalitions were composed of fewer parties in 2008 than in 2006.

Source: Electoral archive of the Italian Interior Ministry, www.elezionistorico. interno.it.

per cent in 2006 to 8.3 per cent in 2008, while the PDL took 37.4 per cent of the vote. This made the PDL the largest single party in Italy, over four points ahead of the newly formed centre-left PD, which received 33.2 per cent. The gap between the two main coalitions was even greater, with the centre-right achieving 46.8 per cent of the vote and the centre-left (whose coalition contained far fewer parties than in 2006) managing just 37.6 per cent.

The margin of victory helped the centre-right coalition to secure over half of the seats in both the Chamber of Deputies and the Senate. This was crucial for governability given the combination of Italy's perfect bicameralism (Cotta and Verzichelli, 2007: 142–147) and the electoral system adopted in 2005 (which has different rules for the assignment of the majority bonus in the Chamber of Deputies and the Senate). The problems this combination can create had been clearly seen during Romano Prodi's 2006–2008 government, when the centre-left coalition had a comfortable advantage in the Chamber but a majority of just two in the Senate. This, predictably, made its brief time in office extremely difficult since it only required a handful of absences or defections to leave it short of votes. There were no such concerns for the PDL–LN alliance in 2008 given that, as we can see from Figures 5.6 and 5.7 (overleaf), it held 344 out of 630 seats in the Chamber of Deputies and 174 out of 315 seats in the Senate.

Berlusconi thus returned to office in 2008 with clear majorities in both houses of parliament and fewer coalition partners to manage than had been the case both in 1994 and 2001. Of course, unlike 2001, this time his

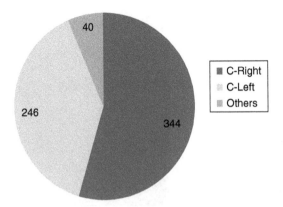

Figure 5.6 Composition of the Chamber of Deputies after the 2008 general election.
Source: Electoral archive of the Italian Interior Ministry, www.elezionistorico.
interno.it.

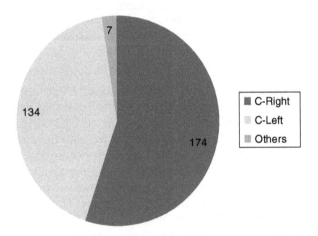

Figure 5.7 Composition of the Senate after the 2008 general election.
Source: Electoral archive of the Italian Interior Ministry, www.elezionistorico.
interno.it.

government's survival was dependent on the LN, which Roberto D'Alimonte (2008: 24) rightly described as 'the big winner of these elections'. Not only did the LN achieve its highest vote share since 1996 (when it ran alone), but it also increased its number of votes in absolute terms by almost 1.3 million compared to 2006. Moreover, and of particular interest to us, is that this increase in support for the Lega came largely at the expense of the PDL. As a study of vote flows by the Istituto Cattaneo (2008) shows, many of the new votes for the LN were cast by northerners who had voted for FI and AN in 2006. Despite some sections of the media and centre-right politicians pushing the story that the LN's rise was in large part due to its taking votes from the Left (and the far-Left in particular), this is a myth. Rather, what Paolo Natale (2007) has termed the 'light loyalty' of voters in the Second Republic prevailed once again in 2008 on both sides, with those who switched loyalties tending either to move between parties *within* the former centre-right and centre-left blocks or deciding not to vote.

Switzerland 2003

As mentioned several times, 2003 was a landmark year for the SVP. We have already discussed in Chapter 4 how the party's leading figure, Christoph Blocher, was elected by parliament to the Federal Council in December of that year, as the party finally secured a second seat in the seven-member government (at the expense of the CVP). While the product of a series of factors, Blocher's appointment mainly reflected the fact that the October 2003 election marked the completion in just eight years (and two federal elections) of the SVP's ascent from its long-standing status as the fourth strongest party to the most-voted single party in the country. As Figure 5.8 shows, although the rise of the SVP had already begun at the 1995 election, it remained behind the FDP, SPS and CVP that year. However, having surpassed the FDP and CVP to share first place with the SPS on 22.5 per cent in 1999, the SVP in 2003 increased its share by 4.2 percentage points to take 26.7 per cent of the vote – the best performance by any Swiss party in a federal election since 1943. By contrast, the two main centre-right parties which had long dominated Swiss

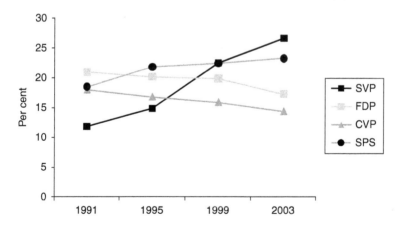

Figure 5.8 Vote shares of the four main Swiss parties (SVP, FDP, CVP, and SPS) in National Council elections, 1991–2003.

Source: Swiss Confederation Federal Statistics Office: http://www.portal-stat.admin. ch/nrw/files/fr/01.xml and http://www.politik-stat.ch/nrw2011CH_it.html.

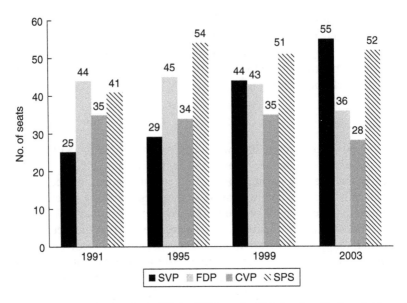

Figure 5.9 Seats of the SVP, FDP, CVP, and SPS in the National Council, 1991–2003.

Source: Swiss Confederation Federal Statistics Office: http://www.portal-stat.admin. ch/nrw/files/fr/01.xml and http://www.politik-stat.ch/nrw2011CH_it.html.

politics, the FDP and the CVP, suffered their worst results since proportional elections were introduced in 1919 (Hardmeier, 2004: 1151).

The 2003 results translated into an 11-seat increase for the SVP in the National Council, making it the largest party in the Chamber for the first time in its history. As Figure 5.9 shows, while the SPS had retained its position as the largest party in terms of seats in 1999 (despite the SVP drawing level with it in percentage terms), in 2003 the SVP nudged past it, gaining 55 seats compared to the SPS's 52. Both of them, however, were well ahead of the FDP and CVP, which took 36 and 28 seats respectively. Notwithstanding the SVP's success, it is worth remembering that – unlike the PDL and LN in the Italian case – the party still remained very much in a minority in the Swiss parliament. As we can see from Figure 5.10, the SVP's 55 seats only accounted for just over a quarter of those available in the National Council, so it could still easily be outvoted by alliances between the other main parties. On the other hand, this seat distribution also allowed the party to say that – while it was now the single greatest force – it was still acting as the minority opposition to the mainstream establishment majority of the FDP, CVP, and SPS. This, of course, was a tactic unavailable to the PDL–LN alliance in Italy.

The 2003 election thus saw the continuation of the remarkable rise of the SVP and the decline of the FDP and CVP. As we might expect, these trends

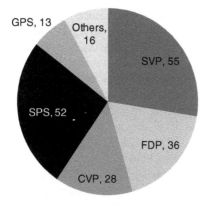

Figure 5.10 Seat distribution in the National Council after the 2003 election.

Note: The total number of seats is 200.

Source: Swiss Confederation Federal Statistics Office: http://www.portal-stat.admin. ch/nrw/files/fr/01.xml and http://www.politik-stat.ch/nrw2011CH_it.html.

are linked. In the 2003 federal election edition of the Swiss Electoral Study (Selects), Peter Selb and Romain Lachat (2004: 14–16) estimate that 13.7 per cent of those who voted for the FDP and 6.8 per cent of those who voted for the CVP in 1999 supported the SVP in 2003 – both of these figures are higher than any of the flows towards the SVP from other parties or from those who had abstained. In geographical terms, the most interesting aspect of the SVP's performance in 2003 was the increase of its vote share in Romandie (the French-speaking cantons). Sibylle Hardmeier (2004: 1151) notes that, in these areas, 'whereas in 1999 only 8.7 per cent of the voters chose the SVP, in 2003 the number increased to 18.4 per cent'.

Second-order elections

SVP

As explained previously, subnational elections in Switzerland are not second-order elections akin to regional elections in Italy, Länder elections in Germany or by-elections in the UK. We will therefore not discuss them in any depth here. Nonetheless, it does seem useful to briefly note their outcomes since, as Selb (2006) suggests, at least some cantonal elections may provide 'snapshots of national trends in party support'. In the case of the SVP between 2003 and 2007, the evidence is very clear that – whether or not results were influenced by Blocher's actions in government – the party certainly did not suffer overall at cantonal and municipal levels during those years. On the contrary, it fared better at both levels than the other three main parties (FDP, CVP, and SPS) with whom it governed in the Federal Council. As Figure 5.11 illustrates, although the total number of seats held by the SVP in cantonal parliaments declined very slightly from 571 to 568 during the four years, the other three main parties performed much worse. As a result, from having been the fourth largest party at the end of 2003 in terms of seats at cantonal level, by the end of 2007 the SVP held more seats at this level than any other party. It is also worth noting that the number of seats held by the SVP in cantonal governments during these four years increased from 17 to 18. Finally, the party also performed well at municipal level during the four years that Blocher was in the national government. If we look at Figure 5.12, which shows the number of municipal assembly seats held by the four main parties on 1 January 2004 and 1 January 2008, we can see that the SVP gained 101 seats during the period – more than any of the other three main parties. Thus, once again, there is no indication of the SVP being punished due to its actions at national level during the 2003–2007 period.

PDL and LN

Unlike the Swiss subnational elections, the 2009 EP and 2010 regional elections in Italy can be fully considered 'second-order' elections, for the reasons outlined previously. Before discussing these, however, there are a couple of points worth bearing in mind. First, as explained earlier, these elections occurred after the beginning of the Great Crisis in Europe (i.e. post-autumn 2008). In other words, they took place at a time when, across Western Europe, incumbent parties were suffering even more than normal at the ballot box. Given that Italy has been one of the worst-hit Eurozone countries, we would expect to find – all things being equal – that voters punish the governing parties, as those in countries like Spain, Greece, and Ireland have done.

Second, when comparing the results of the 2009 EP elections with those in 2004 or the 2010 regional ones with those in 2005, it is important to note the change in the Italian electoral cycle that was caused by the early fall of Prodi's centre-left government in 2008. This had the effect of shifting the two main second-order elections in Italy from the latter half of the national government's mandate to the first half. For example, during the 2001–2006 Berlusconi government, the 2004 EP elections took place three years after the general election and the 2005 regional elections took place four years after. However, in the case of Berlusconi's 2008–2011 government, the EP elections were held just one year after the general election and the regional elections two years after. This is important since the timing of second-order elections during an electoral cycle has an impact on their outcome, due to the fact that most governing parties at national level enjoy a 'honeymoon', or at least a 'grace' period, before they begin to lose ground in second-order elections. As Reiner Dinkel (1977) found in his study of the relationship between federal and state elections in West Germany, 'the further away that a Land election took place from a federal election, the worse the federal government parties performed' (Jeffery

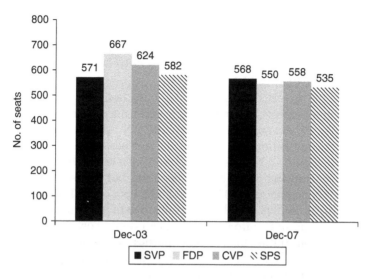

Figure 5.11 Seats held by the main Swiss parties in cantonal parliaments, December 2003 vs December 2007.

Source: Swiss Confederation Statistical Office: http://www.portal-stat.admin.ch/nrw/files/fr/03.xml.

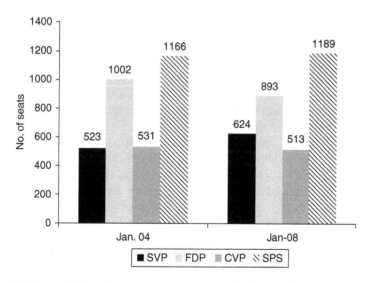

Figure 5.12 Seats held by the main parties in municipal assemblies, January 2004 vs January 2008.

Note: Only municipalities in towns with more than 10,000 inhabitants have been considered.

Source: 'Élections en Suisse': http://www.strabon.ch/elections/index2.htm.

and Hough, 2003: 201). This trend would reach a low point at the exact mid-term of the party's period in national office, before improving shortly prior to federal elections – thus creating what Charlie Jeffery and Daniel Hough (2003: 204) term 'dinkel curves'. Following this logic and, again, all things being equal, we ought therefore to expect the 2010 regional elections to be those in which the PDL and LN fare worst.

Let us take the two elections in order. Although both parties campaigned – albeit to different extents – based on their performance together in government, the 2009 EP election saw the PDL and LN run separately, given the nature of that competition (for example, the two parties are not in the same EP group). As Figure 5.13 shows, the PDL's 35.3 per cent share was 2.1 points less than its general election result (37.4 per cent), but almost 3 points higher than FI and AN's combined 2004 EP result (32.4 per cent). The party's slight decline compared to 2008 was almost entirely due to its dropping 4 points in the South where, as an Istituto Cattaneo (2009) study showed, it mostly 'lost' votes to abstentions (rather than to other parties). In the rest of the country, the PDL share remained almost exactly the same as in the previous year's general election. Even allowing for a 'honeymoon' effect, this still seems a commendable result for the majority party in a Eurozone government during the crisis. It is also worth noting here that the PDL's main rival, the PD, performed very poorly, declining from 33.2 per cent in 2008 (and 31.1 per cent in 2004) to 26.1 per cent in 2009 – again unusual for the major opposition party during the crisis. As for the Lega Nord, the EP election was an unquestionable success. Its result of 10.2 per cent was its best ever in a national-level election – just above the 10.1 per cent it received when it stood alone at the 1996 general election. As we can see from Figure 5.13, the party improved by almost two points on its 2008 result and by more than five points compared to its performance in the 2004 EP election.

The Lega focused its campaign on 'its success and effectiveness while in government', in particular stressing its role in the fight against illegal immigration (Bressanelli *et al.*, 2010: 115). We can see this, for example, by the party's use of posters in 2009, such as one showing a boatload of Africans aboard a ship with the message above it: 'we stopped the invasion' – a clear reference to Roberto Maroni's work as Interior Minister and the security decrees (see Chapter 6). The PDL also appealed to voters on the basis of its actions in government, although to a lesser extent. For example, one of its campaign postcards said: 'I will vote for him because he knows how to handle crises: illegal immigrants, waste, earthquakes, Alitalia' (see Appendix 1, years 2008, 2009). The 'him' in the message refers to Berlusconi, who was, yet again, very firmly at the heart of the PDL's campaign. Despite obviously having no intention of taking up a seat in the EP, Berlusconi stood in all five macro-regional constituencies and people were urged to vote first for him and only then for the local candidate. His central role was further 'enhanced' by news stories – including his wife's decision to divorce him following revelations about his alleged relationship with an underage girl from Naples – which emerged in the

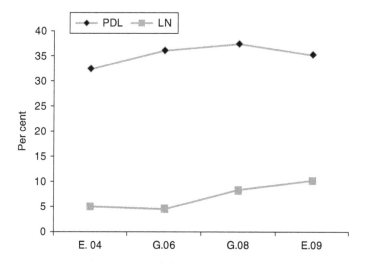

Figure 5.13 PDL and LN in European Parliament and general elections, 2004–2009.
Note: The 2004 and 2006 PDL results are the totals of FI and AN vote shares in those elections.
Source: Electoral archive of the Italian Interior Ministry: www.elezionistorico. interno.it.

election run-up. However, these controversies appeared to have little effect on the PDL's performance.

The 2010 regional elections were obviously closer to the theoretical mid-point of the five-year legislature, since they took place at the end of March 2010 – almost two years after the general election. Nonetheless, despite this being a time when the 'honeymoon' is usually well and truly over for national governing parties (not to mention that the crisis in Europe was still in full swing), these elections were a clear success for the PDL–LN coalition. The term 'coalition' here is important since, unlike the 2009 EP election, the two parties ran together in the 2010 regional elections and agreed on coalition presidential candidates in each region (at least in those central and northern regions where the LN was also present). Elections were held in 13 regions, with 41 million citizens eligible to vote (Corbetta, 2012: 155). They thus represented an important national contest for the parties and coalitions. The elections took place against a backdrop of scandals concerning Berlusconi (See Appendix 1, year 2009). Once again, his response to this was to put himself at the centre of the campaign, both through his increased presence on television (far more than any other party leader) and his appeal to voters to 'take sides' for or against him (Cornia, 2010). However, in line with what we have said above, Berlusconi presented himself very much as the leader of a successful governing coalition rather than simply of the PDL. This was also reflected

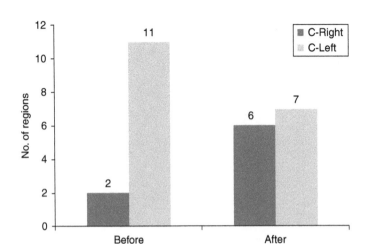

Figure 5.14 Regions governed by centre-right and centre-left coalitions, before and after the 2010 regional elections.

Source: Electoral archive of the Italian Interior Ministry: www.elezionistorico. interno.it.

in the main national centre-right campaign slogan: 'help the government of deeds to win'.

To get an idea of the overall performance of the PDL–LN coalition in 2010, the best way is to look at how many regions it controlled before and after these elections. As we can see from Figure 5.14, the balance in terms of regions governed by the centre-right and centre-left changed considerably, with the centre-right winning four regions from the centre-left (Piedmont, Lazio, Campania, and Calabria) and losing none. Moreover, as Piergiorgio Corbetta (2012: 163) notes, 'the population of the six centre-right regions is twice that of the seven centre-left regions' so we can say that, after the 2010 elections, over half of Italians now lived in regions governed by the centre-right.

In terms of specific party shares, the PDL received 29.6 per cent of votes cast in 2010 – a slight increase on FI and AN's combined total of 29.3 per cent in the 2005 regional elections (the previous time the same regions voted). It is also worth noting, however, that the PDL's 2010 result is significantly less than the 35.3 per cent it received in the same 13 regions at the 2009 EP elections (Ceccarini *et al.*, 2012: 61). As in 2009, again there were no such problems for the LN which, as Tronconi (2010: 582) observed, 'can rightfully claim to be the real winner of these elections'. Simply put, the 2010 regional elections were a triumph for the party. Not only did it increase its vote share to record levels across the North, achieving 35.2 per cent in Veneto and 26.2 per cent in Lombardy, but LN representatives (running as the candidates of the PDL–LN coalition) became presidents of two key northern regions for the first time

(Piedmont and Veneto). Indeed, in a sense, the first major 'victory' of the LN in these elections was that it was able to exert enough leverage on the PDL to secure the coalition's regional presidential candidatures for both Roberto Cota in Piedmont and Luca Zaia in Veneto. These were very significant concessions, especially given that the PDL had long been far stronger electorally than the LN in Piedmont and that Giancarlo Galan of the PDL held the regional presidency in Veneto (although unhappy, he was persuaded to step aside by the offer of a ministry in Rome). Zaia subsequently won easily in Veneto with 60 per cent of the vote and the Lega surpassed the PDL in that region for the first time, taking 35.2 per cent compared to the PDL's 24.7. Meanwhile in Piedmont, as an Istituto Cattaneo (2010) study shows, it was the personal vote for Cota which was decisive in the centre-right's extremely narrow victory.

To conclude this section, we can say that the PDL–LN coalition fared well in the two 'second-order' elections which took place during its time in national office. Of course, there were significant differences as regards individual party performances: the PDL did lose some votes, while the LN made very impressive gains. Nonetheless, when seen against the background not only of what usually happens to incumbents in second-order elections in Western Europe, but also that of a continent in which governing parties were taking heavy beatings at most elections (and often with no honeymoon period whatsoever), these results of the PDL–LN both as individual parties and, especially, as a coalition, are striking. It would be remiss of us not to note that, in the May 2011 local elections (when *c.*25 per cent of the electorate was eligible to vote), the PDL and the Lega suffered significant losses compared to their performances in these cities between 2008 and 2010 (Ceccarini *et al.*, 2012: 66; See also Appendix 1, year 2011). Notwithstanding this final drop in support before their government was replaced six months later by Monti's technocratic administration, however, we consider the record of the PDL and Lega Nord in elections during their time in office from 2008 to 2011 to be, overall, a positive one.

Post-incumbency general elections

Italy 2013

As explained earlier, it is problematic to consider the Italian general election held on 24–25 February 2013 as a normal 'post-incumbency' election for the PDL–LN alliance given that their government resigned in November 2011 (see Appendix 1, year 2011). Of particular relevance to our reading of the subsequent general election results is that, during the 14-month period between the fall of the PDL–LN government and the election: (1) the PDL supported the Monti administration along with the centre-left PD and centrist UDC (although the PDL was by far the most critical of the three parties); (2) Berlusconi took a back seat for much of the first year of the Monti government's time in office, but returned to centre stage in late 2012, when he decided to withdraw PDL support for Monti and to stand once again as the leader of the centre-right coalition at the 2013 election; (3) the LN remained in opposition for the full duration of the Monti government, thus bringing the PDL–LN alliance to an end (at least at national level). This was only re-established in January 2013, in the run-up to the general election that was held in February of the same year, when the PDL agreed to support Roberto Maroni's candidature as president of the Lombardy region (for which early elections were held on the same days as the general election); (4) in April 2012, it emerged that magistrates were investigating the misuse of public funds within the LN by Bossi and members of his family. This led to the leader's resignation on 5 April and his replacement by Maroni on 1 July of the same year; (5) the Movimento Cinque Stelle (M5S – Five-Star Movement), led by the comedian and activist Beppe Grillo, rapidly emerged as one of the major forces in Italian politics, particularly after April–May 2012 (Bartlett *et al.*, 2013: 21–28).

What transpired was the second most volatile general election of recent decades in Western Europe. Using Pederson's index of electoral volatility, we find an increase from 9.5 and 9.7 at the 2006 and 2008 Italian general elections to 41.3 in 2013 (Chiaramonte and Emanuele, 2013; Pedersen, 1979). This was second only to the May 2012 election in Greece, which registered a score of 42.3 (Hanretty, 2013). As Figure 5.15 shows, the PDL dropped 15.8 percentage points – and over six million voters (equivalent to half its electorate) – compared to 2008. Its main opponent, the PD, which had been expected to fare better, declined by almost eight points from 33.2 to 25.4 per cent (Bobba and McDonnell, 2013). The LN also did very poorly, shedding over 1.6 million votes – more than half the total it had received in 2008 – and slipping from 8.3 to 4.1 per cent (see Figure 5.15). It is important to note, though, that there was a very satisfying silver lining for the party since Maroni was elected president of the Lombardy region, meaning that the Lega had gained the presidencies of the three largest northern regions in just three years – a very considerable achievement for a regionalist party of its size.

There was also a silver lining for the PDL: while its result and that of the PDL–LN coalition were well down on 2008, so too was that of the centre-left. This is because, as we can see from Figure 5.16, Italy moved from being a strongly bipolar system in 2008 to a tripolar one in 2013, thanks to the remarkable debut general election result of the M5S, which received 25.6 per cent of the vote. Combined with the peculiar effects of Italy's electoral system, this set of results meant that the centre-left secured a majority in the Chamber of Deputies, but not in the Senate. Given the M5S's unwillingness to co-operate with the other parties and the broad agreement about the undesirability of fresh elections, the only possible solution was therefore a grand coalition between the PDL and PD. This duly occurred, after much turmoil and debate, when the PD's deputy leader, Enrico Letta, was appointed prime minister at the end of April 2013 (see Garzia, 2013: 1096–1098). While the PDL took up several key ministries in the new government, the Lega, again, returned to opposition.

As in 2008, the PDL again did best in the South, where it took 26.7 per cent of the vote. However, it lost many votes both there and in the rest of the country. As Fabio Bordignon and Fabio Turato (2013: 87) show, in 2008 the

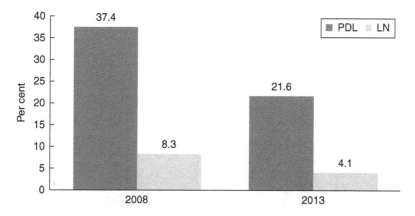

Figure 5.15 PDL and LN results in the 2008 and 2013 Italian general elections.
Source: Electoral service of the Italian Interior Ministry: http://elezioni.interno.it/.

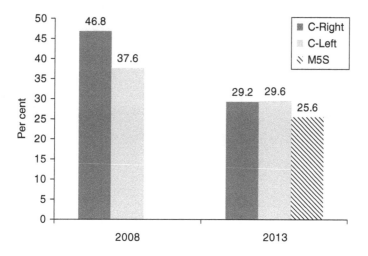

Figure 5.16 Main coalition results in the 2008 and 2013 Italian general elections.
Source: Electoral service of the Italian Interior Ministry: http://elezioni.interno.it/

PDL had come first in 67 of Italy's 110 provinces, mostly in the South but also in many parts of the north-west. In 2013, by contrast, it was the top party in just 17 provinces, all of them in the South except for the province of Como in the far North. Only 49 per cent of those who voted for PDL in 2008 did so again in 2013, with 18 per cent supporting the M5S and 11 per cent abstaining (Bordignon and Turato, 2013: 92). The LN also suffered heavy losses. Roberto Biorcio and Alice Securo (2013: 132) find that only 31 per cent of those who voted for the Lega in 2008 did so again in 2013, with 25 per cent voting for M5S and 10 per cent abstaining. Interestingly, despite the many upheavals in

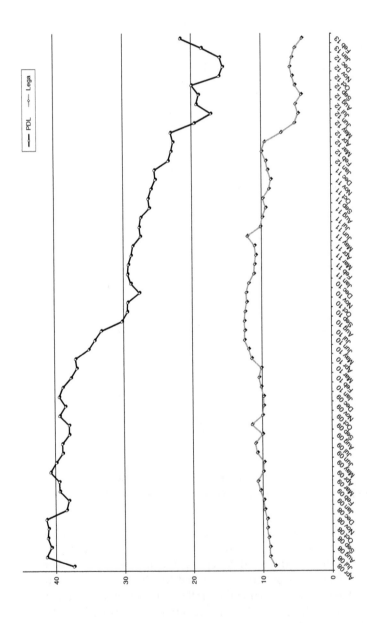

Figure 5.17 Average PDL and LN results in main opinion polls, April 2008–February 2013.

Note: All points in the graph display the averages of voting intention surveys for particular months, with the exceptions of April 2008 and February 2013, when general elections were held (we use the actual election data for these two months).

Source: Data concerning the parties are calculated using the averages of voting intention surveys conducted by the main Italian polling houses (Cfi, Crespi, Datamonitor, Demopolis, Demos, Digis, Emg, Euromedia, Fullresearch, Ipr, Ipsos, Ispo, Lorien, Piepoli, Swg, Tecne). These can be accessed at http://www.sondaggipoliticoelettorali.it/.

voting behaviour, the 'light loyalty' (Natale, 2007) which characterized previous elections seems at least partly present in 2013 as voters still did not tend to cross from centre-right to centre-left (or vice versa) in great numbers: both groups, however, were willing to transfer their support to the M5S.

As we have said, given the time gap between the end of the PDL–LN government in November 2011 and the general election in February 2013, it is difficult to consider this election entirely as a regular post-incumbency one. To gain a better idea of voter support for the PDL and LN during the period when they were in office, we decided to consider opinion poll data on the two parties. In addition to providing us with an idea of how the public saw the parties while they were in government, this also sheds considerable light on the general election results. Most noticeably, as Figure 5.17 shows, it seems fairly evident that the LN's performance in February 2013 had a lot to do with the scandal which had struck the party the previous year and very little to do with its time in government. In fact, during the years it was in office, the party never dropped below the 8.3 per cent it had received at the 2008 general election. Even in November 2011 when the government fell, the Lega was still at 8.6 per cent (its lowest point of the entire incumbency period). Moreover, during its initial months back in opposition in late 2011 and early 2012, the party rose again in the opinion polls. As we can clearly see from Figure 5.17, it is only once the scandal broke in April 2012 that the LN slump began, with the party swiftly dropping in just a couple of months to 4.6 per cent in June 2012 – the level at which it more or less remained until the general election. On the basis of these figures, it thus seems mistaken to attribute the party's general election result to its actions in government. Rather, the LN's poll results while in office seem extremely good.

The same is not true for the PDL, however. As we can see from Figure 5.17, it enjoyed an extended honeymoon and did not drop below its April 2008 general election result of 37.4 per cent until March 2010 when it scored 36.8 per cent. After a slight rise in April 2010, it began to fall rapidly. By August 2010, it had slipped to 30.2 per cent and it would continue to decline, almost without interruption, for the rest of its time in office. When considering the PDL's poll results, we thought it might be interesting to check the relationship between the governing parties' average poll figures and monthly consumer confidence trends, especially given the PDL's focus on the economy (see Chapters 2 and 6). We can see these in Figure 5.18 (overleaf), which looks at the variation of PDL and Lega poll results, along with that of the consumer confidence index (CCI), from the parties' scores in April 2008 and consumer confidence levels at the time of the 2008 election. As we suspected, after the PDL's long 'honeymoon period' ended in early 2010, the party's poll results mirrored fairly closely the decline in consumer confidence. By contrast – and in line with that party's 'delegation' of the economy to the PDL – the LN's results seem to be much less affected by consumer confidence trends.

Switzerland 2007

Like the 2013 general election in Italy, the Swiss federal election in October 2007 was also one of the most dramatic in that country's history. From the campaign

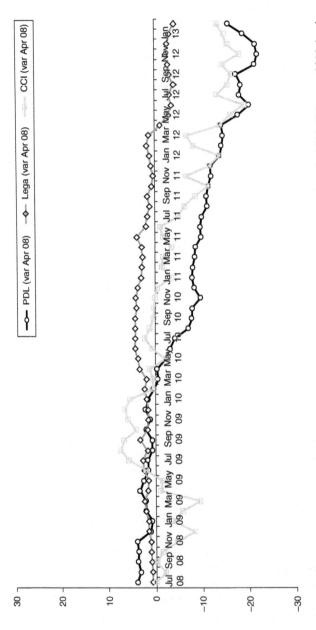

Figure 5.18 PDL and LN voting intentions and consumer confidence monthly trends, July 2008–February 2013 (variation on April 2008).

Note: All points in the graph display the averages of voting intention surveys for particular months, with the exception of February 2013, when the general election was held (we use the actual election data for this month). All points regarding party support display the variation from the April 2008 general election results. The CCI line shows the variation from its value in April 2008.

Source: Data concerning the parties are calculated using the averages of voting intention surveys conducted by the main Italian polling houses (Cfi, Crespi, Datamonitor, Demopolis, Demos, Digis, Emg, Euromedia, Fullresearch, Ipr, Ipsos, Ispo, Lorien, Piepoli, Swg, Tecne). These can be accessed at http://www.sondaggipoliticoelettorali.it/. The data for the Consumer Confidence Indicator (seasonally adjusted data) are taken from Eurostat: epp.eurostat.ec.europa.eu.

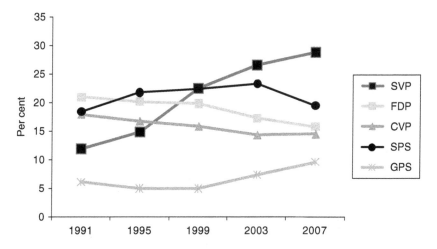

Figure 5.19 Vote shares of the five largest Swiss parties in National Council elections, 1991–2007.

Source: Swiss Confederation Federal Statistics Office: http://www.portal-stat.admin. ch/nrw/files/fr/01.xml and http://www.politik-stat.ch/nrw2011CH_it.html.

to the results to the aftermath, events which were highly unusual for Swiss politics occurred one after another. The first of these was that the elections were framed and fought, at least in part, as a referendum on Blocher. As Hanspeter Kriesi (2012: 840) says, in the month before the election, the SVP 'organized its entire campaign around its leader' and 'covered the whole country with gigantic posters showing its leader and the corresponding slogan'. The slogan referred to is 'Strengthen Blocher! Vote SVP!' and reflected the fact that, for the first time, a party had chosen to put a federal councillor at the centre of its election campaign communications (Burgos *et al.*, 2011: 90–91). The key message was that, despite Blocher's presence in government, the SVP remained an outsider which was still fighting against – and being attacked *by* – the establishment. In particular, it was claimed that all the other major parties were anxious to remove Blocher, i.e. not just the SPS and the Grüne Partei der Schweiz (GPS – Swiss Green Party), who were openly calling for him not to be re-elected to the Federal Council (Dardanelli, 2008: 749). This strategy was backed by an SVP campaign which was said to have cost a record amount (Milic, 2008: 1150).

The second unusual element of the election were the results: the SVP came first with both the highest percentage vote (28.9 per cent) and the largest number of National Council seats (62) of any party since proportional representation was introduced in 1919 (although given the SVP's excellent results in 1999 and 2003, this was perhaps not so unusual). As we can see from Figure 5.19, the SVP increased its share by 2.2 percentage points compared to 2003 and gained seven extra seats (Figure 5.20 overleaf). Figure 5.19 also shows that the gap between the SVP and the second-placed SPS widened

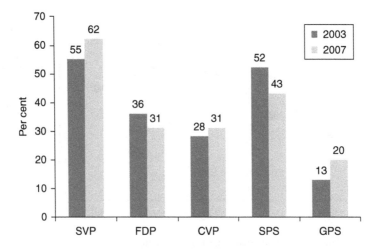

Figure 5.20 Seats of the SVP, FDP, CVP, SPS, and GPS in the National Council, 2003 vs 2007.

Source: Swiss Confederation Federal Statistics Office: http://www.portal-stat.admin. ch/nrw/files/fr/01.xml and http://www.politik-stat.ch/nrw2011CH_it.html.

Table 5.3 Seats won by the four main parties in the Council of States, 1991–2007

	1991	*1995*	*1999*	*2003*	*2007*
SVP	4	5	7	8	7
FDP	18	17	17	14	12
CVP	16	16	15	15	15
SPS	3	5	6	9	9

Sources: http://www.politik-stat.ch/srw2011CH_it.html and http://www.portal-stat. admin.ch/nrw/files/fr/02.xml.

from 3.4 to 9.4 percentage points while, as we can see from Figure 5.20, the SVP's 62 seats in the National Council was equal to the total of those held by the two parties which had once dominated centre-right politics, the CVP and the FDP. The SVP was thus the clear winner of this election, along with the GPS, which was the sole other party to significantly increase both its vote share and number of National Council seats (for this reason, we have chosen to include it in figures 5.19 and 5.20). Due to the SVP and GPS gains and the losses of their rivals, the three parties which had dominated Swiss politics for decades – the FDP, CVP, and SPS – now held just over half (105) of the 200 National Council seats (down from 116 in 2003). Indeed, the total vote share of these three parties in 2007 was less than half, at just 49.8 per cent, down from 55 per cent in 2003. Finally, as promised earlier in this chapter, we should note the results in the Council of States election – although, for the reasons explained previously, we do not consider these in our analysis. The only aspect worth noting, for our purposes, is that the SVP did not suffer any major losses between 2003 and 2007, with its number of seats reduced just by one (see Table 5.3).

Once again, the main 'victim' of the SVP in the National Council elections was the FDP. The 2007 federal election edition of the Swiss Election Study (Selects) by George Lutz shows that 10 per cent of those who voted for the FDP in 2003 supported the SVP in 2007, while 5 per cent of those who had voted for the CVP also did so (Lutz, 2008: 17). In geographical terms, the most interesting aspect of the SVP's performance was, as had already been apparent in 2003, the increasingly national character of its support. Not only did it score over 30 per cent in many German-speaking cantons, but it received *c.* 20 per cent in French-speaking ones (Church, 2008: 613). There were several individual cantonal results which are worth noting here. One is the party's performance in the canton of Berne – long considered the home of the moderate, traditional SVP – where it increased from 29.6 per cent in 2003 to 33.6 per cent in 2007. In other words, despite Blocher's actions being very unlike those of previous federal councillors from the Bernese wing of the party, the voters in that canton did not punish the SVP. More striking, perhaps, were the party's results in the two largest French-speaking cantons of Vaud and Geneva, where it scored 22.4 per cent and 21.1 per cent, respectively, making it the most-voted single party in each canton (in 2003 it had received 20.3 per cent in Vaud and 18.3 per cent in Geneva, thus finishing second in both).

The final unusual aspect of the 2007 federal election was of course its aftermath, by which we mean the chain reaction of Blocher's failure to be re-elected to the Federal Council in December, the SVP's decision not to recognize Eveline Widmer-Schlumpf and Samuel Schmid as legitimate SVP federal councillors and, following that, the party's move into opposition. This brief and tumultuous period is discussed in Chapter 4, so we do not need to go over it at length now. What is important to stress here is that, although what happened may have been largely the product of Blocher's actions during his four years in government, we should not lose sight of the fact that – irrespective of how the other parties reacted in 2007 to Blocher's participation in the Federal Council – the *voters* did not punish the SVP. On the contrary, as we have seen, after a campaign which revolved around Blocher and his presence in government, support for the SVP rose to record levels.

Conclusion

This chapter began by recalling that governing parties of all ideological types in coalitions in Western Europe tend to pay an electoral price for participation in office (Rose and Mackie, 1983; Müller and Strøm, 2006; Nannestad and Paldam, 1999) and that 'average losses have become progressively larger over the last few decades' (Narud and Valen, 2008). We then considered the limited evidence presented so far in the literature concerning the electoral effects of participation in government on populist parties (Buelens and Hino, 2008;

Van Spanje, 2011; Akkerman and de Lange, 2012) and concluded, based on a re-examination of cases in Austria, the Netherlands, and Denmark, that an overly negative view of this has so far prevailed. In particular, as we noted, there is little from these cases to suggest that collaboration with mainstream parties will inevitably have long-term detrimental electoral effects for populists. This set the scene for the rest of the chapter in which we looked in detail at the electoral performances of the SVP relevant to its 2003–2007 period of incumbency and those of the PDL and LN relevant to their time in government between 2008 and 2011. There is no need at this point to restate all that was said with regard to the specific pre-incumbency, second-order and post-incumbency elections in the two countries. Rather, we will recap our main findings as regards electoral performances.

In sum, on the basis of the evidence presented, we can safely say that the SVP did not pay any price at the ballot box either during or after its participation in government. It did not suffer losses at subnational level and, far more importantly, it achieved not only its best ever result in the 2007 National Council election, but the best result of any Swiss party since 1919. As we noted, Blocher's actions in government may subsequently have been punished by the other main parties when they did not re-elect him to the Federal Council, but the voters provided no such sanction. Even allowing for the caveats stated earlier concerning the meaning and implications of government participation in Switzerland, the SVP is a clear example of populist incumbent electoral success. In the Italian case, in addition to general elections, we also looked closely at two second-order elections: the 2009 EP election and the 2010 regional ones. We concluded that, particularly when seen against the backdrop of the post-2008 crisis in Europe (when governing parties almost everywhere were punished by voters), the performances of the PDL and LN in these second-order elections can only be viewed positively. This is especially so if we consider the PDL–LN as a coalition rather than just as individual parties. Both parties eventually lost heavily in 2013 but, as we explained, the opinion poll data presented show that the LN's general election performance had far more to do with events after its time in office than with those during it. In general, therefore, the experiences of both the Lega Nord and the SVP in government recall the conclusion by Eoin O'Malley (2010: 558) regarding junior coalition partners in Ireland that this type of party 'can survive and even thrive in government where it delivers on a "signature" policy and gains credit for having done so' (O'Malley, 2010: 558). As we will see in the next chapter, both parties did indeed focus on delivering specific 'signature' policies which were in line with their core ideologies and the expectations of those within their parties (see Chapter 7).

The case of the PDL is different since, after the end of its long honeymoon period in early 2010, it did indeed begin to lose public support. We suggested that this decline may be linked to the fact that it had stuck its colours so strongly to the flag of economic revival. As Wouter van der Brug, Cees van der Eijk, and Mark Franklin (2007) have shown, bad economic conditions tend to hurt larger parties in coalitions more so than junior partners, particularly where responsibility for economic policy is clear – something that was certainly the case in the PDL–LN government. This also links to the finding by Narud and Valen (2008: 398) that parties which hold the Finance Ministry (as the PDL did) are more likely to be held accountable for the poor state of the economy than other coalition members. In the next chapter, we will closely examine the PDL's emphasis on the economy while in office and its failure to deliver on this issue (although, as Chapter 7 shows, those within the party thought differently). For now, however, we can say that, on the whole, the cases we have presented in this chapter demonstrate that it is by no means a given that office is electorally damaging for populists. On the contrary, and especially when it is not their first time in government, populist parties may be well able to maintain, and even increase, their support.

Notes

1 As we noted in the introductory chapter, although the FPÖ had been in government before its transformation into a populist party in the 1980s, its time in office after 2000 was its first *as a populist party* in power.
2 According to a Megafon poll in late December 2013, the Danish People's Party was at 18.5 per cent. See: http://www.megafon.dk/default.asp?Action=Details&Item=362 (accessed January 2014); Another polling house, Voxmeter, had the party scoring at least 15 per cent in the last five weeks of 2013. See: http://www.voxmeter.dk/index.php/meningsmalinger/?lang=en (accessed January 2014). Indeed, a Yougov poll in mid-December 2013 put the party at 20 per cent. See: http://www.b.dk/berlingske-barometer (accessed January 2014).
3 Italy is divided into 20 regions, of which 15 are 'ordinary statute' (Piedmont, Lombardy, Veneto, Liguria, Emilia-Romagna, Tuscany, Umbria, Marche, Lazio, Abruzzo, Molise, Campania, Puglia, Basilicata, Calabria) and five, which have greater powers under the Constitution, are 'special statute' (Friuli Venezia Giulia, Sardinia, Sicily, Trentino-South Tyrol, and Aosta Valley). See: http://www.interno.gov.it/mininterno/export/sites/default/en/themes/state-local_authority_relations/The_Regions.html.

Bibliography

Akkerman, T. and de Lange, S. (2012) 'Radical Right Parties in Office: Incumbency Records and the Electoral Cost of Governing', *Government and Opposition*, 47 (4), 574–596.

Albertazzi, D., McDonnell, D., and Newell, J. (2011) '*Di lotta e di governo*: The Lega Nord and Rifondazione Comunista in Office', *Party Politics*, 17 (4), 471–487.

Bartlett, J., Froio, C., and McDonnell, D. (2013) *New Political Actors in Europe: Beppe Grillo and the M5S*, London: Demos UK.

Biorcio, R. and Securo, A. (2013) 'Il paradosso della Lega Nord', in Diamanti, I. (ed.), *Un Salto nel Voto*, Rome: Laterza.

Bobba, G. and McDonnell, D. (2013) 'Italy Passes a No-Confidence Verdict in the Centre-Left', *Policy* Network. Available at: http://www.policy-network.net/pno_detail.aspx?ID=4349&title=Italy+passes+a+no-confidence+verdict+in+the+centre-left, 4 March 2013 (accessed October 2013).

Bordignon, F. and Turato, F. (2013) 'Il Popolo della libertà: un Pdl-meno-P', in Diamanti, I. (ed.), *Un Salto nel Voto*, Rome: Laterza.

Bosco, A. and McDonnell, D. (2012) 'Introduction: The Monti Government and the Downgrade of Italian Parties', in Bosco, A. and McDonnell, D. (eds), *From Berlusconi to Monti*, New York: Berghahn.

Bressanelli, E., Calderaro, A., Piccio, D., and Stamati, F. (2010) 'Italy', in Gagatek, W. (ed.), *The 2009 Elections to the European Parliament: Country Reports*, Florence: European University Institute.

Buelens, J. and Hino, A. (2008) 'The Electoral Fate of New Parties in Government', in Deschouwer, K. (ed.), *New Parties in Government: In Power for the First Time*, Oxford: Routledge.

Burgos, E., Mazzoleni, O., and Rayner, H. (2011) *La formule magique, conflits et consensus dans l'élection du Conseil fédéral*, Lausanne: Presses Polytechniques Romandes.

Caramani, D. (2004) *The Nationalization of Politics. The Formation of National Electorates and Party Systems in Western Europe*, Cambridge: Cambridge University Press.

Ceccarini, L., Diamanti, I., and Lazar, M. (2012) 'The End of an Era: The Crumbling of The Italian Party System', in Bosco, A. and McDonnell, D. (eds), *From Berlusconi to Monti*, New York: Berghahn.

Chiaramonte, A. and Emanuele, V. (2013) 'Volatile e tripolare: il nuovo sistema partitico italiano'. Available at: http://cise.luiss.it/cise/2013/02/27/volatile-e-tripolare-il-nuovo-sistema-partitico-italiano/, 27 February 2013 (accessed October 2013).

Church, C. (2008) 'The Swiss Elections of 21 October 2007: Consensus Fights Back', *West European Politics*, 31 (3), 608–623.

Colomer, J.M. (2012) 'Firing the Coach: How Governments are Losing Elections in Europe', *Democracy & Society*, 10 (1), 1–6.

Corbetta, P. (2012) 'The 2010 Regional Elections in Italy: Another Referendum on Berlusconi', *South European Society and Politics*, 17 (2), 155–173.

Cornia, A. (2010) 'Una campagna elettorale molto poco regionale', in Baldi, B. and Tronconi, F. (eds), *Le elezioni regionali del 2010*, Bologna: Il Mulino.

Cotta, M. and Verzichelli, L. (2007) *Political Institutions in Italy*, Oxford: Oxford University Press.

D'Alimonte, R. (2008) 'Il verdetto elettorale', in *ITANES: Il ritorno di Berlusconi*, Bologna: Il Mulino.

Dardanelli, P. (2008) 'The Swiss Federal Elections of 2007', *Electoral Studies*, 27 (4), 748–751.

Dinkel, R. (1977) 'Der Zusammenhang zwischen Bundes-und Landtagswahlergebnissen', *Politische Vierteljahresschrift*, 18 (3), 348–360.

Garzia, D. (2013) 'The 2013 Italian Parliamentary Election: Changing Things so Everything Stays the Same', *West European Politics*, 36 (5), 1095–1105.

Hanretty, C. (2013) 'The Most Volatile Western European Election Ever?'. Available at: http://chrishanretty.co.uk/blog/index.php/2013/02/25/the-most-volatile-western-european-election-ever/, 25 February 2013 (accessed November 2013).

Hardmeier, S. (2004) 'Switzerland', *European Journal of Political Research*, 43 (7–8), 1151–1159.

Heinisch, R. (2008) 'Austria: The Structure and Agency of Austrian Populism', in Albertazzi, D. and McDonnell, D. (eds), *Twenty-First Century Populism: The Spectre of Western European Democracy*, Basingstoke: Palgrave Macmillan.

Istituto Cattaneo (2008) 'Un'analisi dei flussi elettorali'. Available at: http://www.cattaneo.org/pubblicazioni/analisi/pdf/Analisi%20Cattaneo%20-%20Flussi%20elettorali%202008%20(15%20maggio%202008).pdf (accessed October 2013).

Istituto Cattaneo (2009) 'I flussi elettorali tra le elezioni politiche del 2008 e quelle europee del 2009'. Available at: http://www.cattaneo.org/pubblicazioni/analisi/pdf/Analisi%20Istituto%20Cattaneo%20-%20Flussi%20elettorali%202008-2009%20(24%20giugno%202009).pdf (accessed October 2013).

Istituto Cattaneo (2010) 'Personalizzazione e bipolarismo diminuiti nel 2010'. Available at: http://www.cattaneo.org/pubblicazioni/analisi/pdf/Analisi%20Istituto%20Cattaneo%20-%20Voto%20regionale%202010%20-%20Personalizzazione%20del%20voto%20(30.3.2010).pdf (accessed October 2013).

Jeffery, C. and Hough, D. (2003) 'Regional Elections in Multi-Level Systems', *European Urban and Regional Studies*, 10 (3), 199–212.

Kriesi, H. (2012) 'Personalization of National Election Campaigns', *Party Politics*, 18 (6), 825–844.

Kriesi, H. (2014) 'The Political Consequences of the Financial and Economic Crisis in Europe: Electoral Punishment and Popular Protest', in Bermeo, N. and Bartels, L.M. (eds), *Mass Politics in Tough Times: Opinions, Votes, and Protest in the Great Recession*, Oxford: Oxford University Press, 297–333.

Lachat, R. (2006) 'A Tale of Two Councils. Explaining the Weakness of the SVP in the Upper House of the Federal Parliament', *Swiss Political Science Review*, 12 (4), 77–99.

Loughlin, J. and Bolgherini, S. (2006) 'Regional Elections in Italy: National Tests or Regional Affirmation?', in Hough, D. and Jeffery, C. (eds), *Devolution and Electoral Politics: A Comparative Exploration*, Manchester: Manchester University Press.

Lucardie, P. (2008) 'The Netherlands: Populism versus Pillarization', in Albertazzi, D. and McDonnell, D. (eds), *Twenty-First Century Populism: The Spectre of Western European Democracy*, Basingstoke: Palgrave Macmillan.

Luther, R. (2011) 'Of Goals and Own Goals: A Case Study of Right-wing Populist Party Strategy for and during Incumbency', *Party Politics*, 17 (4), 453–470.

Lutz, G. (2008) *Elezioni Federali 2007: Partecipazione e decisione di voto*, Lausanne: Selects – FORS. Available at: http://forscenter.ch/wp-content/uploads/2013/10/selects_07_i.pdf (accessed October 2013).

McDonnell, D. and Newell, J. (2011) 'Outsider Parties in Government in Western Europe', *Party Politics*, 17 (4), 443–452.

Maghalhães, P.C. (2012) 'Economy, Ideology and the Elephant in the Room: A Research Note on the Elections of the Great Recession in Europe'. Available at: http://ssrn.com/abstract=2122416 or http://dx.doi.org/10.2139/ssrn.2122416 (accessed October 2013).

Massetti, E. and Sandri, G. (2013) 'Italy: Between Growing Incongruence and Region Specific Dynamics', in Dandoy, R. and Schakel, A. (eds), *Regional and National Elections in Western Europe: Territoriality of the Vote in Thirteen Countries*, Basingstoke: Palgrave Macmillan.

Milic, T. (2008) 'Switzerland', *European Journal of Political Research*, 47 (7–8), 1148–1155.

Müller, W.C. and Strøm, K. (eds) (2006) *Coalition Governments in Western Europe*, Oxford: Oxford University Press.

Nannestad, P. and Paldam, M. (1999) 'The Cost of Ruling. A Foundation Stone for Two Theories', Working Paper No. 1999-9, Department of Economics, University of Aarhus. Available at: ftp://ftp.econ.au.dk/afn/wp/99/wp99_9.pdf (accessed October 2013).

Narud, H. and Valen, H. (2008) 'Coalition Membership and Electoral Performance', in Strøm, K., Müller, W.C., and Bergman, T. (eds), *Cabinets and Coalition Bargaining: The Democratic Life Cycle in Western Europe*, Oxford: ECPR/Oxford University Press.

Natale, P. (2007) 'Mobilità elettorale e "fedeltà leggera": i movimenti di voto', in Feltrin, P., Natale, P. and Ricolfi, L. (eds), *Nel segreto dell'urna: un'analisi delle elezioni politiche del 2006*, Turin: UTET.

O'Malley, E. (2010) 'Punch Bags for Heavyweights? Minor Parties in Irish Government', *Irish Political Studies*, 25 (4), 539–561.

Pedersen, M. (1979) 'The Dynamics of European Party Systems: Changing Patterns of Electoral Volatility', *European Journal of Political Research*, 7 (1), 1–26.

Reif, K. and Schmitt, H. (1980) 'Nine Second-Order National Elections. A Conceptual Framework for the Analysis of European Election Results', *European Journal of Political Research*, 8 (1), 3–44.

Rose, R. and Mackie, T. (1983) 'Incumbency in Government: Asset or Liability?', in Daalder, H. and Mair, P. (eds), *Western European Party Systems: Continuity and Change*, London: Sage.

Schmitt, H. (2005) 'The European Parliament Elections of June 2004: Still Second-Order?', *West European Politics*, 28 (3), 650–679.

Selb, P. (2006) 'Multi-Level Elections in Switzerland', *Swiss Political Science Review*, 12 (4), 49–75.

Selb, P. and Lachat, R. (2004) *Elezioni 2003: L'evoluzione del comportamento elettorale*, Zurich: Institut für Politikwissenschaft. Available at: http://www2.unil.ch/selects/IMG/pdf/Elezioni2003.pdf (accessed October 2013).

Tronconi, F. (2010) 'The Italian Regional Elections of March 2010. Continuity and a Few Surprises', *Regional and Federal Studies*, 20 (4–5), 577–586.

Tronconi, F. and Roux, C. (2009) 'The Political Systems of Italian Regions between State-wide Logics and Increasing Differentiation', *Modern Italy*, 14 (2), 151–166.

Van der Brug, W., van der Eijk, C., and Franklin, M. (2007) *The Economy and the Vote: Economic Conditions and Elections in Fifteen Countries*, New York: Cambridge University Press.

Van Spanje, J. (2011) 'Keeping the Rascals In: Anti-political-establishment Parties and Their Cost of Governing in Established Democracies', *European Journal of Political Research*, 50 (5), 609–635.

6   Pledges vs actions in government

In Chapter 1, we justified the need to assess the performance of populist parties in power and took issue with the dominant scholarly view of these parties, which argues that they can be neither 'durable nor sustainable parties of government' (Mény and Surel, 2002: 18) and 'will usually fade fast' (Taggart, 2004: 270). Nonetheless, we are well aware that taking office is fraught with danger for populists. This is both a matter of substance (in particular, achieving policy success) and form (e.g. adopting the right communication strategy and being able to 'sell' the inevitable compromises of coalition government to those within the party and the electorate at large).

In this and the following chapter, we discuss the above issues. First, in the present chapter, we identify the pledges made in the three selected parties' manifestos concerning their key themes prior to entering government (in the case of the SVP, in 2003; in those of the LN and PDL, in 2008). Second, we assess the extent to which these pledges were subsequently fulfilled, in order to ascertain whether or not populists delivered what *they* promised. Our conclusion will be that, although the extent to which the three parties in this study were successful in government varied, we have found no evidence that they were *inevitably* destined to fail. Nor is it the case that they had to renounce their identity and key policy proposals.[1] Having completed this analysis, in Chapter 7 we will show that the party leaders managed to keep their representatives and members on board, convincing them that they were doing a good job in government. In other words, these parties were successful overall in selling their achievements and in justifying setbacks to those within them.

We will assess the performance of populist parties in government by starting with Italy, before then considering the Swiss case.

The Lega Nord

The fundamental objectives of the Lega Nord have not changed significantly since its creation, and can be summarized as follows: (a) achieving greater northern autonomy; (b) defending the people from its 'enemies' – essentially criminals and migrants (whether from southern Italy in the 1980s, Africans and Albanians in the 1990s, or Muslims after 11 September 2011). The study of the party's key documentation (see Chapter 3) and strategic communication (Albertazzi and McDonnell, 2010: 1329–1335), in addition to the analyses of interviews with LN members and representatives and the survey of members and sympathizers conducted for this study (see Chapter 7), all underline the centrality of these themes. The LN's performance in government between 2008 and 2011 will therefore be assessed by considering what the party has done in policy terms on these issues, starting with the 'freedom' of the North.

Greater northern autonomy

One of the LN's main aims after the 2008 election was securing the approval of a fiscal federalism reform, seen as a first step to achieving federalism. Fiscal federalism was duly passed on 30 April 2009 (the 42/2009 framework law) and immediately hailed by the LN as a 'turning point in history' (Lega Nord, 2009a: 4). However, when the law is compared with what was called for in the party's election manifesto, it appears in fact to be a timid reform.

The desirability of federalism has always been predicated by the *leghisti* mainly on financial grounds. The 'Resolutions' passed by the 'Parliament of the North' in 2008 – which, according to the former Interior Minister, Roberto Maroni, should be regarded as the official party manifesto for the 2008 election (see http://www.youtube.com/watch?v=ulprGndDP9o, accessed 29 May 2013) – included the demand that Italian regions be allowed to keep 90 per cent of the tax revenue raised within their borders for a period of ten years.[2] This, it was argued, would allow northern regions to finance essential, but costly, infrastructure projects. At the end of this period, regions would continue to retain the same percentage provided they took responsibility for a share of the public debt (Parlamento del Nord, 2008). This latter proposal is patently unconstitutional and was not turned into law.[3] What the 2009 legislation introduced, however, was the principle of some limited 'autonomy of taxation' at all subnational institutional levels (city councils, provinces, and regions) – to be achieved through the levying of 'own taxes' by subnational administrations and a share of the proceeds from revenue taxes (Art. 2). By ensuring that services offered by local administrations were paid for, at least in part, through local taxes, the new law aimed at encouraging citizens to monitor how their money was being spent, thereby increasing accountability. This principle was perfectly consistent with the LN's ideology. However, it was contradicted by initiatives taken by the coalition government, both before and after Law 42/2009 was passed. For instance, shortly after the government was sworn in, it abolished the municipal property levy (ICI) – a property tax paid by local residents – and compensated for the loss of revenue with transfers from central government.[4] In addition, the autonomy of subnational administrations was reduced by three subsequent emergency decrees to tackle the worsening financial crisis of the post-2008 period: the *Disegno di legge*

(Dl – Legislative Decree) 78/2010, the Dl 98/2011, and the Dl 138/2011. These cut the resources available to subnational administrations by *c.* 12 per cent (Ambrosanio and Bordignon, 2011), thus dealing another heavy blow to the application of federalist principles and indeed prompting one commentator to liken the Dl 98/2011 to a 'bomb' thrown at the 'process of implementation of fiscal federalism' (Zanardi, 2011).[5] There has therefore been a noticeable discrepancy between the principle of federalism and financial autonomy championed by the 2009 legislation and what the government actually *did* in the 2008–2011 period, by cutting resources to subnational administrations.

The Law 42/2009 also established an 'equalizing fund' which was designed to guarantee a minimum level of services in all regions. This again appears problematic from the perspective of the LN. The law envisaged a specific set of rules and regulations for the attribution of supplementary resources and special aid to regions 'in which the regional tax revenue per inhabitant ... is less than the average national tax revenue per inhabitant' (Art. 9) (read: southern regions). The stated aim of this was to reduce 'the interregional differences of tax revenue per inhabitant' (ibid.). In its 'Resolutions', the LN had accepted that an equalizing fund would need to be introduced (Parlamento del Nord, 2008). After all, article 119 of the Constitution stipulates that any financial autonomy granted to subnational administrations must be mitigated by the establishment of such a fund, in order to protect poorer regions. The devil, however, was in the detail, and specifically the size and scope of this fund. Dl 68/2011 (one of the decrees implementing the new legislation) stated that the fund had to guarantee *full* and *complete* coverage throughout Italy of essential services such as health, education, and local transport, which together make up 80 per cent of regional expenditure (Muraro, 2011). In addition, as Emanuele Massetti (2012: 143) explains: 'high levels of national solidarity are strengthened by the provisions of Legislative Decree No. 88/2011, which restates the objective of economic convergence between regions'. In short, as Gilberto Muraro (2011) has said, to get the reform passed, the LN had to settle for what he terms 'high solidarity federalism'. The clear implication of this is that northern Italy would not enjoy the type of fiscal autonomy called for in the LN manifesto. If the LN's intention was to 'produce an ambitious reform that would tackle many of Italy's structural problems – in particular public spending inefficiency, low political accountability, excessive cross-regional financial redistribution, and excessive tax burdens' (Massetti, 2012: 143), and grant considerable financial autonomy to 'all levels of government' (Lega Nord, 2009b: 3), then the results achieved while the party was in power between 2008 and 2011 were clearly more modest.

Despite these shortcomings, however, the legislation did introduce some changes in line with those indicated by the LN's pre-election manifesto. These included the important stipulation that pre-defined 'standard' costs and 'standard' requirements were to be used in place of the *spesa storica* (historic expenditure) as the criteria for deciding funding levels for essential services.[6] This was obviously meant to increase efficiency – although, arguably, it is simplistic to assume that the same services can be provided at the same cost everywhere in a country, without taking into account the infrastructure available, local conditions, etc. (Viesti, 2010: 735–736). If intelligently applied, however, this aspect of the reform clearly has the potential to impact positively on how resources are administered at subnational level. Therefore, one could contend that – while obviously not the revolutionary reform claimed by the LN – 'fiscal federalism' may be seen as a first, tentative, but potentially significant, step towards a much more 'complete' federalism to be achieved in the future. In short, some degree of change *was* delivered by this reform: first, the link between local taxation and provision of local services was established – although only on paper, and despite the government introducing cuts that, in actual fact, hit subnational administrations; second, the foundations for fostering efficiency were laid through the introduction of the principle of 'standard' costs and expenditures. For all the Lega's rhetoric, however, the law only constituted a modest step forward.

Law and order and immigration

While the realization of fully fledged federalism therefore remained a long-term and complex goal, the other key theme for the Lega, *la sicurezza* ('security', understood as the defence of 'the people' against migrants and criminals), offered the party more immediate opportunities for straightforward and spectacular – albeit, in reality, usually just symbolic – gains. Before and after the 2008 election, the LN made several headline-grabbing proposals that did not come to pass but nonetheless generated considerable publicity for the party, such as the suggested introduction of special classes in schools for immigrant children, a halt to all immigration for two years, restricted access for illegal immigrants to social services, and a long series of other repressive proposals. Moreover, it also launched controversial campaigns that attracted the attention of the international media, such as the one in the town of Coccaglio in 2009 against illegal immigrants (disturbingly dubbed 'White Christmas' by the local LN mayor) (Hooper, 2009). As for its actions in national government after 2008, the LN championed a barrage of hard-line measures against immigration, such as the *respingimenti* and the census of Romany people resident in Italy. The *respingimenti* – meaning 'rejections' of boatloads of mainly African migrants trying to reach Italy by crossing the Mediterranean sea – became frequent in the run-up to the June 2009 European Parliament (EP) elections. They were found on 23 February 2012 to be in violation of article 3 of the European Convention on Human Rights by the European Court of Justice (ECJ) (Polchi, 2012). As for the census and fingerprinting of members of the Romany community (including children) that started shortly after the 2008 election, it was severely criticized by the General Secretary of the Council of Europe (CoE) in June 2008, by the Commissioner of the same institution the following month, and by a motion passed in the EP, again in July. In short, the LN repeatedly promoted initiatives that caused international outcries, with the apparent aim of generating publicity and establishing issue ownership over the themes of law and order and immigration (Albertazzi and McDonnell, 2010). This is not surprising, since a key aspect of the party's discursive strategy has always been to equate 'laxity' towards migrants/foreigners with increased crime and insecurity, despite the link between the two being unproven (Pinotti *et al.*, 2009; Boeri, 2010).

For our purposes, it is necessary to consider the proposals concerning *la sicurezza* made by the LN in its 2008 pre-election manifesto. The most prominent of these were: (a) the introduction of heavier punishments for a series of offences alleged to be linked to migration, such as prostitution; (b) the legalization of the *ronde*, i.e. associations of volunteers conducting patrols in cities and towns; (c) making it compulsory for Muslims to hold religious gatherings and celebrate rites in Italian (presumably to facilitate the work of the secret services as they eavesdropped on such events); (d) granting permits for the building (or enlargement) of mosques only following local referendums; (e) giving mayors the right to expel illegal migrants; and (f) banning the construction of Roma traveller camps, even when these were not on illegal sites.[7] The question for us here, as in the case of federalism, is how many of these proposals were actually turned into law. As we will see, although the legislation sponsored by the Lega and the party manifesto were inspired by the same principles (first and foremost the idea that a safer society could be created through greater repression and crime control), actual results were modest.

The main focus of our analysis will be the 'security package' – high-profile legislation on 'security' issues – that was championed by the LN and passed in July 2009. The 'package' (Law 94/2009) – a complex and heterogeneous document covering a wide variety of themes and crimes – was sold by the LN to its electorate as a comprehensive set of measures that would make the country safer (Cota, 2009). The first thing to note is that, of the pre-election proposals made by the LN on this issue, only two became law: the introduction of heavier punishments for a series of offences (ranging from graffiti to insulting public officials to organized crime) and the legalization of the *ronde*. However, the latter measure had hardly any impact. This was, first, since very few *ronde* ever came into existence (Polchi, 2010) and, second, because point 40 of article 3 of the law (concerning the *ronde*) was declared 'partially illegitimate' by the Constitutional Court in June 2010 (due to its being in conflict with the Constitution) (*Il Giornale*, 2010). In short, the *ronde* offered yet another example of the LN engaging in symbolic politics through the introduction of measures of dubious constitutional legitimacy.

Of the measures contained in the 'security package', the one that attracted most attention had not in fact been listed in the party manifesto: the introduction of the 'crime of illegal immigration' (meaning that those without valid residence permits could be given prison sentences). However, this norm was thrown out by the ECJ on 28 April 2011 because it was deemed to be in conflict with the European directive on the repatriation of illegal immigrants (*La Repubblica*, 2011). This aside, it can be argued that the LN introduced legislation relevant to only a few of those measures proposed in its mani-festo (perhaps knowing that many of them would also have fallen foul of the Constitutional Court or international law). However, the party undoubtedly acted both in government and in parliament in ways that were fully consistent with the approach to immigration and law and order advocated before the election. As for the practical consequences of the legislation introduced while the LN was in power – for example, whether the number of migrants, espe-cially illegal migrants, declined and whether crime figures fell – the results are contradictory. Importantly, the 'security package' was immediately followed by an amnesty for 300,000 people, which did reduce the number of illegal migrants, but only by legalizing their presence in the country – the second amnesty of this kind passed by the centre-right in less than a decade, and the sixth in Italy since the late 1980s (Ambrosini, 2010). Moreover, for all the talk about 'rejections' of boatloads in 2009, the overall number of foreigners living in Italy steadily increased (Caritas/Migrantes, 2009, 2011; Istat, 2011). As for the question of whether the 'security package' and, more generally, the measures sponsored by the LN made Italy safer, data published by the Italian Istituto nazionale di statistica (Istat – National Institute of Statistics) show that the overall number of crimes reported to the police between 2008 and 2010 did in fact decline (dropping from 2,709,888 to 2,621,019) (Istat, 2010b; also Censis, 2011: 529–530). However, it is simplistic to attribute this trend exclusively to the approval of the 'package'. Nonetheless, although the decrease was modest (not to mention the fact that the figures represent the number of *reported* crimes), this result could arguably be brandished as a suc-cess by the centre-right government and the LN in particular (as the sponsor of the new legislation).

Whether one considers the legislation advocated by the LN or what the party could claim its outcomes to be, the Lega's achievements in govern-ment thus appear to have been limited. Concerning *la sicurezza*, it delivered only a few of the measures it had talked about before the 2008 election, and what it delivered was sometimes thrown out by the courts. As far as legisla-tion was concerned, however, the LN did not betray the essentially repres-sive approach to law and order which it had always advocated and it did make some progress on themes dear to the party, particularly federalism. As for actual government actions, in some cases, such as the cuts imposed on local administrations and the amnesty for illegal migrants, the party none-theless went along with measures wholly contradicting its alleged objectives in government.

The Popolo della Libertà

The most high-profile initiatives taken by the PDL in government concerning issues that the party, as opposed to the LN, could be said to 'own', were the following: (a) the launch of two reforms, the first presented in June 2008 to make the public administration more efficient, and the second in August/

September 2008, introducing major changes to the education system; (b) the approval of several bills between 2008 and 2011 containing measures that politicians could use to avoid attending court trials, arguably aimed at helping the PM Silvio Berlusconi and some of his close associates in some of the trials in which they were involved at the time (Albertazzi and Mueller, 2013: 356–357). For instance, in July 2008 the 'Alfano' law granted immunity to the four highest offices of the state, including the PM (it was later struck down by the Constitutional Court); in November 2009, a proposal was deposited in the Senate for the introduction of the 'short trial', a norm setting a time limit of six and a half years to legal proceedings, which would have helped Berlusconi in no less than three of his trials; phone wiretaps were restricted in 2010; and so on. In addition to these, the government also passed several one-off measures specifically to fight the effects of the economic crisis, such as, for instance, the introduction in late November 2009 of a 'social card' worth €40 per month for the poorest citizens, one-off payments for families in need and measures to aid those without fixed-rate mortgages (see Appendix 1 for more detail).

These initiatives aside, however, we believe that the performance of the Berlusconi government during these years should be assessed with reference to its economic record, since the promise that Forza Italia, and its successor the PDL, would deliver a 'new Italian miracle' (Forza Italia, 2001: 77) had always been the core message delivered to voters by Berlusconi's party. In line with this, among the seven 'missions for the future of Italy' listed in the PDL's 2008 manifesto (explaining what a PDL-led government would do), 're-launching economic growth' had been given pride of place as number one on the list, while 'supporting families' was second. The manifesto stated that both these 'missions' were to be accomplished thanks in part to a reduction of the tax burden. Further down the list (although obviously linked to the first 'mission'), the reduction of the public debt was also cited (again to be achieved not by raising taxation, but by means of an extended privatization programme).[8] The (repeated) promise to reduce the overall tax burden was consistent with the party's contention that growth is spurred not by a 'large' state but by private companies benefiting from the increased spending power of citizens. So much so, that the introduction to the 2008 manifesto ended with the words: 'we will never put our hands in people's pockets' (PDL, 2008), a pledge which, as we will see in Chapter 7, Berlusconi kept repeating during his time in office and which members and representatives of his party felt he had indeed been able to fulfil.

In the light of the above, in this chapter we will assess the PDL's performance in government by considering the extent to which it managed to deliver not only economic growth but also a reduction in the public debt and the burden of taxation. Assessing the latter two promises will be relatively straightforward, since the data is readily available. However, 're-launching economic growth' is a quite general and vague pledge to evaluate, so we will consider a variety of indicators here, such as variations in the following: (1) gross domestic product (GDP); (2) average GDP per person; (3) average disposable income; (4) the unemployment rate; (5) competiveness; and (6) productivity. The first four indicators will allow us to assess Italy's economic performance and, crucially, see how this impacted on the finances of families and individuals (and the latter's chances of being in employment); the latter two are equally important, since weak productivity and a lack of competiveness have slowed Italy's recovery in recent decades quite considerably (see below). As always, our main focus will be the period between May 2008 and November 2011; however, we will also make frequent references to the entire decade between 2001 and 2011, given that the country was governed by the centre-right under Berlusconi during eight of those 11 years. Our overall conclusion will be that the PDL failed to deliver on every single one of its promises made in 2008 – the only possible exception being taxation, on which a firm conclusion cannot be reached (see below). Whatever the impact of external factors from 2008 onwards might have been (and it was certainly considerable), the fact remains that, during a decade dominated by FI/PDL – and, more specifically, under the 2008–2011 Berlusconi government – Italians became poorer, more indebted, no more competitive globally and more likely to be unemployed (particularly if they were young).

Re-launching economic growth

The second half of Berlusconi's 2008–2011 period in office was characterized by serious economic difficulties for Italy. As the country's economic performance was judged to be too weak to generate the revenue needed to service – or, ideally, even reduce – its vast sovereign debt (hovering around 120 per cent of GDP in those years), and given the uncertainty caused by the international financial crisis, bond markets in 2011 began to worry about Italy becoming insolvent. As a result, yields for its bonds soared through the 7 per cent ceiling that had previously signalled the need for Greece, Ireland, and Portugal to be bailed out. With external pressure mounting on his government and his majority collapsing, Berlusconi eventually resigned in November 2011, opening the way for the former European Union (EU) Commissioner Mario Monti to become PM and lead a government able to command wide support in parliament (see Appendix 1).

In reality, none of Italy's problems in 2011 were new, but their impact on Italy's economy had indeed been exacerbated by the financial crisis. They were: lack of competitiveness and productivity; a very large sovereign debt draining resources away from investment; widespread family ownership of companies, leading to a reluctance to float these on the stock exchange (in turn making it difficult for them to grow in size); insufficient investment in research and innovation (Toniolo, 2011; OECD, 2013a). Last, but not least, Italy badly needed a wide-ranging reform of the tax system, as it was blighted by widespread tax avoidance (Istat, 2010a), combined with a very high tax burden imposed on those who actually *were* paying their taxes. Faced with these formidable challenges, the Berlusconi government took a series of piecemeal initiatives on the economy, but managed neither to put together an overarching, coherent, and convincing economic strategy, nor to initiate any major structural reforms (Boeri, 2009; Giannini, 2010). The PM thus contented himself with passing one-off measures, such as the ones mentioned in the preceding section of this chapter: (a) the abolition of a property tax on people's primary homes (ICI) shortly after the government took office in 2008, as well as tax amnesties (Giannini, 2010) – all allegedly aimed at spurring growth by fostering consumption; and (b) a series of emergency decrees responding to the financial crisis (the Dl 78/2010, the Dl 98/2011, and the Dl 138/2011), which simply tried to balance the books by cutting expenditure (for instance, those of the public administration and the health and education systems), increasing some taxes (such as VAT), and decreasing transfers to subnational administrations. However, the PDL-led government did not address any of Italy's structural problems in this period (Bordignon, 2010; Boeri and Bordignon, 2010; Boeri, 2011). So, while the Italian economy had already been performing badly (as we will see below), this process of decline clearly accelerated between 2008 and 2011, due to a combination of worsening international circumstances and government inaction.

Let us consider the evidence. According to research conducted on behalf of the Bank of Italy, between 1973 and 1992 Italy's per capita GDP had risen to 76 per cent of that of the USA and, by 1992, the convergence with Western Europe was 'virtually complete' (Toniolo, 2011: 33). The beginning of the 1990s, however, saw a reversal of that trend and, by the time of Berlusconi's resignation in 2011, this had taken 'the ratio between Italian and US per capita GDP back to its 1973 level of 64 per cent' (ibid.: 34). With regard to the specific period of 2000 to 2010, Italy's average growth, measured by GDP at constant prices, 'was just 0.25 per cent a year' (*Economist*, 2011a). This made it the third-worst performer in the world over the decade, ahead of just Haiti and Zimbabwe. Since Italy's population was growing in the same period (mainly thanks to immigration), overall GDP growth at the levels mentioned above (+0.25 per cent a year) actually meant that Italy's national income per head was *shrinking* (Emmott, 2013: 79). This is clearly shown by Figure 6.1 (overleaf), which compares Italy's average annual growth in real GDP per capita with that of the 33 member countries of the Organisation for Economic Co-operation and Development (OECD).[9] As the figure makes plain, no OECD country performed as badly as Italy during the first decade of the new century.

As for the years 2008–2010, despite the PM's promises of a 'new economic miracle', OECD figures show Italy's overall GDP shrinking (from USD 1,990.5 bn to USD 1,908.6 bn [based on purchasing power parity – PPP]), and GDP per capita contracting too (from USD 33,269 bn to USD 31,563 bn [PPP]) (OECD, 2012). By the time of Berlusconi's resignation in 2011, Italy's GDP – which had shrunk considerably throughout 2008 – had not yet returned to its pre-crisis levels (Istat, 2012c: Fig. 1). Rather, it continued to shrink in both 2012 and 2013 (OECD, 2013a: Table 1). Not unexpectedly, therefore, data concerning average disposable income show that this also fell

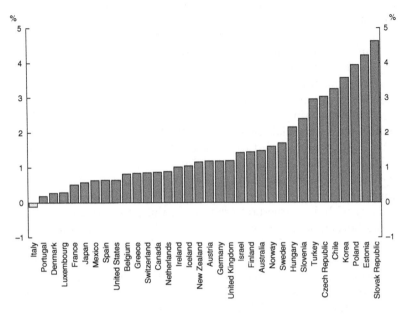

Figure 6.1 Average annual growth in real GDP per capita, 2000–2011

Source: OECD (2013), *OECD Economic Surveys: Italy 2013*, OECD Publishing. http://dx.doi.org/10.1787/eco_surveys-ita-2013-en.

between 2000 and 2009 (from €20,917 to €20,043) (Istat, 2012a: 221), with purchasing power declining by 5 per cent between 2007 and 2011 (Istat, 2013a: Table 1.4). In part, this was due to employers offering fixed-term con-tracts to new employees (which translated into low pay and a lack of job security). In a 2007 report on Italy, the OECD claimed that 'over 40% of new jobs in recent years have been on a fixed-term basis' (OECD, 2007: 32). As a result, the total number of *lavoratori precari* ('precarious workers', as they are known in Italy) was estimated to amount to 18 per cent of the workforce by the end of 2010 (*La Voce*, 2010). Although the introduction of more flex-ible contracts had served to reduce unemployment since the beginning of the decade, this started to increase again under the 2008–2011 Berlusconi gov-ernment. In November 2011, shortly before Berlusconi stepped down, Italy's unemployment rate was 8.8 per cent, as opposed to 6.9 per cent in May 2008 when he took office (Istat, 2012b).[10] In addition, youth unemployment rose by ten percentage points in the same period (from *c.*21.4 per cent in May 2008 to 31.2 per cent in November 2011) (ibid).

The data concerning the state's finances do not offer a rosier picture as, by the time the Berlusconi government resigned, Italy was still the most indebted EU member state in absolute terms, and the second most indebted (after Greece) as a percentage of GDP. As Table 6.1 shows, Italy's debt as a

Table 6.1 Italy's GDP, sovereign debt, and debt as percentage of GDP (2000–2012)

Year	GDP (million euros)	Debt (million euros)	Debt/GDP
2000	1,198,292	1,300,269	108.5
2001	1,255,738	1,358,351	108.2
2002	1,301,873	1,368,897	105.1
2003	1,341,850	1,394,339	103.9
2004	1,397,728	1,445,826	103.4
2005	1,436,379	1,514,409	105.4
2006	1,493,031	1,584,096	106.1
2007	1,554,199	1,602,107	103.1
2008	1,575,144	1,666,584	105.8
2009	1,526,790	1,763,629	115.5
2010	1,556,029	1,842,826	118.4
2011*	1,578,497	1,907,392	120.8
2012*	1,565,916	1,988,658	127.0

Notes: * indicates provisional data.
Sources: Istat, 2012a and 2013b.

percentage of GDP had been reduced in the first three years of the previous Berlusconi government (between 2001 and 2004), but rose again in the last two (2005 and 2006). By 2007, the debt had been reduced to 103.1 per cent of GDP (under Romano Prodi's centre-left government), thus reaching the more manageable levels last seen in 1992 (Istat, 2012a: 281). However, by 2011, the debt had gone back up again, to 120.8 per cent. Even in this respect, therefore, Berlusconi and his parties could not claim to have performed well.

The country's competiveness and productivity provided further cause for concern. As *The Economist* (2011b) pointed out: 'whereas productivity rose by a fifth in America and a tenth in Britain in the decade to 2010, in Italy it fell by 5 per cent'. It also noted that Italy was ranked in eightieth position in the World Bank's 'Doing Business' index, and forty-eighth in the World Economic Forum's competitiveness rankings (ibid.). While labour productivity had grown very slightly (by 0.1 per cent a year) during the 2001–2006 Berlusconi government, it rapidly shrank by 0.8 per cent a year between 2006 and 2009, i.e. under the premiership of Prodi, and then Berlusconi (*Economist*, 2011c). Mario Draghi, the Governor of the Bank of Italy who became president of the European Central Bank in 2011, made the following statement in his final speech as Governor to the Italian central bank's shareholders:

> In the course of the past ten years, Italy's gross domestic product has increased by less than 3 per cent; that of France, with about the same population, by 12 per cent. The gap perfectly reflects the difference in hourly productivity – stationary in Italy, up by 9 per cent in France. Italy's disappointing result applies to the country as a whole, North and South alike.
>
> cited in Emmott (2013: 104–105)[11]

Table 6.2 Italy's tax burden as percentage of GDP

Year	OECD	Eurostat	Istat
2001	42.0	41.5	41.0
2002	41.4	40.8	40.5
2003	41.8	41.3	41.0
2004	41.0	40.7	40.4
2005	40.8	40.3	40.1
2006	42.3	42.0	41.7
2007	43.4	43.0	42.7
2008	43.3	43.0	42.6
2009	43.4	43.3	43.0
2010	43.0	42.8	42.6
2011	42.9	42.8	42.6

Sources: OECD, 2009, 2013b, 2013c; Eurostat, 2013; Istat, 2012a, 2013b.

In sum, the main party of government during the 2001–2011 decade presided over a process of decline that visibly affected all the indicators considered so far. A survey published on 29 December 2011 found that, not surprisingly, 50 per cent of Italians expected the country's economic situation to worsen in 2012 (compared to only 30 per cent who had expressed the same fear the previous year), while 44 per cent thought the same of the economic prospects of their own family (compared to 18 per cent a year before) (Ispo, 2011). Indeed, the 2013 Annual Report published by Istat on Italy's economy and society began with a reference to the 'decidedly negative trend of the Italian economic cycle in 2012' (Istat, 2013a: 1).

Given the economic context summarized above, reducing the burden of taxation would have been a stunning achievement on the part of the 2008–2011 Berlusconi government. On this point, the data vary, with Istat stating that the tax burden as a percentage of GDP in 2011 was equivalent to that in 2008, and both the Statistical Office of the European Communities (Eurostat) and the OECD indicating that it had been slightly reduced (see Table 6.2). Arguably, therefore, the PDL can take comfort from these data. However, if we look at the 2001–2011 period as a whole, the conclusion remains stubbornly the same (irrespective of the data source): put simply, Italians were paying more tax at the end of the decade than they had been at the beginning.

After the effects of the economic crisis began to be felt, both Berlusconi and the PDL Finance Minister, Giulio Tremonti, attempted to manage expectations and, by January 2010, had dropped the plan to lower taxes, stating that it was not 'realistic' (*Repubblica*, 2010; *Corriere della Sera*, 2010). In line with these admissions, the emergency measures passed the following year to stabilize Italy's accounts included the raising of many taxes, as the PDL itself had to acknowledge (PDL, undated: 7). However, and importantly for us here, some of these taxes only started to bite after the PDL-led government gave way to the Monti government in 2011 (see Appendix 1, year 2011).

To conclude, the data presented in this section tells a very consistent story: that of a party failing to deliver on *all* the key promises it had made to voters in 2008 (with the only possible exception being the overall tax burden between 2008 and 2011, for which we have contradictory data). This seems to confirm the most pessimistic claims found in the literature concerning the inability of populists to deliver when in power. On the contrary, however, our next party, the Schweizerische Volkspartei (SVP – Swiss People's Party) appeared much better able to deliver for their electorate between 2003 and 2007. As we will see, this was also due to the fact that they had been more skilful in choosing their pledges in the first place. The final part of this chapter will therefore focus on the experience of SVP, which in many ways stands in stark contrast to that of the PDL in Italy.

The Schweizerische Volkspartei

As we saw in Chapter 4, the SVP began a process of radicalization during the 1980s which subsequently paid off heavily in electoral terms. Although the party has distinctive policies on a variety of issues – some of which have characterized it for a long time (it has consistently advocated a reduction of the tax burden, for instance, as well as policies in support of Swiss agriculture) – the two, interrelated, themes that have been at the heart of its communication strategy since the 1980s are the following:

1   preserving the country's ordered and prosperous way of life, as well as its culture, from those who are said to pose a threat from *within*. These are, first, the 'elites' and, second, immigrants (especially Muslims), 'fake' asylum seekers and criminals (with the latter three categories often conflated);
2   preserving the country's independence, autonomy, prosperity, neutrality, and alleged 'uniqueness' from *external* threats, such as international bodies (primarily the EU, with its various institutions, and the United Nations (UN)), and foreign powers (e.g. the governments of Germany and the United States). The latter have often been accused of meddling in Switzerland's affairs and trying to put pressure on it.

The party's key documents (such as the 2003 and 2007 manifestos), our interviews with party members and representatives, and the survey we conducted of party members and sympathizers fully support the claim that the party's position and actions on the above themes largely define the 'new' SVP's identity.[12] The performance of the SVP in government between 2003 and 2007 will therefore be assessed with reference to these. As regards the first theme, we will discuss the party's achievements concerning migration, asylum seeking, and law and order. In the case of the second, we will focus mainly on the EU, as it was against the threat allegedly posed by it to the country's independence that the SVP mainly sought to act during the 2003–2007 period.

In line with our approach when discussing Italian populists in the previous sections, we will take the SVP *at its own word* and discuss the extent to which it managed to deliver what the party itself had promised.

Asylum, immigration, and law and order

In the period preceding Christoph Blocher's election to the Federal Council (the Swiss governing executive), the SVP argued that three interrelated problems had had a negative impact on the Swiss asylum system: first, the sheer number of people claiming asylum in the country, which the party considered excessive; second, the fact that too many asylum seekers were said to be economic migrants in disguise (and were therefore accused of abusing the asylum system as well as its welfare provisions); third, the fact that the costs related to dealing with asylum were regarded as being disproportionate (Blocher, 2003). In line with the party's approach to these problems, the Swiss were asked to vote in November 2002 on an initiative launched by the SVP called 'Against the Abuse of Asylum Rights'. By far the most controversial aspect of this initiative was the proposal that people entering Switzerland from a safe country would no longer be allowed to apply for asylum. Due to Switzerland's location as a land-locked state surrounded by European countries, this measure would have brought the number of asylum seekers reaching Switzerland by land down to zero, thus also cutting to near zero the *overall* number of people allowed to seek asylum in the country. Interestingly, although the SVP lost this ballot, it was defeated by the narrowest of margins (49.9 vs 50.1 per cent, but with a majority of cantons supporting it). The result fits with a general pattern noted in recent years, whereby large sections of the electorate side with the SVP in direct democratic votes (and against the parties they normally vote for), especially when the issues being debated have to do with migration, asylum, and law and order.

Buoyed by this 'honourable' defeat, the SVP re-presented the very same proposal in its 2003 election manifesto (SVP, 2003: 37). Moreover, the party also advocated the following: (1) the acceleration of asylum procedures, in order to expel unsuccessful applicants quickly; (2) the immediate expulsion of asylum seekers who are convicted of crimes; (3) the reduction of the over-all costs of the asylum system (ibid.: 36). Having entered government and become Minister of Justice and the Police (with responsibility for asylum matters), Blocher drafted a reform of the system which was not only very much inspired by these ideas, but was tightened up and made more stringent before being passed by a series of SVP-sponsored amendments. In the end, the legislation included: (a) an obligation on asylum seekers to prove their identity solely by producing official papers (if they were unable to do so, their case would not be considered); (b) measures making it harder for applicants to prove their status as 'refugees'; (c) the shortening of the period during which applicants could appeal against asylum application refusals (from 30

Table 6.3 Total number of asylum applications in Switzerland and cost of the asylum system

Year	2002	2003	2004	2005	2006	2007
Applications	26,678	21,037	14,248	10,061	10,537	9,638
Cost (million francs)	n.d.	985	969	884	829	808

Sources: Bundesamt für Migration, quoted in Fibbi, 2008: 209; EJPD, 2007: 12 and 14.

to 4 days); and (d) the abolition of welfare payments to asylum seekers whose applications were unsuccessful (EJPD, 2004; Sidler, 2007: 1130). While (a) and (b) made it more difficult for asylum seekers to lodge an application (the objective of this being to reduce their numbers), (c) and (d) were designed to accelerate asylum procedures and bring down their costs – again in line with the approach set out in the SVP's manifesto. Unlike the initiative on asylum voted upon in 2002, this time the reform passed the direct democratic test when, in 2006, an overwhelmingly majority of 68 per cent rejected a referendum called by the Left to repeal it (Sidler, 2007: 1130).

The two linked objectives of decreasing the number of would-be asylum seekers and reducing the costs of the system can also be assessed in terms of the actual results achieved under Blocher's watch as Minister of Justice and the Police. The data available show that, not only was there a very substantial drop in the number of asylum applications during his time in office, but the overall costs of the system also decreased, albeit to a less impressive degree. Table 6.3 provides the data for the 2002–2007 period.

As far as asylum is concerned, therefore, the SVP appears to have performed well while Blocher was in government, since it introduced legislation that was perfectly in line with the pledges it had made in its 2003 manifesto, as well as overseeing a reduction both in the number of applications for asylum and in the costs of the system.[13] It is also worth mentioning that the savings achieved on asylum came in addition to those gained by Blocher through the merger of two previously separate administrative divisions of his ministry (see Appendix 2, year 2004; also Chapter 7).

Like the LN, the SVP has constantly conflated law and order and migration issues, by blaming foreigners for the increase in the number of crimes (especially violent ones) which was noted before Blocher became a minister (see, for instance, Blocher, 2007). One of the most high-profile and radical proposals concerning law and order listed in the SVP's 2003 manifesto was that of expelling whole families of foreign repeat young offenders (SVP, 2003: 51). This was meant to have a deterrent effect on the criminals themselves and force their families to keep a close eye on what they were up to. In line with this approach, on 18 December 2006, the party tabled four parliamentary motions on law and order, which included motion 06.483 (on the expulsion of foreign residents whose children commit serious crimes) and motion 06.484 (on the expulsion of foreign residents who commit certain crimes). Not unexpectedly, these motions failed to attract the necessary support in parliament.[14] This being the case, three and a half months before the 2007 federal election, the party started collecting the signatures required to put these proposals directly to the people. In the process, the SVP also caused an international outcry, since it publicized the initiative through a poster depicting three white sheep kicking a black sheep against a backdrop of the Swiss flag (see Appendix 2, year 2007). Eventually, in 2010 (i.e. after the period we are mainly concerned with here), having dropped the idea of deporting the *parents* of offenders, the SVP won an initiative on 'The deportation of criminal migrants' with a majority of 52.9 per cent. According to this, foreign nationals would be immediately expelled if convicted of certain crimes. Since the other three governmental parties and the federal authorities had recommended a 'no' vote, this victory again strengthened the SVP's claim that it had been the only one defending the views of the majority.

One initiative and two referendums voted upon in 2004 provide further examples of the uncompromising strategy on law and order and immigration matters adopted by the party, as they all saw the SVP stand alone against the other governmental parties, and win. In the first case – an initiative introducing 'life imprisonment for non-treatable extremely violent criminals and sex offenders' – 56.2 per cent of voters and a large majority of cantons supported the SVP, which had launched it; in the second and third cases, two referendums (backed by the government and a parliamentary majority) designed, respectively, to facilitate the naturalization of second-generation foreigners and make naturalization automatic for third-generation ones were rejected by voters. Consistent with the principles guiding its actions on migration during those years, the SVP had opposed both proposals (SVP, 2004; Milic, 2005). It is important to note here that, despite being a member of the collegial federal government, Blocher was often very reluctant to defend the governmental line when it came to popular votes on these matters. This, as we will see in Chapter 7, constituted a considerable break with the country's political culture, while signalling very clearly to the electorate where the SVP's minister stood on crucial issues (Skenderovic and Mazzoleni, 2007: 98–100). Finally, in addition to the popular votes just mentioned, the SVP launched an initiative in May 2004 to give Swiss municipalities the option to maintain local ballots to decide on the naturalization of foreigners (and without giving failed applicants the chance to appeal). This was rejected by voters in June 2008.

The SVP can therefore be said to have won several battles on asylum, immigration, and law and order during Blocher's time in office between 2003 and 2007. Not only did it fulfil some of its promises (Bornschier, 2010: 164), but, even when it failed, it acted in ways that were very consistent with the letter and spirit of its 2003 election manifesto. As we will see in the next section, the party's initiatives on the EU were not as successful in the same period. Even here, however, and despite losing all votes, the SVP could still claim to have fulfilled its pre-election promises, as the discussion below will show.

Switzerland and the EU

In its 2003 federal election manifesto, the SVP stated that it wanted Switzerland to remain outside the EU, proposed the use of referendums for ratification of international treaties (including those with the EU), expressed its opposition to signing the Schengen and Dublin agreements, and said that freedom of movement for citizens of countries that were about to join the EU should be delayed until the Swiss had an opportunity to vote on the matter (SVP, 2003: 43). Importantly, however, since it was conscious of being in a minority of one within the government on these issues, the party said only that it was committing itself to fighting *for* its positions but stopped short of promising that it would definitely achieve any specific and concrete results.

Direct democracy has played a major role in the SVP's attempts to oppose the federal government on EU-related issues in recent decades and was widely used in this period too. The first vote on Switzerland's relationship with the EU following Blocher's entry into government was held on 5 June 2005. This was a referendum launched by the party and the Aktion für eine unabhängige und neutrale Schweiz (AUNS – Campaign for an Independent and Neutral Switzerland) which aimed to reverse the government's decision to sign up to the Schengen/Dublin agreements. The party had argued that border controls with neighbouring countries – removed under Schengen – were necessary to keep Switzerland safe, and that signing up to Schengen was just another step towards further integration with the EU (Milic, 2006: 1275–7). This vote was lost by the SVP, with 54.6 per cent of voters siding with the executive on the matter.

The second vote on the EU was held on 25 September 2005 and concerned an initiative launched by the Schweizer Demokraten (SD – Swiss Democrats), a small right-wing party, with support from the SVP, which sought to block the extension of the right to free movement to citizens of those (mainly central and Eastern European) countries that had joined the EU in May 2004. The SVP had unsuccessfully opposed this extension in parliament. In the end, 56 per cent of voters again sided with the government (and all major parties except the SVP), and the initiative was rejected. Interestingly, on this issue the SVP itself was divided for the first time in many years, as some within the party (including both its federal councillors, Blocher and Samuel Schmid) backed the governmental line. This caused consternation within the SVP, especially due to Blocher's decision to officially side with the government. Far from hiding the divisions within the party, the SVP went as far as terming them a 'split' (SVP, 2005: 15). Although painful, this difference of opinion did not lead to the departure of any of the party's representatives, nor did it have any enduring consequences.[15]

The third vote on European matters was held on 26 November 2006: this was a referendum backed by the SVP and again opposed by all other major political parties (importantly, it was also opposed by all major business organizations) (Sidler, 2007: 1131). It proposed revoking Switzerland's pledge to contribute one billion francs to a fund set up to facilitate the economic development of the ten new EU member states – a pledge made by the government as part of its bilateral negotiations with the EU. Although the SVP lost this referendum too, it was another case of honourable defeat, since only 53.4 per cent of voters backed the executive's position.

In conclusion, as far as actual results are concerned, the SVP achieved little on EU-related matters between 2003 and 2007, since it lost the referendums/initiatives it launched/supported. It was also unable to change the executive's strategy on Swiss–EU relations. Nonetheless, as mentioned above, the party consistently opposed what it saw as negative developments in the relationship between Switzerland and the EU, thereby fulfilling its manifesto commitments on the matter. The fact that, on the issue of freedom of movement, its federal councillors officially took a different view from the rest of the party does not invalidate this claim, since it is widely accepted in Switzerland that ministers must sometimes defend positions their parties object to, and which the latter may seek to reverse by putting issues directly to the people (see Chapter 7 for a discussion of this). Our assessment of the SVP's failed attempts to reverse the decisions taken by the executive on EU-related matters during those years is thus that these were perfectly consistent with both the letter and the spirit of the SVP's 2003 election programme and therefore constituted a fulfilment of the party's pledges.

Conclusions

As we have shown in this chapter, the three parties were not equally successful in delivering on the promises they had made before entering government. In sum, the SVP can be said to have done well overall, the LN achieved only partial results (and, in some cases, supported government initiatives that contradicted what it had said it wanted), and the PDL failed to deliver on all fronts.

The success of the SVP was particularly apparent on asylum and law and order, as we have just shown. Here, not only did the party consistently focus on the pledges it had made, but – after the approval of the legislation sponsored by its minister, Blocher – it could also claim to have overseen a fall in the number of asylum applications and a reduction in the burden placed on the country's finances by the asylum system. Having convinced the other governmental parties to accept its priorities on asylum and pass a reform very much inspired by its proposals, the SVP then proceeded to defeat them in a popular vote when they refused to sing to its tune on the issue of 'criminal migrants'. However, in the 2003–2007 period, the party was not successful on all its key themes, since it lost a series of high-profile votes on EU-related matters. Even on 'Europe', however, the SVP could at least claim to have acted in accordance with the 2003 manifesto and to have delivered on its promises, since it had avoided pledging the introduction of any specific legislative measures (unlike the LN, which had done so on federalism and immigration), or the achievement of specific *results* (as the PDL had done on the economy). More cautiously, the SVP had only committed to stubbornly opposing certain developments in Switzerland's relationship with the EU. And this it certainly did.

As for the LN, while the party's glass of government participation can only be judged partially full, its impact on the executive was not irrelevant either. There is no doubt that the Lega in government managed to focus almost entirely on its key themes of federal reform and immigration/law and order from day one and that it was also very quick in delivering some sort of results on these. Moreover, a number of the principles established by the LN's fiscal federal reform (such as the introduction of 'standard' costs and requirements) were indeed innovative. This was despite the reform itself being timid, and despite many other government measures posing a powerful threat to the spirit and letter of federalism during those years. In sum, although the LN claimed to have sparked a revolution on federal matters after 2008 (Lega Nord, 2009b), the evidence is clear that this was not the case; however, the party did achieve some results nonetheless. As for migration and law and order, the legislation championed by the LN and the initiatives taken by its Minister of the Interior, Roberto Maroni, often provided examples of purely 'symbolic politics' (Cento Bull, 2009: 143). These included the introduction of the soon-forgotten (and not fully constitutional) *ronde*, and only partially fulfilled the pledges made in the party's manifesto. As for what actually happened during those years regarding the number of migrants and crimes, results were, again, mixed: while the number of legal migrants living in Italy increased between 2008 and 2011 (also thanks to an amnesty passed by the government), there was a small reduction in the number of crimes, something which could be presented as a success.

Finally, and following its third stint in power, the FI/PDL's glass of government participation appeared to be desperately empty. As we have demonstrated, not only was Berlusconi's party unable to unambiguously fulfil *any* of the key promises it had made, but it presided over developments (such as the considerable deterioration of Italy's economic performance throughout the first decade of the twenty-first century and the acceleration of this trend between 2008 and 2011) that went in the *opposite direction* to what the party had promised it would deliver. Rather than turning Italy's ship round, as he had said only he could do, Berlusconi steered it straight at the rocks, increasing its speed for good measure. This is demonstrated by the worsening of all economic indicators in the country between 2008 and 2011, as well as the state of its public finances. At least to the extent that fulfilling its promises mattered to the party, the PDL was therefore unwise in promising it would deliver very substantial *results* (unlike, for instance, the LN or the SVP) – and ones that depended too heavily (when not entirely) on external factors, over which the party obviously had no control. So, while the LN, for instance, had championed legislation on federalism and immigration knowing that the

PDL would be forced to support it in the interests of coalition stability, the PDL promised it would deliver growth and prosperity – achievements that would have been hostages to fortune *even* in better times. By 2011, the PDL's leader Berlusconi had become a prisoner of his own rhetoric, and no attempt to lower the expectations of the Italian public could by itself suffice. Having based much of his appeal since the creation of Forza Italia in the 1990s on the claim that he could make the country considerably more prosperous, and having placed this promise right at the heart of his communication strategy, Berlusconi's failure became painfully obvious throughout 2011, and was sealed by his resignation on 12 November.

Nonetheless – and despite the PDL's experience – the evidence presented in this chapter shows that there are no reasons why populists should *inevitably* be condemned to fail in government and be unable to deliver on their pledges. On the contrary, our analysis demonstrates that these parties do not necessarily need to renounce their identity and policies when in power and that sticking to their core proposals can bring at least some measure of success – when circumstances are not overwhelmingly unfavourable and when pledges are realistic (something which, of course, can be said of *any* party). As we will see in the next chapter, however, whether party members and representatives regard their party as successful may be unrelated to the analysis of 'dry' figures and relevant legislation that we have presented here. Despite everything said above, therefore, not only did the members and representatives of the SVP and the LN interviewed for this book express satisfaction with what their parties had achieved in government in the periods under consideration (and compared it favourably with other periods), but even PDL members and representatives sounded surprisingly upbeat. It is now time therefore to focus on how the experience of populists in government has been interpreted by those who make up the fabric of their organizations, i.e. their members and representatives. This we will do in the next chapter.

Notes

1 Like all parties, populist parties are obviously not entirely the makers of their own destiny. However, and again like all parties, they should know this and keep it in mind when drafting their manifestos. We are not concerned in this chapter with the extent to which external circumstances may have affected these parties' ability to deliver on the promises they had made, but only with whether they achieved what they said they would.

2 The 'Parliament of the North' is an assembly of LN representatives originally created in 1995. Arguably, it is yet another means through which the party engages in symbolic politics, by creating institutions devoid of actual power parallel to those of the central state. When talking about the 2008 election manifesto, we will be referring to the 'Resolutions' passed by this 'Parliament'.

3 It is common for the LN – and other populist parties – to propose laws that they know to be unconstitutional or in contrast with European law, thus finding themselves in a win–win situation: even if a measure cannot be passed, the claim can always be made that the rules have been written by national or supranational elites so that they can ignore the people's will.

4 Berlusconi promised the abolition of ICI during both the 2006 and 2008 campaigns. As we will see in Chapter 7, its elimination in 2008 was hailed by many PDL members and representatives as a very important achievement.

5 For an analysis of the measures passed in 2010, see Bordignon (2010) and Boeri and Bordignon (2010), and for those passed in 2011, see Boeri (2011) and the just-mentioned Zanardi (2011).

6 The 'historical expenditure' yardstick means that state transfers for the provision of specific services are allocated according to how much these have cost in region X in the past. However, this creates a situation whereby those regions which have spent more in comparative terms continue to receive more. Hence, the system ends up rewarding inefficiency and overspending. By contrast, if the cost of service provision is decided in advance – and only that amount is provided by the state – then a virtuous circle should be created since regional administrations would be discouraged from wasting money, as this would no longer result in larger state transfers in the future.

7 Measures such as the prohibition of the use of languages other than Italian during public events (extended to everybody, however, not just Muslims) and the closure of mosques that did not fully comply with building and health and safety regulations were implemented by some northern Italian councils (Ambrosini, 2012: 75–82).

8 The size of the public debt is arguably a formidable obstacle to growth in Italy, given the considerable amount of resources that are needed to service it and that could instead be invested in stimulating the economy and supporting productive activities.

9 The majority of the OECD's 34 members are very advanced economically. Hence, comparisons with the OECD average are extremely useful to assess an industrialized country's economic performance.

10 Overall averages mask sharp gender, age, and geographical variations.

11 According to Eurostat (2011: Table 1.4), the situation was even more dramatic, as their data shows Italian hourly productivity decreasing throughout the decade.

12 As discussed in more detail in Chapter 7, we asked a sample of SVP respondents which issues had attracted them to the party. We found that the two related categories of 'immigration' and 'Swiss independence' – chosen, respectively, by 76 and 57.5 per cent of interviewees – were by far the most cited.

13 It is worth noting here that, in his interview with us, Fulvio Pelli, former president of the Freisinnig-Demokratische Partei der Schweiz (FDP – The Free Democrats), a liberal party, said that fluctuations in the number of would-be refugees during those years had in fact been determined by external factors (for instance, the Kosovo crisis), rather than anything the Swiss government had done. Moreover, it could also be argued that, since the new legislation only took effect in 2008, the fall in applications seen after Blocher's entry into government could not have been caused by it. A counter-argument would be that the mere presence of a Minister of Justice and the Police who was working tirelessly to 'toughen up' the system must have deterred 'fake' asylum seekers from trying their luck in the country, a thesis that will be discussed at more length in Chapter 7. Interesting as these discussions certainly are, they fall outside the remit of this chapter, as we have explained in note 1. Rather, what matters to us here is that, under Blocher's watch as the minister in charge of asylum affairs, the SVP's stated aims on asylum were met, and that this could be presented as a success to the electorate (as Blocher subsequently did – see EJPD, 2007). Equally, and whatever the impact of the international financial crisis on the Italian economy, Berlusconi presided over a considerable worsening of the economic and financial situation in Italy, as we have seen above, when he had promised to achieve the very opposite.

14 Like the LN (Albertazzi and McDonnell, 2010), the SVP sometimes puts forward proposals that have no chance of being approved in parliament. This seems designed to demonstrate that it is in a minority of one in consistently 'speaking up' for the people on controversial issues. By proposing to punish 'A' for the deeds of 'B', motion 06.483 was clearly not in line with the principles of justice enshrined in most democratic legal systems and, as such, had no chance of receiving the backing of the other governing parties.

15 Blocher sent conflicting messages on the topic of 'free movement' during his years in office, and was widely seen by SVP supporters as having been forced to oppose this initiative against his will, due to the rules of concordance (see Chapter 7). Indeed, while he had officially opposed the initiative mentioned above, he also stated in public that he did not fully agree with the government on Schengen and that the executive should have acknowledged its internal divisions on the issue (Blocher, 2005).

Bibliography

Albertazzi, D. and McDonnell, D. (2010) 'The Lega Nord Back in Government', *West European Politics*, 33 (6), 1318–1350.

Albertazzi, D. and Mueller, S. (2013) 'Populism and Liberal Democracy: Populists in Government in Austria, Italy, Poland and Switzerland', *Government and Opposition*, (48) 3, 343–371.

Ambrosanio, M.F. and Bordignon, M. (2011) 'Un patto col diavolo', *La Voce*. Available at: http://www.lavoce.info/un-patto-col-diavolo/, 28 July 2011 (accessed 27 October 2014).

Ambrosini, M. (2010) 'Solo parole nella lotta alla clandestinità', *La Voce*. Available at: http://www.lavoce.info/solo-parole-nella-lotta-alla-clandestinita/, 2 November 2010 (accessed 27 October 2014).

Ambrosini, M. (2012) 'Separati in città: Le Politiche locali di esclusione degli immigrati', *La Rivista delle Politiche Sociali*, 1, 69–88.

Blocher, C. (2003) 'Dichiarazione personale sulla mia candidatura a consigliere federale'. Available at: http://www.blocher.ch/en/articles/dichiarazione-personale-sulla-mia-candidatura-a-consigliere-federale.html, 7 November 2003 (accessed 27 October 2014).

Blocher, C. (2005) 'La svizzera nel contesto Europeo. Discorso di commemorazione del 60 anniversario della fine della guerra tenuto l'8 maggio 2005'. Available at: http://www.ejpd.admin.ch/ejpd/it/home/dokumentation/red/archiv/reden_christoph_blocher/2005/2005-05-08.html, 8 May 2005 (accessed 3 April 2013).

Blocher, C. (2007) 'Kriminalität, Sicherheit, Ausländer: eine Standortbestimmung'. Referat von Bundesrat Christoph Blocher an der Informationsveranstaltung SVP, 8. Juni 2007, in Riehen BS. Available at: http://www.ejpd.admin.ch/ejpd/de/home/aktuell/reden---interviews/reden/archiv/reden_christoph_blocher/2007/2007-06-08.html, 17 March 2007 (accessed 27 October 2014).

Boeri, T. (2009) 'La Finanziaria light e il maxiemendamento che verrà', *La Voce*. Available at: http://www.lavoce.info/la-finanziaria-light-e-il-maxiemendamento-che-verra/, 22 September 2009 (accessed 27 October 2014).

Boeri, T. (2010) 'Immigrazione non è uguale a criminalità', *La Voce*. Available at: http://www.lavoce.info/immigrazione-non-e-uguale-a-criminalita/, 2 February 2010 (accessed 27 October 2014).

Boeri, T. (2011) 'I numeri della manovra approvata dal Parlamento', *La Voce*. Available at: http://www.lavoce.info/i-numeri-della-manovra-approvata-dal-parlamento/, 7 September 2011 (accessed 27 October 2014).

Boeri, T. and Bordignon, M. (2010) 'I veri numeri della manovra', *La Voce*. Available at: http://www.lavoce.info/i-veri-numeri-della-manovra/, 1 June 2010 (accessed 27 October 2014).

Bordignon, M. (2010) 'Regioni e enti locali', *La Voce*. Available at: http://www.lavoce.info/regioni-ed-enti-locali/, 14 June 2010 (accessed 27 October 2014).

Bornschier, S. (2010) *Cleavage Politics and the Populist Right. The New Cultural Conflict in Western Europe*, Philadelphia: Temple University Press.

Caritas/Migrantes (2009) *Immigrazione – Dossier Statistico 2009*, Rome: Idos.

Caritas/Migrantes (2011) *Immigrazione – Dossier Statistico 2011*, Rome: Idos.

Censis (2011) *45o Rapporto sulla situazione sociale del Paese*, Rome: Censis.

Cento Bull, A. (2009) 'Lega Nord: A Case of Simulative Politics?', *South European Society and Politics*, (14) 2, 129–146.

Corriere della Sera (2010) 'Tasse giù solo con la ripresa'. Available at: http://archiviostorico.corriere.it/2010/gennaio/24/Tasse_giu_solo_con_ripresa_co_8_100124018.shtml, 24 January 2010 (accessed 15 June 2012).

Cota, R. (2009) 'Così abbiamo mantenuto le promesse fatte', *La Padania*, 15 May 2009.

Economist, The (2011a) 'Oh for a new risorgimento', 9 June 2011.

Economist, The (2011b) 'The man who screwed an entire country', 9 June 2011.

Economist, The (2011c) 'For ever espresso', 9 June 2011.

EJPD – Eidgenössisches Justiz-und Polizeidepartement (2004) 'Teilrevision des Asylgesetzes: Bundesrat beschliesst Ergänzungs-und Änderungsanträge für den Zweitrat', Press release, 25 August.

EJPD (2007) 'Vier Jahre im Bundesrat – Bilanz einer Legislatur von Bundesrat Christoph Blocher. Folien'. Available at: http://www.ejpd.admin.ch/content/ejpd/de/home/dokumentation/mi/2007/2007-12-28.html, 28 December 2007 (accessed 6 June 2013).

Emmott, B. (2013) *Good and Bad Italy*, New Haven and London: Yale University Press.

Eurostat – Statistical Office of the European Communities (2011) *Europe in Figures. Eurostat Yearbook 2011*, Brussels: EU Commission.

Eurostat (2013) 'Main national accounts tax aggregates'. Available at: http://appsso.eurostat.ec.europa.eu/nui/show.do, 8 May 2013 (accessed 6 June 2013).

Fibbi, R. (2008) *12. Asylpolitik und Migrationsfragen, Schweizerisches Jahrbuch für Entwicklungspolitik*, (27) 1, Geneva: Institut de hautes études internationales et du développement. Available at: http://www.sjep.revues.org/85, 29 March 2008 (accessed 8 June 2013).

Forza Italia (2001) *Una storia italiana*, Milan: Mondadori.

Giannini, S. (2010) 'Due anni di governo: politica di bilancio', *La Voce*. Available at: http://www.lavoce.info/due-anni-di-governo-politica-di-bilancio/, 26 April 2010 (accessed 27 October 2014).

Giornale, il (2009) 'Sicurezza, ronde bocciate parzialmente da Consulta: "Non per disagio sociale"'. Available at: http://www.ilgiornale.it/news/sicurezza-ronde-bocciate-parzialmente-consulta-non-disagio.html, 24 July 2010 (accessed 27 October 2014).

Hooper, J. (2009) 'Italian Town Where a White Christmas is a Police Matter', *The Guardian*, 20 December 2009.

Ispo – Istituto per gli Studi sulla Pubblica Opinione (2011) 'Sondaggio Politico-Elettorale: Critiche alla Manovra da un Italiano su Due'. Available at: http://www.sondaggipoliticoelettorali.it, 29 December 2011 (accessed 15 February 2012).

Istat – Istituto Nazionale di Statistica (2010a) 'La misura dell'economia sommersa secondo le statistiche ufficiali, anni 2000–2008'. Available at: http://www3.istat.it/salastampa/comunicati/non_calendario/20100713_00/, 13 July 2010 (accessed 26 May 2013).

Istat (2010b) 'Delitti denunciati dalle forze di Polizia all'autorità giudiziaria – anno 2010'. Available at: http://www.istat.it/it/archivio/50144, 11 January 2012 (accessed 15 January 2012).

Istat (2011) 'Report: la popolazione straniera residente in Italia'. Available at: http://www.istat.it/it/archivio/39726, 1 January 2011 (accessed 27 October 2014).

Istat (2012a) *Noi Italia. 100 Statistiche per capire il paese in cui viviamo. 2012,* Rome: Istat.

Istat (2012b) 'Istat disoccupazione serie storiche, Tabella 1'. Available at: http://dati.istat.it/?lang=it, 31 January 2012 (accessed 20 May 2012).

Istat (2012c) 'Anni 2009–2011. Pil e indebitamento amministrazione pubblica'. Available at: http://www.istat.it/it/archivio/55566, 2 March 2012 (accessed 4 June 2013).

Istat (2013a) *Rapporto Annuale 2013. La situazione del Paese*, Rome: Istat.

Istat (2013b) 'Anni 2010–2012. Pil e indebitamento amministrazione pubblica'. Available at: http://www.istat.it/it/archivio/83796, 2 March 2013 (accessed 3 June 2013).

Lega Nord (2009a) *Cronistoria della Lega Nord. Dalle origini a oggi. Capitolo 12.* Available at: www.leganord.org/index.php/il-movimento/la-nostra-storia/la-storia-della-lega (accessed 25 May 2013).

Lega Nord (2009b) *1 anno di Lega Nord al governo*, Milan: Lega Nord.

Massetti, E. (2012) 'Federal Reform: The End of the Beginning or the Beginning of the End?', in Bosco, A. and McDonnell, D. (eds), *Italian Politics – From Berlusconi to Monti*, New York, Oxford: Berghahn.

Mény, Y. and Surel, Y. (eds) (2002) *Democracies and the Populist Challenge*, London: Palgrave Macmillan.

Milic, T. (2005) 'Switzerland', *European Journal of Political Research*, (44) 7–8, 1203–1210.

Milic, T. (2006) 'Switzerland', *European Journal of Political Research*, (45) 7–8, 1275–81.

Muraro, G. (2011) 'Federalismo regionale: La rivoluzione può attendere', *La Voce*. Available at: http://www.lavoce.info/federalismo-regionale-la-rivoluzione-puo-attendere/, 5 April 2011 (accessed 14 October 2014).

OECD – Organisation for Economic Co-operation and Development (2007) *OECD Economic Survey of Italy 2007*, 4 June 2007.

OECD (2009) *Country statistical profile: Italy 2009*. Available at: http://www.oecd-ilibrary.org/economics/country-statistical-profile-italy-2011_csp-ita-table-2011-1-en, 18 January 2012 (accessed 1 February 2012).

OECD (2012) *Country statistical profiles: Italy 2011–2012*. Available at: http://www.oecd-ilibrary.org/economics/country-statistical-profile-italy-2011_csp-ita-table-2011-1-en, 6 April 2009 (accessed 1 February 2012).

OECD (2013a) *OECD Economic Surveys – Italy 2013*. Available at: http://www.oecd.org/eco/surveys/italy-2013.htm, May 2013 (accessed 3 June 2013).

OECD (2013b) *OECD Factbook statistics. Country Statistical Profiles: Key tables from OECD*. Available at: http://dx.doi.org/10.1787/csp-ita-table-2013-1-en, 28 February 2013 (accessed 10 June 2013).

OECD (2013c) *OECD Factbook statistics. Country Statistical Profiles: Key tables from OECD*. Available: http://dx.doi.org/10.1787/csp-ita-table-2013-2-en, 15 November 2013 (accessed 6 January 2014).

Parlamento del Nord (2008) *Risoluzioni, 2 March 2008*, Milan: Lega Nord.

PDL – Popolo della Libertà (undated) *Il Governo Berlusconi. Le Principali Realizzazioni (maggio 2008 – ottobre 2011)*. Available at: http://www.pdl.it/libri/le-principali-realizzazioni/le-principali-realizzazioni.pdf, (accessed 27 October 2014).

PDL (2008) *7 missioni per il futuro dell'Italia*. Available at: http://www.slideshare.net/FORZASILVIO/7-missioni-per-il-futuro-dellitalia, (accessed 27 October 2014).

Pinotti, P., Buonanno, P., and Bianchi, M. (2009) 'Crimini e immigrati', *La Voce*. Available at: http://www.lavoce.info/crimini-e-immigrati/, 3 February 2009 (accessed 14 October 2014).

Polchi, V. (2010) 'Il flop delle ronde padane. Dopo un anno ce n'è una sola', *La Repubblica*. Available at: http://www.repubblica.it/politica/2010/09/12/news/il_flop_delle_ronde_padane_dopo_un_anno_ce_n_una_sola-6989688, 12 September 2010 (accessed 13 September 2010).

Polchi, V. (2012) 'Strasburgo, l'Italia condannata per i respingimenti verso la Libia', *La Repubblica*. Available at: http://www.repubblica.it/solidarieta/immigrazione/2012/02/23/news/l_italia_condannata_per_i_respingimenti-30366965, 23 February 2012 (accessed 27 October 2014).

Reinhart, C. and Rogoff, K. (2009) *This Time is Different: Eight Centuries of Financial Folly*, Princeton, NJ: Princeton University Press.

Repubblica, la (2010) 'Tasse, scontro governo-opposizione? Berlusconi: "Non le riduco". Pd: "Irresponsabile"', *La Repubblica*. Available at: http://www.repubblica.it/economia/2010/01/13/news/tasse-taglio-1929643, 13 January 2010 (accessed on the same day).

Repubblica, la (2011) 'Ue: "Clandestini non punibili con carcere". Maroni: "Rischio espulsioni impossibili"', *La Repubblica*. Available at: http://www.repubblica.it/esteri/2011/04/28/news/corte_ue_boccia_reato_di_clandestinit-15471497, 28 April 2011 (accessed on the same day).

Skenderovic, D. and Mazzoleni, O. (2007) 'Contester et utiliser les règles du jeu institutionnel', in Mazzoleni, O. *et al.* (eds), *L'Union Démocratique du Centre: Un Parti, Son Action, Ses Soutiens*, Lausanne: Éditions Antipodes.

Sidler, A. (2007) 'Switzerland', *European Journal of Political Research*, (46), 7–8, 1127–1133.

SVP – Schweizerische Volkspartei (2003) *Piattaforma Elettorale 2003–7*, Berne: SVP.

SVP (2004) *Rapport annuel 2004*, Zurich: SVP.

SVP (2005) *Rapport annuel 2005*, Zurich: SVP.

Taggart, P. (2004) 'Populism and Representative Politics in Contemporary Europe', *Journal of Political Ideologies*, 9 (3), 269–288.

Toniolo, G. (2011) *Italy and the World Economy, 1861–2011*, Rome: Banca d'Italia.

Viesti, G. (2010) 'Il federalismo difficile', *Il Mulino*, 5, 730–8.

Voce, la (2010) 'Meno Lavori, Più Precari', *La Voce*. Available at http://www.lavoce. info/meno-lavori-piu-precari/ 1, 22 December 2010 (accessed 27 October 2014).

Zanardi, A. (2011) 'Una bomba sul federalismo fiscale', *La Voce*. Available at: http://www. lavoce.info/una-bomba-sul-federalismo-fiscale/, 28 July 2011 (accessed 27 October 2014).

7 Members' and representatives' reactions to government participation

In the previous two chapters we have considered the consequences of government participation for populists in electoral terms (Chapter 5) and the extent to which they managed to deliver on their key election pledges while in office (Chapter 6). Given the aims of our book, we now examine how the experience of populist parties in government was perceived by their representatives and members.[1] In doing so, we are aware that this means entering a rarely explored terrain within political science. Indeed, despite some renewed interest in party members during the 1980s and 1990s (discussed by van Haute, 2011: 10), the micro level of parties remains very much neglected. As Knut Heidar (2007: 8) observed, 'what is known about peoples' motivations for joining a party is scattered; there is no generally acknowledged typology for peoples' motivations'. Likewise, there are few studies available that investigate 'the reasons for remaining a member or for leaving a party' (van Haute, 2011: 21).[2] Both Emilie van Haute (2011) and Heidar (2007) have therefore called for more comparative research to be done on party members so that we can better understand both what drives them and how they conceive of their experiences within their parties.

More specifically, scholars have proposed 'typologies' for activists of 'extreme right parties' (a category that only partially overlaps with our own), according to political backgrounds and the extent to which activists adhere to the party's ideology (Klandermans and Mayer, 2006; Linden and Klandermans, 2007; Goodwin, 2010); however, we still know very little about how members and representatives of populist parties view their parties and what they think of their parties' experiences in government. As far as Italian and Swiss populist parties are concerned, this chapter goes some way towards filling that gap by examining: (a) what members and representatives thought of their party in office, especially whether or not they believed it had delivered on its key pre-election promises; (b) what they thought of their government partners and how well they believed their party had related to them. Exploring these questions will allow us to insert a crucial piece in the larger puzzle of how government participation is experienced and perceived within populist parties. As we will see, and perhaps not unexpectedly, our own assessment of the extent to which these parties were able to deliver on their pre-electoral pledges while in government (see Chapter 6) diverges considerably from the views of their members and representatives. An important conclusion of this chapter is therefore that the three parties were generally successful in convincing their members and representatives that they were delivering on their promises and that government participation could, in the end, pay off (regardless of their very different degrees of success in fulfilling their pledges). To discuss all this in detail, we will now cover the three parties in turn – first the LN, then the PDL, and, finally, the SVP. In each case, we will start by discussing what members and representatives thought of the experience of their party in government, and then we will consider how they assessed its relationship with its government partners.

Populists in government: the view from within

The Lega Nord

As the junior component of a two-party coalition, the Lega Nord (LN – Northern League) was faced with the important task of convincing its larger partner, the Popolo della Libertà (PDL – People of Freedom), to make concessions on policy when they renewed their electoral alliance, eventually leading to the formation of another Silvio Berlusconi-led government in 2008. These concessions were necessary to show that the LN had not 'sold out' for the sake of accessing power and that there were limits to the extent to which it was willing to sacrifice its policies for the sake of office. Moreover, in order to justify making the inevitable compromises of office, the LN needed to remain vigilant during its time in government, ensuring that the agreements negotiated with the PDL were implemented.

As we have discussed in Chapter 6, the LN was indeed successful, not only with respect to putting its key themes of greater northern autonomy and immigration and law and order firmly and consistently at the centre of government actions (particularly during the first two years in office), but also in being seen to constantly lead the executive on these themes. In short, having specialized in a few key policy areas which were not the main concern of its ally– a strategy that Nicole Bolleyer (2007: 123) suggests should be adopted by all small parties taking part in coalitions – the LN was then successful in reinforcing its 'issue ownership' over these themes while in government (see Budge and Farlie, 1983; Petrocik, 1996; van der Brug, 2004).

In this section, we rely on data collected through a combination of quantitative and qualitative methods to assess the extent to which LN representatives and members: (a) were satisfied with the experiences of their party in power; (b) thought it had managed to deliver on its pledges; and (c) believed the relationship it had established with the PDL was beneficial to it (or not). We will therefore consider the results of a questionnaire we distributed to a

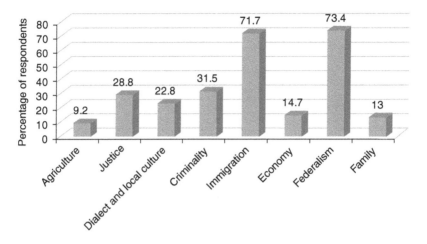

Figure 7.1 'What led you to vote for the LN? Indicate the three most important themes'

Note: Respondents were asked to indicate up to three main themes. Only those categories that were listed by at least 5 per cent of respondents are shown. Total valid responses out of 206: 184.

random sample of LN members and sympathizers at the annual rally held in Pontida on 14 June 2009, and complement this with the analysis of a series of group and one-to-one interviews with LN members and representatives conducted in various locations across northern Italy.[3] On the basis of our research, we will uncover the 'views from within' the LN while the party was in government.

The most important finding of the questionnaire was that the great majority of members/sympathizers – at least the kind who were committed enough to take part in an event such as the annual Pontida gathering –fully accepted the LN's narrative concerning its place in government and were satisfied with the party's actions. To start with, when respondents were asked the three main reasons why they voted for the Lega, the most cited categories were 'federalism' (73.4 per cent of respondents), 'immigration' (71.7 per cent) and 'criminality' (31.5 per cent) (see Figure 7.1). This shows that there was clear and direct correspondence between what the party stressed in its communications at the time and what respondents said attracted them to it. In addition – and particularly relevant to our discussion in this chapter – a very similar picture emerged when respondents were asked to identify the areas in which they believed the LN had achieved success since entering government (see Figure 7.2 overleaf).[4]

Importantly, therefore, not only did a majority of members/sympathizers state that they were most interested in the areas the party was campaigning on, but they also thought it had been successful in government in those same areas.

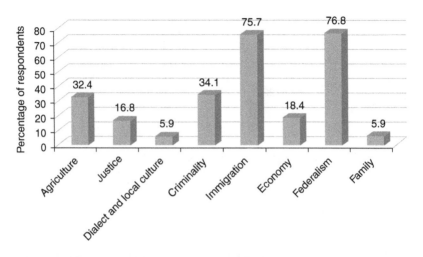

Figure 7.2 'In what areas do you think the LN has achieved important successes in the last year? Indicate the three most important'

Note: Respondents were asked to indicate up to three main areas. Only those categories that were listed by at least 5 per cent of respondents are shown. Total valid responses out of 206: 185.

Not surprisingly, when asked whether they were satisfied overall with the LN's performance in government, the majority of respondents said that indeed they were. What is unexpected, however, is the degree of consensus that there was on this question: 97 per cent of respondents said they were either 'very', or at least 'reasonably' satisfied (see Figure 7.3). This is even higher than the already buoyant figure of 80.5 per cent who stated they were satisfied with the party's previous governmental experience of 2001–2006 (see Figure 7.4).

Our interviews with LN representatives and members echoed the questionnaire's findings. Two-thirds of party representatives told us that the LN had achieved success on at least one of its key themes (federalism and immigration/criminality), and, of these, the great majority believed the party to have been successful on both. The reason for this, according to many representatives and members, was that the party had grown up considerably since its days as a protest party (presumably a reference to the 1990s) – something that many noted had been well illustrated by the very professional behaviour of LN representatives in government (particularly the Minister of the Interior, Roberto Maroni).[5] For instance, member 8 from the Veneto region defined Maroni as 'a very capable person', praised the policy of *respingimenti* (rejections of boatloads of mostly African illegal migrants trying to reach Italy – see Appendix 1, year 2009), and argued that the latter was proof of the extent to which the LN had managed to change the government's approach to law and order. Never before had these boats been sent 'back to their sender', as he

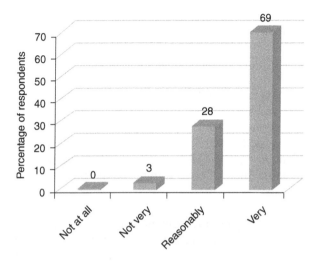

Figure 7.3 'How happy are you with what the Lega has done in government in the last year?'

Note: Tot = 100. Total valid responses out of 206: 202.

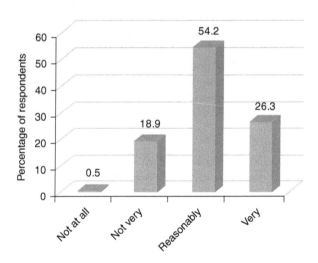

Figure 7.4 'How happy are you with what the Lega did in government between 2001 and 2006?'

Note: Tot = 99.9. Total valid responses out of 206: 190.

put it. Others, such as member 5 from Piedmont, also expressed satisfaction with what the party had achieved on immigration, and cited an agreement signed with Libya in 2008 (designed to reduce the number of attempted crossings from Africa to Europe) as proof of the LN's effectiveness in government.

According to member 10 from Veneto, therefore, the image of the *leghisti* ('those of the Lega Nord') was starting to change because of the skills demonstrated by LN representatives in government:

> this rock-solid image of the *leghista* who is a bit ignorant ... not very cultured, not fit and able to be a politician has collapsed. This wall of hypocrisy which all the mass media built around our movement has collapsed ... precisely because we have someone like Maroni, Castelli, and lots of other people here in Veneto ... like Luca Zaia who has been phenomenal for this region and has performed miracles for the farming community. People have seen that our representatives are credible, they have seen that when they begin a battle, they follow it through to the end as they have promised.

In their interviews, representatives sang from the same hymn sheet concerning the LN's place in government, the quality of its ministers, its effectiveness in driving the government's agenda and its ability to get what it wanted. According to Marino Finozzi, President of the Veneto Regional Council Chamber, Maroni had understood how worried Italians were about criminality (particularly in the North) and had acted swiftly, thereby allowing people to start hoping that things would eventually get better. Federico Razzini, a regional councillor in the Friuli Venezia Giulia region, saw the fight against illegal immigration, of which Maroni was the undisputed symbol, as no less than 'essential for the survival of the social and cultural identity of Italy, and particularly of Padania [i.e. Northern Italy]'. Representatives were also in agreement with members concerning the new-found respectability of the LN. For instance, Pietro Fontanini (president of the Province of Udine) said to us that the actions of LN ministers, whom he termed 'very effective policy-makers':

> have transformed our image into one which is increasingly that of a mature party. And the people now see in us a party which is not just about protest and opposing, but which can govern.

Federal reform was the other main area in which members thought the party had achieved success. When talking to us, members praised the importance of the legislation on fiscal federalism passed in 2009 (defined by member 6 from Piedmont as the realization of a 'dream') and the speed with which it had been approved (that is, within a year of the government taking office, as member 3 from Piedmont reminded us – see Appendix 1, year 2009). Representatives made similar claims when talking about this subject. Hence, for Finozzi, federalism was no less than the party's 'mission', while for Oreste Rossi (a regional councillor from Piedmont), it was the objective justifying the party's very existence. Furthermore, Razzini argued that the introduction of the principle of 'standard' costs and 'standard' expenditures (see Chapter 6) was essential to achieving a decrease in the future burden of taxation on northerners (an important objective for the LN since its foundation).

Besides being successful in government, interviewees felt that the LN had also been very effective in managing its relationship with the PDL – despite respondents generally expressing a very unfavourable judgement about this party in interviews. Although, for reasons of space, we are unable to expand here on what respondents thought of the PDL (but see Albertazzi, 2013), a very brief discussion of this is necessary in order to shed light on how the relationship between the two parties was seen to work by their members.

Criticism was levelled at the PDL by LN interviewees mainly for the following reasons: first, it was said to lack the organization of a 'proper' party, as well as genuine roots at local level (thereby allegedly relying on the resources of its leader rather than on the commitment of a well-organized network of members);[6] second, it was said to lack a clear ideological identity; third, too many within the PDL were said to have been members of the 'old' First Republic political class, which was not to be trusted. In other words, as far as its weaknesses were concerned, the PDL was said to be the very opposite of the LN (and interviewees did not find anything positive to say about it, except, as we will see below, that it had given their party what it wanted). For instance, Fontanini said to us that the PDL would end up 'exploding' without its leader, while member 12 (from Veneto) talked of its 'implosion', saying that 'after Berlusconi, there will be nothing left'. For Lorenzo Fontana, a city councillor from Verona, the PDL was 'a plastic party, which does not exist on the ground', while LN members similarly defined it as: 'a chaos, a minestrone' (member 14, from Veneto), a 'mixture' (member 3) and a 'hotchpotch' (member 5 from Piedmont). As for the PDL's relationship with the old political class, Franco Manzato (vice-president of the Veneto regional government) bluntly stated that the PDL was 'the First Republic', a view that very much tallied with that of grassroots respondents, many of whom made frequent references to the party which had been the fulcrum of the political system for over 40 years before Berlusconi's decision to enter politics, i.e. the Democrazia Cristiana (DC – Christian Democracy). For member 3, therefore, 'Forza Italia [from which the PDL originated] carries the DNA of the old DC', while member 18 from the Veneto region argued that 'they think they are still like the old DC'.

Being associated with the PDL was thus something LN respondents admitted to resenting; however, interestingly, they deemed it as essential in order to achieve the party's goals (especially federalism). Indeed, interviewees appeared to have fully embraced the idea that working with Berlusconi's party – and accepting the painful compromises that this entailed – was the only way to get results. In our view, this is a clear indication that the LN's internal communications concerning the gains and compromises of office – a thorny issue for a party that claims it is very different from the traditional political class – were effective and persuasive in this period.[7] From MPs and senators right down to local grassroots members, the argument used by LN respondents to justify the party's permanence in government alongside the PDL was always the same – and was even expressed using the exact same words at times. We consider this to be a key finding which contradicts the simplistic portrayal of LN members as mindless radicals unable to accept compromises and only focused on 'voice'.

One emblematic example is the case of the bailouts in 2009 for the highly indebted local councils of Rome and the Sicilian cities of Catania and Palermo (see Appendix 1, year 2009). In truth, there were never any doubts that a government headed by a party like the PDL with a large following in central and southern Italy would have had to find a solution to these councils' financial woes. However, for the LN, it was obviously hard to justify the intervention of the government in these instances, since they were seen by the party as the worst examples of typically spendthrift and wasteful southern councils. Referring to this matter, the vice-president of the LN group in the Chamber of Deputies, Manuela dal Lago (from Veneto) said to us:

> our explanation to the activists was fairly obvious … within a majority coalition there is give-and-take, and in the end, what we have gained [i.e. the quick approval of measures on federalism and law and order] is far more than what we have given.

We found this account repeated right down the party ranks. For instance, when asked about these bailouts, the Piedmont regional councillor, Claudio Dutto, said: 'the reasoning behind it is that this is the price to be paid in order to obtain federalism', while member 5 said to us that: 'if you stay out of government, you cannot do anything. I mean, you'll end up like Rifondazione Comunista or similar oddballs.' In short, as member 12, summing up the prevailing logic on the issue in a local branch group discussion, said:

> [the Lega] has realized that if you want to be up there [i.e. in office] you have to be with someone else. And, to be with someone else, you have to give up something. Not everything, but something.

Despite the difficult compromises, LN respondents appeared to believe that the relationship between the two parties had functioned satisfactorily, for two main reasons. First, and importantly, the PDL was said to have fully accepted the priorities of the LN; second, the central place within the LN occupied by its charismatic founder-leader, Umberto Bossi, meant that he was able to act as the 'guarantor' of the alliance for the grassroots and could continue to do so in the foreseeable future. On the first point, and summing up the views of many we talked to, the LN leader in the Friuli Venezia Giulia Regional Chamber, Danilo Narduzzi, said that Berlusconi 'generally always kept his word'. In addition, LN respondents appeared to place their trust in what they considered Bossi's superior vision of political machinations (see Chapter 3) and his expertise in managing the Lega's alliance strategy.

Therefore, Federico Bricolo, president of the LN group in the Senate, said: 'Our Federal Secretary, Umberto Bossi, has always been able to find the right path, the right mediation'. So much so that, for Manzato, the agreement had not even been between two parties but between two people: Bossi and Berlusconi. As he put it: 'our guarantee is Bossi. Full stop'. The two leaders, who were at loggerheads for much of the second half of the 1990s, were seen by LN respondents to have developed a close relationship in later years. For Claudio Dutto, a Piedmont regional councillor, '[Bossi's] relationship with Berlusconi was already good in the last five years, and now has improved further', while member 1 from Piedmont claimed that: 'Bossi and Berlusconi speak to each other on the phone at least a couple of times a day. They have a relationship based on mutual collaboration and mutual trust'.

It is worth noting here that the two leaders had already worked well together under the previous centre-right government, between 2001 and 2006 (Albertazzi and McDonnell, 2005: 956). During this period, in return for his support for 'devolution' and refusal to condemn Bossi's more controversial stances and comments, Berlusconi had received unswerving backing from the Lega on issues of personal interest to him, such as the reform of the justice system and media regulation. The evidence shows that this *entente* (and its guiding principles) was again present between 2008 and 2011, and, crucially, was *seen* to be again present by people within both parties. Therefore, after 2008, the PDL once again voted in favour of legislation the LN wanted on law and order and immigration and federalism (see Chapter 6 and Appendix 1, year 2009). Moreover, it supported the LN's bid to gain the governorships of key northern regions, such as Piedmont and Veneto (see Appendix 1, year 2010). In return, Prime Minister Berlusconi received rock-solid backing in parliament from the Lega on issues such as the laws curbing the power of the judiciary that were passed in that period and those aimed to protect Berlusconi from the ongoing investigations being pursued against him (see Appendix 1, years 2008 and 2010).[8] Indeed, the relationship between the two parties appeared to be so strong for so long (of course, so essential to Berlusconi's chances of staying in power), that the PM seemed to care more about the success of the centre-right coalition as a whole than that of the party he had founded. As Guido Possa, a PDL Senator from Lombardy, put it to us in a revealing comment:

> I think Berlusconi views the Lega as being part of us. So we don't clash over ideas very much. We are two parts, two co-existing political groups that he does not see as being in competition.

Indeed, when interviewed on the current affairs television programme 'Porta a Porta' on 3 June 2009 (shortly before the European Parliament (EP) elections that year), Berlusconi said that not only was he in favour of the PDL playing a supporting role to help LN candidates become governors of important northern regions, but he was not even concerned by the possibility of the LN

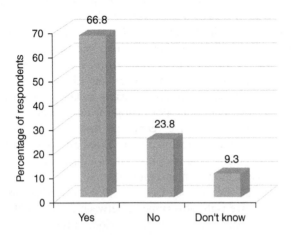

Figure 7.5 'Has the Lega Nord had to make difficult compromises (or "swallow bitter pills") in the last year?'
Note: Tot = 99.9. Total valid responses out of 206: 193.

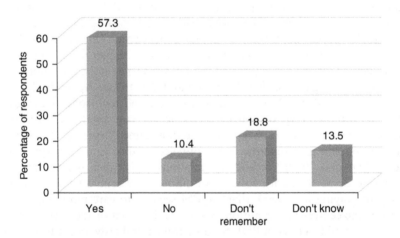

Figure 7.6 'Did the Lega Nord have to make difficult compromises (or "swallow bitter
pills") when in government between 2001 and 2006?'
Note: Tot = 99.9. Total valid responses out of 206: 192.

gaining more votes than the PDL in some areas of the North. Since, for the
reasons explained above, the relationship between the two parties was widely
judged to have worked by LN respondents, in the end – and despite more
LN members believing that the Lega had had to make difficult compromises
between 2008 and 2009 than during the previous experience in government
(see Figures 7.5 and 7.6) – the same members were also more satisfied with

what the LN had achieved in the post-2008 period in government than in the preceding one, as we have shown above (see Figures 7.3 and 7.4 on page 135). It is therefore fair to conclude that a majority of *leghisti* whom we spoke to considered the relationship with the PDL to have been beneficial to their party and cause.

As we will see in the next section, the alliance between the two parties was also regarded as advantageous by PDL respondents. Despite expressing reservations about the LN (as well as admiration for the way it communicated and was led), PDL interviewees appeared to believe that the relationship between the two parties had worked well overall, and that the LN had behaved as a very loyal ally.

The Popolo della Libertà

The PDL, we have argued, was a personal party (see Chapter 2; also McDonnell, 2013) which belonged to its founder Berlusconi and whose appeal relied heavily on the claim that he could do for Italy what he had done for himself: in a word, make the country prosperous. Even more important than the PDL's key themes of low taxation and being 'pro-business', therefore, was the idea that Berlusconi was offering to put the management and leadership skills he had acquired in the private sector at the disposal of the nation. As Berlusconi himself claimed, a year after returning to power: 'you have a government led for the first time by a businessman and a team of Ministers that are so efficient they seem like members of a board of directors' (*La Repubblica*, 2009a). Usefully for the PDL, after the 2008 election it emerged as by far the largest party in what was fundamentally a two-party coalition; as such, it held key posts within government, including the premiership and the Ministry of Finance and the Economy. Moreover, the LN–PDL coalition enjoyed a large majority in parliament (see Chapter 5). The financial crisis notwithstanding, therefore, the PDL certainly could not claim it lacked the numbers or the freedom of manoeuvre within the coalition to fulfil the campaign pledges it had made.[9] However, as we have seen in Chapter 6, it utterly failed to deliver. Consistent with what we did in the preceding section, here we discuss whether that failure was perceived to be such within the PDL itself and how respondents saw their party's relationship with the LN. We do so on the basis of a rich series of one-to-one and group interviews with PDL members and representatives. As we will see, and contrary to our own assessment, the tendency was for interviewees to speak highly of what they thought their party had achieved in government. However, when they were asked to discuss what had not gone to plan for the PDL (i.e. the setbacks and the compromises), we found that, unlike the case of representatives and members of the LN, a coherent narrative appeared to be lacking.

To start with, there was widespread agreement among our respondents concerning the government's ability to handle successive emergencies and manage a series of crises. These were, in particular: the waste-management emergency in Naples, peaking in the summer of 2008, the powerful earthquake that struck the Abruzzo region in April 2009, and the acute financial crisis of 2008–2009, leading to global economic decline (concerning these events, see the respective years in Appendix 1).[10] Particularly in the period leading up to the 2009 EP election (which, as we have seen in Chapter 5, went well for the centre-right), very high-profile members of the government, including the PM, had regularly appeared on national television to defend the government's record in dealing with these crises.[11] In our interviews, we found that the arguments put forward by PDL leading figures concerning the alleged successes of the government in this period had been fully accepted within the party.

PDL respondents felt that, in addition to handling crises well, the government had been especially effective in two areas: the management of the economy, cited by almost half of the representatives and a quarter of members, and the alleged reduction of the burden of taxation, mentioned by roughly half of the representatives and members. Among the latter group of respondents, 70 per cent of representatives and 50 per cent of members referred specifically to the removal of a property tax paid by local residents, the municipal property levy ICI.[12] However, as far as taxation is concerned, we also found some discordant opinions within the party (see below). Interestingly, these mirror the discordance of views among different organizations which provide official data on the Italian economy (see Chapter 6, Table 6.2).

Let us consider the views of our respondents in more detail, beginning with their responses about how the government had handled emergencies and crises. According to member 27 from Piedmont, whose views are emblematic of the answers we got more generally, Berlusconi had always had the misfortune to become PM at the worst possible times, since all his governments had been affected by crises immediately after taking office:

> unfortunately, we have been quite unlucky, because every time we have got into government, all sorts of things have happened. When Berlusconi entered government for the first time in 1994, they hit him with the famous notification that he was under investigation. Then he was forced to resign because the Lega withdrew from the coalition. He entered government in 2001 and 9/11 happened; he returned to government in 2008 and a terrible international crisis occurred … we can say that the trend is for him to always take office … in the worst moments.

Despite the government finding itself operating in unfavourable circumstances, according to our respondents it had conducted itself very well, achieving considerable results (for instance, in the aftermath of the 2009 Abruzzo earthquake). For example, member 3 from the Liguria region said:

> even though he [Berlusconi] has been criticized and so on … providing people with homes in just three months [following the earthquake] is something that probably nobody before has done, because there are

earthquake victims from Belice [an area struck by an earthquake in 1968] who are still living in huts and prefabs. Then, you know, the situation which he has had to tackle has not been easy or simple. Unfortunately the crisis is still with us, no doubt about that.

When talking about the earthquake, member 7 from the Liguria region also stressed that the current government compared favourably with previous ones due to its efficiency. As he stressed: 'we have done lots of things! We have really done lots of things!' PDL representatives expressed the exact same views. For instance, according to Piergiorgio Cortellazzo, a Veneto regional councillor, although Italy was 'always in crisis', this time at least the government had been able to exercise its authority – for instance by mobilizing the army to help resolve the rubbish crisis in Naples. Similarly, Maurizio Bucci, a Friuli Venezia Giulia regional councillor, defined the response to the earthquake as:

> a demonstration of great efficiency and, in particular, of great decision-making ... the Berlusconi government, with great courage, stripped everyone else of their power and said: 'out of the way everybody, I'm going to handle this', and then sorted it out in record time.

Consistent with this, the tragic events of l'Aquila had provided further proof for some interviewees of the exceptionality of the PM's personal qualities – an assertion that was, again, fully in line with what Berlusconi had been arguing in the months following the disaster.[13] Roberto Cassinelli, a member of the Chamber of Deputies from the Liguria region, thus emphasized the importance of Berlusconi's involvement in the reconstruction effort:

> with a drive that was worthy of the Guinness Book of Records, President Berlusconi personally oversaw the reconstruction work and in a stunningly short period of time we were able to rebuild real houses which respect the basic anti-seismic requirements.[14]

As we have seen, the economy and taxation were also areas in which the PDL was generally said to have done well (although taxation proved more controversial). It is significant that so many respondents chose to mention these topics (both very important to Berlusconi's party), since, during those years, the government was actually clearly failing to deliver what the PDL had promised before the 2008 election as regards the economy (the jury is out on taxation, as we have seen in Chapter 6). The key argument that we encountered in our interviews – and one that was again perfectly in line with what PDL leaders were repeating on television in that period –was that Italy's economy was in good shape and that the country was weathering the storm of the global financial crisis better than other Western economies.[15] Even Carlo Alberto Tesserin, a Veneto regional councillor interviewed in May 2010 who had not shied away from criticizing the party when talking to us, stuck to the official line on financial and economic matters. He thus argued that the government had shown it could:

> react positively to the initial part of the crisis. So this crisis, which is terrible globally, at European level and therefore also nationally, has not been as big in Italy as it has in the United States, especially the financial crisis.

Similarly, for Bucci, interviewed in the same period:

> perhaps the most important element politically has been the careful analysis and management of the public purse, and the management of the state budget. And I have to say that maybe we are not in such a bad position compared to the rest of Europe.

In addition to running the economy well and balancing the books, the PDL-led government was also said to have acted wisely to avoid social conflict, a reference to the package of measures approved in late November 2008 in support of families in need (see Appendix 1, year 2008). Therefore, for member 3 from the Liguria region, '[The government] has largely left untouched those people who did not deserve to be hit ... who struggle to get to the end of the month'. This claim was reiterated to us by other respondents (such as Daniele Cantore, a Piedmont regional councillor); however, it is one that is very much open to debate (see Chapter 6).

Not unexpectedly, given what was said above – and similar to the LN – PDL respondents also expressed considerable satisfaction with the actions of 'their' ministers, in particular the Minister of Finance, Giulio Tremonti. As member 11 from Piedmont said to us, Tremonti had achieved international recognition due to his ability to steer the Italian economy: 'Whenever Tremonti goes abroad they take their hat off to him because of how good he has been', while member 12, again from Piedmont, believed him to have 'balanced the books better than many others [in other countries]'.

Despite being cited by many respondents as a government success, taxation proved a more controversial topic – in line with what we found in Chapter 6. For instance, both member 12 and member 6 (the latter from the Liguria region) candidly admitted that they had not seen any evidence that the burden of taxation had been reduced. Although this 'could not be regarded as a failure on the part of the government', according to member 12, since 'the time is not right' to reduce taxation, the inevitable conclusion was that there had been a discrepancy between pledges and reality. Therefore, although a reduction in the burden of taxation had been 'proclaimed as one of the objectives', member 12 said to us: 'in the end, if I take a look, I can't find any sign of a reduction. Definitely not. Objectively speaking'. Despite this, half of the representatives and half of the members still listed the reduction of taxation among the government's successes, as we have seen above, with many referring specifically to the abolition of ICI. This was a measure of great symbolic importance, as it had been the subject of a much publicized pre-electoral commitment originally made by Berlusconi on national television before the 2006 general election (*Corriere della Sera*, 3 April 2006) – which he lost by a very narrow margin – and repeated in the 2008 campaign. Member 6 from the Liguria region saw the abolition of ICI as the most prominent success of the government, while for member 23 and the MP Nunzia de Girolamo (both from the Campania region), it had also provided proof of Berlusconi's willingness and ability to fulfil his pledges: 'the President made a commitment: that he would abolish ICI. And he did it!' (member 23). However, as the financial crisis in Italy deepened from 2010 onwards, Berlusconi started lowering expectations, and the pledge to reduce taxation was downgraded to a promise not to raise it. Our interviewees appeared to believe that the government was fulfilling this pledge and often simply repeated the PM's exact words when talking about the issue.[16] An emblematic example is that of Piergiorgio Cortellazzo, who said to us:

> having kept a promise to the voters not to increase the tax take, despite the fact that at the same time we have faced a global crisis and lots of banking institutions have defaulted ... *we did not put our hands into the wallets of the Italians* (our emphasis).

As we have seen, therefore, and with the partial exception of taxation, PDL interviewees put forward a consistent narrative concerning the government's successes when talking to us, which appears inspired by claims made by Berlusconi and other PDL leaders in the national media. The same cannot be said of the evaluation by respondents of the problems the party had encountered in government, as well as their analysis of the setbacks. On the contrary, these topics generated a great variety of responses, since not only did the areas that were said to have posed challenges vary according to whom we talked to, but interpretations concerning why these areas had been difficult to tackle also lacked consistency. In short, unlike the Lega Nord, whose representatives and members were almost always 'on message', the PDL did not appear to have invested in 'teaching' its members and representatives how to address questions of this kind. Although, as we have shown, when talking about the executive's alleged successes, respondents could draw on a repertoire of arguments that were being rehearsed by their leaders in the national media, there were simply no corresponding sources of 'inspiration' they could use when discussing the failings of the government, the compromises the PDL had had to make, and what had not gone to plan. In short, a party that relied entirely on its leader to put its message across, and was used to 'deflating' after elections, did not appear to be interested in whether its members and representatives were able to defend the government's record. (In fact, the party had not even put in place the necessary structures at local level to explain political developments to its representatives and members – see Chapter 2).

As for the last topic to be covered in this section – the relationship between governing allies – PDL respondents appeared to share the LN's view that this had worked well. To start with, even the LN's advocacy of the need for federal reform (which had the potential to harm poorer southern Italian regions) seemed widely accepted by PDL interviewees. Fiscal federalism was apparently something that everyone wanted, as member 24 from the Campania region (in the South) said to us. This is not to say that southern PDL respondents did not resent the LN's allegedly exclusive focus on the North and what interviewees saw as its radicalism. They did. However, they also seemed to feel that the PDL had been able to 'contain' the LN's excesses. Thus, the president of the Province of Lecce, Antonio Gabellone, commented that: 'the Lega protects the interests of a particular area and it is clear that ... this implies a loss for the South', while for Walter Liaci, a member of the Lecce city government, the LN would have split the country in two had it been allowed to do so. Importantly, however, very few respondents were willing to question the relationship between the two parties, and no one was able to provide concrete examples of government initiatives promoted by the LN that had penalized some of the PDL's southern constituencies.

Besides focusing too much on the needs of the North, the LN was criticized for its radicalism on issues such as immigration. For instance Mariangela Cotto, the vice-president of the Piedmont Regional Council Chamber, argued that the differences between the two allies were 'clear to everyone! Beginning with the discussion on immigration, which the PDL tries to talk about in terms of greater integration'. Enrico Musso, a Senator from the Liguria region, also criticized the LN's (media-driven) approach to immigration, particularly its fixation with the turning back of boats from Africa. As he observed: 'if someone thinks that security problems are only related to immigrants, well then we're off to a bad start'.

Notably, however, critics only spoke in private about these themes and some revealed that they had been dissuaded by those in the party hierarchy from openly criticizing the LN. As the quick approval of the 'security package' by parliament clearly showed (see Chapter 6), the government was happy to follow the LN's lead on this issue and reap the benefits of being seen to be 'tough' on crime and immigration. Therefore, in public, the PDL was always keen not to differentiate itself too much from the LN on policy, beyond occasional calls for it to moderate the tone (but rarely the substance) of what it said. In short, as far as the business of governing and passing legislation was concerned, the two parties appeared to work well alongside each other, something that was recognized by respondents within both of them. In addition, the LN also elicited feelings of admiration within the PDL (feelings that were not reciprocated, as we have seen above) especially due to the Lega's unity and strong roots at local level. There is no need for us to dwell on this here; however, the following quotes are both emblematic and revelatory of views within the PDL concerning its ally:

Instead of demonising the Lega, we should take a leaf out of its book, even here in the South. What I mean is this: if all the MPs and people with responsibilities in the South focused on what to do for the area, in a responsible manner and leaving aside their own interests, and if they fought a battle inside the institutions with some determination, as they [i.e. LN representatives] do, working as a team for the benefit of the area, it would be much better.

De Girolamo

Well, look, the Lega is a real party, a true party, one of those parties in which members are given training and kept up-to-date. I mean, a real party! (Laughs) One of those parties which existed once upon a time.

member 24

In the end, all but one of the respondents from the PDL who commented about the relationship between the two allies claimed to be optimistic concerning its future, and argued that the LN could be trusted. As member 4 from the Liguria region told us, the LN was:

a faithful ally. Always. Even in the past. It has always been faithful. Whether things go well or not [within the alliance] is not for me to say; however you can always count on a leghista [i.e. a LN member]. There is no doubt about this.

In order to make the alliance work smoothly, ensuring agreements were respected and that the LN's excesses could be 'contained', many respondents said they were relying on their leader Berlusconi, with help from less senior members of government who were power brokers in their own regions. Interestingly, this view mirrored the opinion of LN interviewees concerning the role of their leader, Bossi. In the South, Luigi Mazzei (a Lecce city councillor, and president of the PDL group within the Union of Communes of the Salento area) said to us:

This government is coming under a lot of pressure from the Lega which, since it holds the balance of power, can have a big influence over decisions. Here we rely on the capacity of the Prime Minister who is beyond reproach in terms of how he mediates and is able to calm the more outlandish requests [of the LN].

As proof of Berlusconi's power of persuasion, Mazzei cited the LN's abandonment of separatism and argued that the Minister for Regional Affairs, Raffaele Fitto (the PDL power broker in the region of Puglia), was also standing up for the South in government. Nunzia Brandi (a city councillor from Lecce) expressed the same views, arguing that members of government from the region were 'a big guarantee for us! ... to prevent everything going

to the North'. She also reiterated the role of Berlusconi in acting as guarantor for the South – views also echoed by other respondents, such as Liaci, Vincenzo Barba, a Senator from the region of Puglia, and member 25 from the Campania region.

While, as we have noted in Chapter 2, Berlusconi's leadership was considered essential by many within the party for its very survival, he was also seen as playing a vital role in keeping the PDL and LN together. In other words, Berlusconi was 'the glue' of the coalition and, without him, 'a well-functioning and "organic" alliance like the one we have today with the Lega would be more complicated' (member 27). In essence, one of the interesting findings to emerge from our analysis so far is that both PDL and LN members and representatives believed the alliance between their organizations to have worked, and the party leaders to have been essential to the smooth functioning of the relationship between the two.

As we shall see in the next section, the case of Switzerland is very different, as here the style and behaviour in government of the SVP's prominent leader-turned-minister Christoph Blocher was widely thought to have been an impediment to establishing smooth relations between government partners, rather than facilitating it. Importantly, this view was popular among both Blocher's supporters and foes. We will discuss this finding, and others, in the last section of this chapter, which, as previously mentioned, focuses on the Swiss populists.

The Schweizerische Volkspartei

As mentioned in Chapter 1, Switzerland defies the majoritarian logic of government vs opposition due to the key features of its political system, particularly consociationalism and direct democracy (Albertazzi, 2008). Consociationalism makes it impossible for an opposition to provide a clear alternative to the electorate, since there is no chance that parties will alternate in power and pursue 'their own' programmes when they enter government, given that representatives from the four major Swiss parties always rule together. The role of the opposition is thus 'taken over' by direct democracy, as parties and other organizations put proposals directly to the people when they want to circumvent the executive (even though representatives of their parties may well be in government). This being the case, in asking SVP members and representatives to 'assess' how well their party had done in government when Blocher was a federal councillor (or minister) we were setting a difficult task for them, since it is very hard in Switzerland to disentangle the impact and performance of a specific party in power from those of the others. Nonetheless, some of the initiatives taken by a government may be associated strongly with a party by the voting public and the media, even in this country, especially when a minister invests political capital in pursuing an issue and/or putting legislation forward – an obvious example being the Blocher-initiated reform of asylum legislation discussed in Chapter 6. We therefore asked respondents to reflect critically on the experience of the 'radicalized' SVP (which only entered government via Blocher's election to the federal executive in 2003) (Mazzoleni and Skenderovic, 2007: 96; also Chapter 4) and tell us: (a) whether they thought the party had been able to deliver on some of its key pledges during the 2003–2007 period, and (b) what kind of relationship it had been able to establish with the other parties. The analysis of the answers provided to these questions allows us to make comparisons with the views discussed above concerning how the performance of Italian populists in government had been seen within the LN and PDL.

In terms of the methodology, our discussion of the SVP relies on: (a) the results of a questionnaire that was distributed to a random sample of SVP members and sympathizers attending the Festival of the Family in Berne on 11 September 2011, and (b) a series of group and one-to-one interviews with SVP members and representatives conducted in various locations across Switzerland (for more details, see Chapter 1). We found that respondents were usually satisfied with what the party (and, specifically, Blocher) had achieved in government, and even with how the SVP had engaged with its governing partners – despite Blocher's experience as a minister having come to an abrupt end after only four years, allegedly due, in part, to the way he had related to other ministers.

Let us start by considering some of the quantitative data. As in the case of the LN, one of the questions asked concerned what had led respondents to vote for the SVP. We found that the party's positions on 'immigration' and 'Swiss independence' – chosen, respectively, by 76 and 57.5 per cent of respondents – were by far the most cited (see Figure 7.7). 'Criminality', often overlapping with 'immigration' in the communication of the SVP, also scored

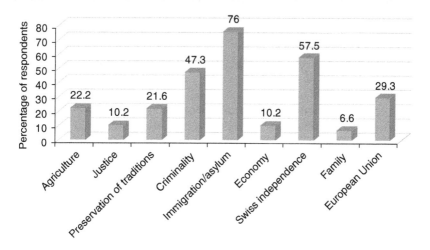

Figure 7.7 'What led you to vote for the SVP? (Indicate the three most important themes)'
Note: Total valid responses out of 203: 167.

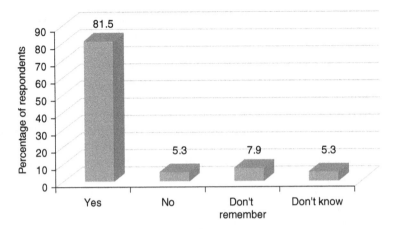

Figure 7.8 'Did the SVP achieve important successes in government between 2003 and 2007?'
Note: Tot = 100. Total valid responses out of 203: 189.

well in its own right, emerging as the third largest category, mentioned by 47.3 per cent of respondents. It is also significant that 'agriculture' was only mentioned by 22.2 per cent of respondents, given the party's origins as a 'Party of Peasants, Craftsmen and Burghers', and its strong roots in non-urban areas (Chapter 4; Albertazzi, 2008).

Just like the case of the LN, therefore, there appeared to be clear correspondence between the themes the party had stressed in its communication of recent years and what respondents said attracted them to it. In addition to this, and again similar to the LN, the overwhelming majority of SVP respondents (81.5 per cent) said that the party had achieved 'important successes' in government between 2003 and 2007 (i.e. when Blocher was a minister). This is shown by Figure 7.8.

Interestingly, when asked to state what these successes were, 58.5 per cent of respondents mentioned specifically the party's initiatives on asylum (including the amendments to the relevant legislation sponsored by Blocher as Minister of Justice and the Police). Not unexpectedly, therefore, 70.6 per cent of respondents said they were either 'reasonably' or 'very' happy with the performance of the SVP in government during the 2003–2007 period, as opposed to only 55.5 per cent who said the same about the most recent period, i.e. between the end of 2008 and mid-2011 when Ueli Maurer was the party's sole federal councillor (see Figures 7.9 and 7.10). In summary, not only did we find that many members/sympathizers had been attracted to the party for the 'right' reasons, but a majority of them also appeared to believe that the SVP had been particularly successful in government during the 2003–2007 period and were satisfied with its performance.

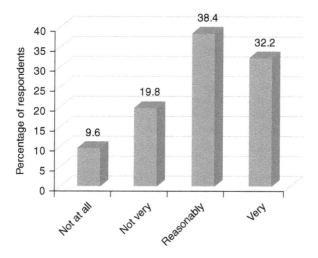

Figure 7.9 'How happy were you with the performance of the SVP in government between 2003 and 2007?'

Note: Tot = 100. Total valid responses out of 203: 177.

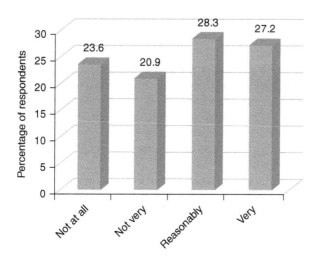

Figure 7.10 'How happy are you with the performance of the SVP in government in the last four years (2008–2011)?'

Note: Tot = 100. Total valid responses out of 203: 191.

That the reform of asylum legislation initiated by Blocher was so popular among questionnaire respondents testifies to his importance (in their eyes) for the party's success in government. This view was confirmed by our interviews with representatives and members. Indeed, not only did a majority of party representatives identify the same areas cited by the survey respondents as those in which the SVP had been successful in government, but two-thirds of them claimed that the introduction of new legislation on asylum had been the most important success of all between 2003 and 2007. Moreover, representatives were also adamant that Blocher had set an example to other federal councillors.

For Ulrich Schlüer, a Zurich member of the National Council, the 2006 referendum which had approved the asylum legislation reform devised by Blocher had been 'the most important item and the most important votation we had in that period [i.e. the 2003–7 years]'. As he said to us, it was:

> a great victory of Mr. Blocher, because it was the first time that a stronger regime was adopted and was adopted even by a very large majority of the population. That was important and it is important to this day.

As already mentioned, this assessment was echoed by the majority of SVP representatives. Interestingly, some of Blocher's opponents interviewed for this book, including those who were very critical of his behaviour in government, conceded that Blocher had been successful in forcing other parties to accept his proposals on asylum and foreigners. Asked whether her party had had to compromise with the SVP in the 2003–2007 period, for instance, Chiara Simoneschi-Cortesi, a member of the National Council from Ticino representing the Christlichdemokratische Volkspartei der Schweiz (CVP – The Christian Democrats), said that this had indeed been the case and cited precisely the legislation on foreigners and asylum seekers as evidence. According to her, the CVP had 'made too many concessions' to Blocher.

Besides sharing the view that Blocher had pushed through the legislation that he (and his party) wanted, SVP members and representatives also credited him with reducing the number of asylum seekers through his actions as federal councillor (something which, as we have seen in Chapter 6, is open to discussion). The opinion of Rolf Siegenthaler (a member of the Zurich City Assembly) on this topic was emblematic, and was shared by several others (for instance, member 3 from Vaud canton). For Siegenthaler, the decrease in asylum claims was due to the effectiveness of the amendments to the legislation sponsored by Blocher and the changed approach to these issues that Blocher had forced the Federal Council to adopt. It was, to put it simply, a Blocher success:

> We are aware of the fact that people who migrate on economic grounds on the asylum track are very much aware of the political wind that blows. For instance, when in Denmark some minister said, or the prime minister even said, that they wanted to reduce immigration substantially, it dropped immediately.

Blocher was also said to have set an example to other ministers since he was believed to have been able to show them that it was possible to shrink the state and run it 'like a business' (as Oscar Freysinger, a Vallais member of the National Council, said to us). In short, according to several of our respondents, Blocher had been the only federal councillor ever to have cut expenses in a ministry rather than raising them.[17] Fabrice Moscheni, the cantonal president of SVP Vaud, put it as follows:

> Suddenly there was one guy that succeeded in decreasing his budget, although all the other ones were saying it was just impossible, and suddenly he showed the way. He showed the example, which means that it is possible. So this old idea that the State has only one direction – to grow – is wrong.

Making claims that were reminiscent of what PDL respondents had said to us about Berlusconi, SVP representatives argued that Blocher had always been an outsider in government. When given the chance, they argued, he had used his experience as a businessman to simply do what he knew was necessary – something widely regarded within the SVP as being revolutionary. Interestingly, this view was shared by the non-SVP politicians and functionaries who agreed to be interviewed for this book. For instance, Tim Frey, the Administrative Director of the CVP, defined Blocher as a 'good organizer' who knew 'how to lead big teams'. According to him, there was no question that Blocher was, and had acted as, 'an entrepreneur' first and foremost. The same view was reiterated to us by several SVP members, who had been impressed by what Ernst Nigg, a member of the Graubünden Cantonal Assembly, defined as Blocher's 'huge efficiency' in government. As member 1 from Thurgau canton explained:

> one also notices that he was a successful businessman, he brought a lot with him from that experience, which obviously he then put into practice in Bern, and immediately focused on how to make the state more efficient .... The consequence of this was that some civil servants had to go and the Department [Blocher's Ministry] was made slimmer and then ... yes, he could work in a more efficient manner.

Moreover, for Johann Durisch, a member of the town assembly in the city of Chur (in the canton of Graubünden):

> the whole organisational cost savings-approach [i.e. reducing expenses in his Ministry], he [Blocher] made that in such a short time that it means an immense point for him. How he rearranged to save money and make it more efficient, that is unique. And all in the interest of the citizen. He said he would do it, and then did it.[18]

Blocher's actions were not just said to be right. Importantly in the context of our discussion, they were also seen as demonstrating his decisiveness and leadership qualities, again recalling the views expressed about Berlusconi by PDL interviewees (see previous section). As Moscheni claimed:

> [Blocher] brought much more clarity and much more leadership in Swiss politics. Swiss politicians are seen as very grey; they don't have to be bad, they don't have to be good. They have to be lukewarm. Nobody sees them. Who is the President? Nobody knows. Blocher came and said 'No; if we want to be successful, we need to have leaders'. And Blocher is a leader. I mean, you dislike him, you like him, but that's it. You cannot say that you forgot him. So he has this leadership, he knows where he goes, he knows why he goes there, he has methodologies and either you are with him or you are not.

Blocher's management skills in government thus appeared to be much appreciated in our interviews: not only had the party supposedly chosen the right themes and objectives during the period under discussion, but, importantly, Blocher was also said to have been the ideal candidate to pursue such themes in his role as a minister. This remained true in the eyes of SVP respondents, despite the fact that, arguably, Blocher's willingness to lead, stand out, and do things 'his own way' had ended up weakening those rules of concordance and collegiality that had governed relations between members of the executive for many years before his accession to government (Skenderovic and Mazzoleni, 2007: 98–101; Mazzoleni and Skenderovic, 2007: 105–106). According to these rules, as Mazzoleni and Skenderovic (2007: 105) explain:

> While the majority system applies to each vote taken inside the government body and while the outcome of that vote remains confidential, once a majority decision has been taken, government members present a common position in public [...]. It is therefore possible that a federal Councillor, who is officially in charge of the policy under debate, must support in a referendum campaign certain policy positions which contradict his personal opinion or the position of his own party.

Keen to mark a new beginning, as far as the style of government was concerned (see Blocher, 2004), Blocher broke these unwritten rules more than once. For instance, although he did officially side with the executive and against his own party on the Schengen/Dublin agreement, as we have seen (see Chapter 6), he was hardly consistent in his support of the government line and let it be known on other occasions that he disagreed with decisions taken by the executive. An example of this is his refusal to provide proper backing to the government on measures facilitating the granting of Swiss citizenship to second- and third-generation foreigners when a referendum was held on the matter in 2004 (see Appendix 2, year 2004), or his insistence that the rules of concordance were being interpreted too strictly. In a much-discussed speech, for instance, Blocher openly advocated letting the public know when there were disagreements between government ministers:

> I really do not understand how a Federal Council can state that the government 'unanimously' supports a decision, when this decision has not been unanimously approved. This is what has happened in the press conference about Schengen [...]. As a result, I feel free to say here: the vote in the Federal Council on joining Schengen was not unanimous and the Federal Council does not unanimously support this project. Any other account of this does not correspond to the truth.
>
> Blocher (2005b)

Helped by the increased mediatization of politics in Switzerland since the 1990s, and the media's eagerness to report disagreements between government members (Albertazzi, 2008: 114–115), Blocher nurtured the public image of a challenger who, although in government, wanted to retain close ties with his party – a 'subversive', as he famously described his role as a federal councillor (Blocher, 2004), and one who was not there to seek 'compromises at all cost' (ibid.). This was a decisive factor complicating the relationship between the SVP and its governing partners – the Freisinnig-Demokratische Partei der Schweiz (FDP – The Free Democrats), the CVP and the Sozialdemokratische Partei der Schweiz (SPS – Swiss Social Democratic Party). Blocher's (often successful) attempts to steal the spotlight – Marina Carobbio, then the SPS vice-president, told us that 'the government revolved around Blocher' in that period – and his way of approaching the rules of concordance, were thus widely credited both inside and outside Blocher's party as an important reason why he failed to be re-elected in 2007. According to Tim Frey from the CVP, for example, the attempt to moderate Blocher by giving him access to power evidently did not work, while for Chiara Simoneschi-Cortesi, also from the CVP, Blocher's inability to adapt to the system of concordance was due precisely to his 'businessman-like' approach to politics:

> He [Blocher] upset the apple cart straight away because, since he was not a politician, but a businessman first and foremost, and a successful businessman, I should add, and therefore someone who always thinks he is right, who thinks he knows everything ... he upset the apple cart also in the Federal Council.
>
> INTERVIEWER: In what way?
>
> SIMONESCHI: There were more leaks, he used to go in front of the press and openly contradict his colleagues.

Importantly, while accepting that Blocher had at times been confrontational in government, SVP respondents seemed to regard this as a significant *achievement* of that period, as it provided clear proof that ministers could do their job without necessarily betraying their values and beliefs in the interest of 'concordance'. As Bruno Amacker, a member of the Zurich City Assembly, put it to us:

> his greatest success was that he became really an active member of the group [the executive] and that he wasn't just in this group to be nice with the others and not stand on the feet of the others. He wasn't afraid of confrontation.

Amacker contrasted this with the behaviour of previous SVP ministers – traditionally from the moderate Bernese branch (see Chapter 4) – saying that these had been much more accommodating towards the other parties. Similar to Amacker, Jedidjah Bollag, another member of the Zurich City Assembly, said that, once in government, Blocher 'didn't quieten down, calm down … It was good to have somebody like him in the government with his ideas', while for Rolf Siegenthaler, also a member of the same assembly, Blocher's approach led to 'real discussions in the Federal Council, not just rubber-stamping, but really discussions about contents'. Finally, according to Amacker, Schlüer, and Eric Bertinat (a member of the Geneva Cantonal Assembly), Blocher's unorthodox and conflictual way of dealing with his government partners was very much part of the explanation of their party's success, insofar as it had confirmed some important and unique features of the SVP, such as the strength of its identity and its willingness to unashamedly and forcefully defend conservative values.

The way Blocher's experience had ended, however (see Chapter 4), had provided proof of the existence of a common front created by all the other governing parties (left, centre, and right) against the SVP, according to our respondents. The reasons for this, we were told, were twofold. First, since support for the CVP, the FDP, and even the SPS had been eroded by the SVP in successive elections (see Chapter 5), these parties were now simply trying to weaken the SVP. For instance, both Jan Koch, a member of the Graubünden Cantonal Assembly, and member 1, put their party's clashes with the FDP down to this. As member 1 said to us:

> if things go well for someone, this happens in every circumstance in life, then envy emerges, and envy poses more dangers than anything else. And the SVP has grown so much, has become large so quickly, and this has generated envy… and no doubt a certain amount of fear, too.

Second, the SVP's competitors were said to have been unable to control the political agenda, as this had been dominated by Blocher's party for some time, and thus allegedly needed to get rid of the key man responsible for the radicalization and extraordinary electoral success of the SVP. Interestingly, even functionaries and representatives from the other governing parties (e.g. Frey and the FDP President Fulvio Pelli) conceded to us that the SVP had indeed held control of the agenda in the country for a long time, especially as far as immigration policy and the EU was concerned. For instance, Frey said that the SVP had forced them to talk about 'issues that we don't like to talk about' (such as immigration and the EU). SVP representatives and members also stated in interviews that their party had been very consistent in pursuing certain strategic objectives and in focusing on key themes. As we were told time and again in exchanges that reminded us of our interviews with LN respondents, this was because the SVP knew what it wanted and was not going to let opposition from the other major parties get in its way. On this point, Casper Baader, a member of the National Council for Basel-Landschaft, argued that SVP supporters and members were perfectly aware of the key ideas and proposals made by their party, and that this strongly distinguished them from the supporters of other parties:

> We have a goal and this goal we have communicated in the course of many years down to the voters; the people know that. We stand for safety [law and order], for independence against entry into the EU, and we are for less taxes; the people understand this. [...] [T]he other parties have problems because they always tackle issues in an isolated way. They do not have founding principles that are known by their voters. [...] [T]he identification with the party [the SVP] is very strong; this is also very important, this is also the cornerstone upon which the party is built. On this basis the representatives in the canton and the members know what to do and what the party stands for. They follow these three points as well.

Despite its alleged coherence and the many qualities that were widely attributed to the party by its members and representatives, it was widely accepted by our interviewees that the SVP had not always gained what it wanted (a situation similar to the case of the LN, as we have seen). Not surprisingly, when asked for examples of setbacks, our respondents often mentioned those concerning Switzerland's relationship with the EU (see Chapter 6). For instance, Fabienne Despot, a member of the Vaud Cantonal Assembly, termed the approval of the Schengen agreements by Switzerland 'a failure', while Hans Ueli Vogt, a member of the City of Zurich Assembly, said it had been a 'huge disappointment'. As we have seen previously, on this occasion both SVP ministers, Schmid and Blocher, had officially sided with the executive (although the latter had not been consistent in his support), thus causing what the party had defined as a 'split'. Unwilling to criticize Blocher about this matter, our respondents often stressed that the split had simply been inevitable, since all ministers were *forced* to follow the rules of concordance. As Hans Fehr, a Zurich member of the National Council, said to us, in the end: 'everybody could see that he [Blocher] did not agree, that he was against Schengen'. Similar claims were made by several other interviewees, such as Moscheni, Durisch, and Koch. The latter said to us:

It was clear on the basis of his appearances back then that he did not support this decision [to sign up to Schengen], but had to 'sell it' nonetheless. And the outcome was then blamed on him and the party, that's clear, this is our system. Collegiality means that you have to stand there and defend the collective decision of the Federal Council.

Evidently, therefore, the rules of concordance and collegiality appeared to our interviewees to be more or less stringent depending on the circumstances. As a result, if Blocher could be praised for having had the courage to break these rules at times, his 'betrayal' of his own party concerning the Schengen/Dublin agreements was condoned due to the need for him to follow the very same rules. In short, the SVP interviewees were still so enthralled by Blocher, even long after he had been ejected from government, that they were very willing to excuse his failure to back the party's position during one of its key struggles of the 2003–2007 period (i.e. Schengen). The reasons Blocher was held in such great esteem within his party had mainly to do with the qualities of 'efficiency' and 'leadership' that respondents felt he had brought to government. These were particularly evident in the way he had dealt with asylum reform, slimmed down his own ministry, related to other councillors and forced the Federal Council to hold open and honest discussions – all without renouncing his values. Therefore, despite the poor results achieved by the party between 2003 and 2007 on issues regarding Switzerland's relationship with the EU, SVP members and representatives usually judged Blocher's experience in government to have been a very positive one overall.

Conclusions

This chapter has presented several key findings of our research. The most important of these is the demonstration of the effectiveness of populist leaders during the selected periods in convincing their members/sympathizers and representatives that they had delivered, or were on course to deliver, on their pre-election pledges. This outcome could not be taken for granted, obviously; indeed, the results of our questionnaire reveal that LN and SVP respondents did not always necessarily judge the performances of their parties when in government in the same terms – the opinions expressed by both groups about periods in office other than those we are examining in this book were less favourable (see above). Having demonstrated in Chapter 6 that, despite their varying degree of success, populist parties in government are not inevitably condemned to fail to introduce policies in line with their key promises, in this chapter we have shown that populist party members/sympathizers and representatives can also be satisfied with their parties' performances in power. In other words, those within populist parties will not necessarily feel betrayed by the inevitable compromises and setbacks that government participation entails. The great esteem in which leaders such as Berlusconi,

Bossi, and Blocher were held within their parties (see Chapters 2–4) and the considerable faith placed in them by our respondents clearly played a role in helping the leadership 'sell' achievements to the grassroots and mid-ranking representatives. This was particularly true in the case of Italy; as for the Swiss populists, despite Blocher's importance in redefining what the 'new' SVP stood for (see Chapter 4), he was never in a position to exercise the influence, and especially command the loyalty, that characterized Bossi and Berlusconi in their country (see Chapters 2–4). Nonetheless, Blocher's actions in government were very much appreciated within the SVP, and his leadership skills were praised by interviewees.

A further important finding of this chapter has been the extent to which LN and SVP respondents consistently sang from the same hymn sheet when asked to justify and discuss the compromises their parties had made and any shortcomings and mistakes they felt had been made during their parties' time in government. As the evidence presented above demonstrates, when populist leaders keep lines of communication open with mid-ranking representatives and members, when they invest in shaping their perceptions of politics and their reactions to events (in short, when these parties take it upon themselves to socialize members and representatives), they *can* cultivate a framework of interpretation of events to be shared by people within the party that is favourable to their permanence in government. This finding contradicts the common stereotypical representation of the members and representatives of populist parties, whereby they are seen as almost mindless 'radicals', exclusively focused on 'voice', and only interested in preserving the 'purity' of their parties' ideologies. On the contrary, our interviews have shown that, within both the LN and the SVP, members and representatives valued the opportunity to achieve some results in government, even if partial, and demonstrated a considerable degree of realism, by fully embracing the notions that: (a) there could be 'no gain without pain', and (b) mistakes and setbacks in government were just inevitable. This also applies to the PDL, despite its respondents being unable to put forward a consistent framework of interpretation concerning the party's failures and setbacks during its time in government. For instance, when talking about the LN, interviewees from the PDL showed awareness of the need to 'put up' with the many aspects of their ally's rhetoric and style that they said were difficult to accept, on the grounds that their main aim in government was to achieve progress on the issues they cared about.

Finally, as regards working as part of a coalition, we have argued that Italian populists were more successful than the SVP in establishing an effective working relationship with other parties in government, and were also perceived to be effective by their members. However, on this point we should note that, between 2008 and 2011, the LN and the PDL obviously only needed to relate to each other. Moreover, they were not very distant ideologically and their interests coincided to some extent. Despite being the smaller of the two in terms of electoral weight and MPs, the LN was generally seen, by interviewees from both parties, as the one that was driving the agenda, punching above its weight, and eroding support from its partner. Nonetheless, PDL respondents appeared convinced that their party had also benefited from being a member of the right-wing alliance, and that Berlusconi had been able to 'tame' the LN's most radical proposals, such as fiscal federalism (see Chapter 6). In fact, according to some interviewees, Berlusconi did not even see the LN as a competitor during those years.

As for the SVP, given the nature of the Swiss political system, it was forced to collaborate with parties that were very distant from it in ideological terms and with which it had no pre-electoral agreement (unlike the case of the LN and the PDL). In the end, the SVP ended up paying a price for challenging the logic of consociationalism, given that Blocher failed to be re-elected to the Federal Council, as we have seen. The SVP may have privileged policies and electoral results over government participation in recent years; however, there is no escaping the fact that Blocher's failure to be re-elected can hardly be 'sold' as a victory and further underlines the SVP's isolation within the Swiss system. Moreover, it is also clear that the SVP's attempt to redefine the rules of the game while Blocher was in government failed. However, importantly for us here, even this setback was not perceived by the party's representatives and members to be the result of major strategic errors. Moreover, it certainly was not widely perceived to be the result of Blocher's own shortcomings. Therefore, in the end, SVP interviewees were still satisfied with their party's performance and achievements in government during the 2003–2007 period, and more specifically with the performance of Blocher.

Notes

1 We employ the following definition of 'party membership': 'an organizational affiliation by an individual to a political party, assigning obligations and privileges to that individual' (Heidar, 2006, cited in Heidar, 2007: 6). We define 'party representatives' as 'those sitting in party groups in representative institutions at subnational (above the borough level), national and EU levels and/or those nominated by the party to governing institutions at subnational (above the borough level), national and EU levels'. Finally, we define sympathizers as 'those who support the aims of a political party, without formally applying for membership of it'.
2 Specifically on the UK, however, see Paul F. Whiteley and Patrick Seyd (2002).
3 A more detailed description of the methodology can be found in Chapter 1.
4 These two questions did not follow each other on the questionnaire. One important reason why the LN was successful in being seen to 'own' the key themes of federal reform and 'immigration/law and order' was the fact that it held the corresponding ministries of Federal Reform and the Interior.
5 According to monthly surveys conducted from May 2008 to December 2009 by IPR Marketing for the newspaper *La Repubblica*, Maroni – widely regarded as the driving force behind the government's initiatives on immigration and law and order (see Chapter 6) – was consistently the highest-scoring minister, with over 60 per cent of Italians each month saying they had 'sufficient' or 'a lot of' faith in him (see http://www.iprmarketing.it/file/image/FidMonitor/2009_12_21_FidMonitor_Min. jpg, accessed 20 January 2010).

6 As shown in Chapter 2, this is a view that the authors of this book, and indeed many PDL members and representatives, also share. In short, the party model adopted by the PDL's founder Silvio Berlusconi is such that active members are not really needed to guarantee its electoral success (McDonnell, 2013). On the contrary, as Gianluca Passarelli and Dario Tuorto (2012: 107–201) convincingly show, and as the authors of this book have also argued in Chapter 3, the LN fosters a very close relationship between its elites and members. LN members thus feel valued, informed, and much relied upon by the party for its success.

7 As Passarelli and Tuorto (2012: 176–177) show, and as our own interviews confirm, LN grassroots members are often heavily involved with the life and activities of the party (indeed, full members have to be, according to the party's statute). As part of this, they regularly meet with party representatives and leaders at all levels (see Chapter 3).

8 We cannot discuss this legislation here, but see Albertazzi and Mueller (2013: 357–359) for an analysis of the extent to which it challenged fundamental principles of liberal democracy. Throughout the years, the LN has provided essential backing in parliament for such legislation in all but a handful of cases (a list of the most important laws can be found in *La Repubblica*, 2009b).

9 During his previous stints in government (i.e. in 1994, and again during the 2001–2006 period) Berlusconi had justified the meagre results achieved by his executives precisely by claiming that his allies 'were not letting him work' (see, for instance, Giannini, 2004).

10 It must be noted that, in these interviews, respondents rarely seemed able to distinguish between the performance of their party in government and that of the government as a whole, perhaps given the key role played by the PDL within the executive.

11 See, for instance, the Minister of the Economy Giulio Tremonti interviewed on 19 April 2009 for the RAI Tre programme 'In Mezz'Ora', and Berlusconi's appearance on the RAI Uno current affairs programme 'Porta a Porta', broadcast on 3 June 2009. Indeed, two years later, not long before resigning to give way to Mario Monti, Berlusconi was still arguing that his government had been able to perform 'miracles' as regards the economy (see *Il Corriere della Sera*, 9 September 2011).

12 For the purpose of this quantification, we have taken into account only members who were interviewed individually, since the dynamics of group interviews make it problematic to assess how many people should be counted as having mentioned a specific theme during a group discussion.

13 In the already-cited episode of 'Porta a Porta' of 3 June 2009 (see note 11), the PM said he had taken it upon himself to oversee the reconstruction effort in l'Aquila, down to the smallest detail (such as taking charge of the procurement of the concrete needed to rebuild the city, thereby drawing on his prior expertise as a property developer). At the final press conference of the G8 held in l'Aquila in July 2009, Berlusconi reiterated this claim once again (see http://www.youtube.com/watch?v=gIBeHhvTYQ8, accessed 20 June 2013). The interview with Cassinelli quoted in this chapter took place in November of the same year.

14 The official title of the PM in Italy is 'president of the Council of Ministers', not to be confused with the Head of State – the president of the Republic.

15 See, for instance, the statements made by Berlusconi and Tremonti at the end of the European Council on 20 March 2009 (Ministero del Tesoro, 20 March 2009), and the claims repeated by the PM in 2010 (e.g. *Il Corriere della Sera*, 7 February 2010). Furthermore, both Berlusconi and Tremonti prematurely stated that the crisis had ended well before the financial markets turned against Italy in mid-2011 (see, for instance, Governo Italiano, 16 May 2009; *La Repubblica*, 29 June 2010).

16 In reality, Berlusconi was just repeating the slogan that had originally appeared in the PDL's 2008 manifesto, i.e. the commitment 'never to put our hands in people's pockets' (for examples of the PM's use of this expression, see *Il Corriere della Sera*, 28 May 2010 and *Il Fatto Quotidiano*, 30 August 2011).
17 See Blocher's decision in 2004 to merge two previously separate administrative divisions of his ministry (see Appendix 2, year 2004).
18 In his speeches, Blocher has always emphasized his background as an entrepreneur, just as Berlusconi has always done (e.g. Blocher's declaration of 7 November 2003, following his selection as the SVP candidate for the 2003 election of the federal executive alongside the previously sole SVP councilor Samuel Schmid: see Blocher, 2003; also Blocher, 2005a).

Bibliography

Albertazzi, D. (2008) 'Switzerland: Yet Another Populist Paradise', in Albertazzi, D. and McDonnell, D. (eds), *Twenty-First Century Populism: The Spectre of Western European Democracy*, Basingstoke: Palgrave Macmillan.

Albertazzi, D. (2013) 'Amici Fragili: The Alliance between the Lega Nord and the Popolo della Libertà as Seen by their Representatives and Members', *Modern Italy*, (18) 1, 1–18.

Albertazzi, D. and McDonnell, D. (2005) 'The Lega Nord in the Second Berlusconi Government: In a League of Its Own', *West European Politics*, (28) 5, 952–972.

Albertazzi, D. and Mueller, S. (2013) 'Populism and Liberal Democracy: Populists in Government in Austria, Italy, Poland and Switzerland', *Government and Opposition*, (48) 3, 343–371.

Blocher, C. (2003) 'Dichiarazione personale sulla mia candidatura a consigliere federale'. Available at: http://www.blocher.ch/en/articles/dichiarazione-personale-sulla-mia-candidatura-a-consigliere-federale.html, 7 November 2011 (accessed 2 April 2013).

Blocher, C. (2004) 'Un anno di consiglio federale. Il bilancio del consigliere federale Christoph Blocher'. Available at: http://www.ejpd.admin.ch/content/ejpd/it/home/dokumentation/red/archiv/reden_christoph_blocher/2004/2004-12-20.html, 20 December 2004 (accessed 1 June 2005).

Blocher, C. (2005a) 'Come imprenditore nel Consiglio federale – un primo bilancio'. Available at: http://www.ejpd.admin.ch/content/ejpd/it/home/dokumentation/red/archiv/reden_christoph_blocher/2005/2005-04-01.html, 1 April 2005 (accessed 3 April 2013).

Blocher, C. (2005b) 'La svizzera nel contesto europeo. Discorso di commemorazione del 60 anniversario della fine della guerra tenuto l'8 maggio 2005'. Available at: http://www.ejpd.admin.ch/ejpd/it/home/dokumentation/red/archiv/reden_christoph_blocher/2005/2005-05-08.html, 8 May 2005 (accessed 3 April 2013).

Bolleyer, N. (2007) 'Small Parties: From Party Pledges to Government Policy', *West European Politics*, (30) 1, 121–147.

Budge, I. and Farlie, D.J. (1983) *Explaining and Predicting Elections. Issue Effects and Party Strategies in Twenty-three Democracies*, London: Allen & Unwin.

Church, C. and Vatter, A. (2009) 'Opposition in Consensual Switzerland: A Short but Significant Experiment', *Government and Opposition*, (44) 4, 412–437.

Corriere della Sera, il (2006) 'Prodi-Berlusconi, duello ad alta tensione'. Available at: http://www.corriere.it/Primo_Piano/Politica/2006/Notizie/Politiche2006/articoli/04_Aprile/03/berlu_prodi.shtml, 3 April 2006 (accessed 27 April 2013).

Corriere della Sera, il (2010) 'Berlusconi: "Le critiche degli industriali? Si rileggano bene il testo della manovra"'. Available at: http://www.corriere.it/politica/10_maggio_28/berlusconi-manovra-canale5_7cb5a620-6a2a-11df-bd58-00144f02aabe.shtml, 28 May 2010 (accessed 27 April 2013).

Deschouwer, K. (2008) 'Comparing Newly Governing Parties', in Deschouwer, K. (ed.), *New Parties in Government: In Power for the First Time*, London: Routledge.

Fatto Quotidiano, il (2011) 'Berlusconi: "Manovra più equa, non abbiamo messo le mani nelle tasche degli italiani"'. Available at: http://www.ilfattoquotidiano.it/2011/08/30/berlusconi-manovra-piu-equa-non-abbiamo-messo-le-mani-nelle-tasche-degli-italiani/154200/, 30 August 2011 (accessed 27 April 2013).

Giannini, M. (2004) 'Il gioco populista del premier in difficoltà', *La Repubblica*, 28 February 2004.

Goodwin, M. (2010) 'Activism in Contemporary Extreme Right Parties: The Case of the British National Party (BNP)', *Journal of Elections, Public Opinion and Parties*, (20) 1, 31–54.

Governo Italiano (2009) 'Berlusconi Russia: crisi è stata un diluvio ora meglio di prima'. Available at: http://www.governo.it/Notizie/Palazzo%20Chigi/dettaglio.asp?d=45556, 16 May 2009 (accessed 19 March 2013).

Heidar, K. (2007) 'What Would Be Nice to Know About Party Members in European Democracies', conference paper presented at the Joint Sessions of the European Consortium for Political Research, Helsinki, 7–12 May 2007.

Klandermans, B. and Mayer, N. (eds) (2006) *Extreme Right Activists in Europe: Through the Magnifying Glass*, New York: Routledge.

Repubblica, la (2009a) 'Berlusconi contro i giudici "estremisti" Anm: "A rischio la democrazia"'. Available at: http://www.repubblica.it/2009/05/sezioni/politica/mills-condannato/berlusconi-conf/berlusconi-conf.html, 21 May 2009 (accessed 22 May 2009).

Repubblica, la (2009b) 'Ecco le leggi che hanno aiutato Berlusconi'. Available at: http://www.repubblica.it/2009/11/sezioni/politica/giustizia-18/scheda-leggi/scheda-leggi.html, 23 November 2009 (accessed on the same day).

Repubblica, la (2010) 'La visita in Brasile: Berlusconi "La crisi è alle spalle gli italiani sanno risparmiare"'. Available at: http://www.repubblica.it/economia/2010/06/29/news/berlusconi_la_crisi_alle_spalle-5261778/?ref=search, 29 June 2010 (accessed on the same day).

Linden, A. and Klandermans, B. (2007) 'Revolutionaries, Wanderers, Converts, and Compliants: Life Histories of Extreme Right Activists', *Journal of Contemporary Ethnography*, (36) 2, 184–201.

McDonnell, D. (2013) 'Silvio Berlusconi's Personal Parties: From Forza Italia to the Popolo Della Libertà', *Political Studies* (61) S1, 217–233.

Mazzoleni, O. and Skenderovic, D. (2007) 'The Rise and Impact of the Swiss People's Party: Challenging the Rules of Governance in Switzerland', in Delwit, P. and Poirer, P. (eds), *Extrême droite et pouvoir en Europe - The extreme right parties and power in Europe*, Brussels: Editions de l'Université de Bruxelles.

Ministero del Tesoro (2009) 'Tg - Conferenza stampa Consiglio Europeo – 20 marzo 2009'. Available at: http://www.tesoro.it/system/modules/it.mef/elements/podcast/box.video.jsp?lob_id=4325, 20 March 2009 (accessed 21 March 2009).

Passarelli, G. and Tuorto, D. (2012) *Lega e Padania*, Bologna: Il Mulino.

Petrocik, J.R. (1996) 'Issue Ownership in Presidential Elections, with a 1980 Case Study', *American Journal of Political Science*, (40) 3, 825–50.

Skenderovic, D. and Mazzoleni, O. (2007) 'Contester et utiliser les règles du jeu institutionnel', in Mazzoleni, O. *et al.* (eds), *L'Union Démocratique du Centre: Un Parti, Son Action, Ses Soutiens*, Lausanne: Éditions Antipodes.

Van der Brug, W. (2004) 'Issue Ownership and Party Choice', *Electoral Studies*, (23) 2, 209–233.

Van Haute, E. (2011) 'Party Membership: An Under-Studied Mode of Political Participation', in van Haute, E. (ed.), *Party Membership in Europe: Exploration into the Anthills of Party Politics*, Brussels: Editions de l'université de Bruxelles.

Whiteley, P. and Seyd, P. (2002) *High Intensity Participation: the Dynamics of Party Activism in Britain*, Ann Arbor, MI: The University of Michigan Press.

8 Conclusions

Populists and power

This book has offered the first detailed and systematic comparative analysis based on original research and extensive fieldwork of the ideologies, organizational models and recent experiences in power of three populist parties: the Popolo della Libertà (PDL – People of Freedom) and the Lega Nord (LN – Northern League) in Italy, and the Schweizerische Volkspartei (SVP – Swiss People's Party) in Switzerland. Aiming, for the first time, to address the question of how sustainable populist parties are in government, the research has considered what the three parties have done as members of executives, their electoral performances before and after incumbency, how leaders were seen by members and representatives while their party was in power, and the reactions of members and representatives to government participation. As we have reiterated at various points, the analysis of Italian and Swiss political developments presented in this book, as well as developments in other European countries over the past decade, demonstrate that claims made at the beginning of the twenty-first century about the episodic and short-lived nature of populism (e.g. Taggart, 2000, 2004; Mény and Surel, 2002) are no longer supported by the available evidence. The same can be said of the charge that populist parties are not sustainable parties of government (e.g. Mény and Surel, 2002: 18). On the contrary, not only have populist parties become crucial political actors in many European countries, but the trend for populism to spread, rather than retreat, continues. Examples of this abound, from the extraordinary success achieved by Perussuomalaiset (PS – The Finns Party) in the 2011 Finnish general election, when its support rose from 4 to 19 per cent (the largest increase of any political party at a general election in Finnish history), to that of the UK Independence Party (UKIP) and the French Front National (FN – National Front) in the 2014 European Parliament (EP) elections, when each became the most-voted single party in their respective countries. Even where their support has dipped sharply, as was the case for the Freiheitliche Partei Österreichs (FPÖ – Austrian Freedom Party) after 2002, their ability to 'bounce back' has provided ample proof of the resilience and durability of populist parties (see Chapter 5). The lesson we must draw from the above is that, while populist parties naturally suffer setbacks from time to time, there is nothing to suggest that they are *destined* to be 'flash-in-the-pan' parties.

As for the sustainability of populists in power, we have a much better opportunity to gather comparative evidence now than was the case 15 years ago, when some of the 'classics' were published that still set the tone of the debate on populism (e.g. the already cited Taggart, 2000 and Mény and Surel, 2002). In recent years, the electoral strength of populists in many countries, coupled with corresponding erosions in support for mainstream parties, has meant that the former have increasingly been accepted as coalition partners by the latter – or have at least been asked to provide parliamentary support for governments. In addition to the cases analysed in this book, and even considering only the last ten years or so, one could mention, for example, the creation of a coalition government in Poland by three populist parties between 2006 and 2007,[1] the Dansk Folkeparti's (DF – Danish People's Party) external support for several governments from 2001 to 2011, the decision by the Partij voor de Vrijheid's (PVV – Party for Freedom) to back the Dutch government between 2010 and 2012, and the participation of the Fremskrittspartiet (FrP – Progress Party) in the Norwegian executive since 2013. It is clearly no longer the case, therefore, as Cas Mudde (2007: 279) observed in the last decade, that 'there have been only a few instances where a populist radical right party had a chance to really implement its policies'.

The objective of this final chapter of our book is therefore to summarize and discuss the answers our research has provided to a series of key questions concerning populists in power. These are as follows:

1. How did the SVP, LN and PDL fare in elections before, during, and after their terms in office? This will be covered in the second section of this chapter ('Electoral losses are not the inevitable price of populist incumbency'), drawing mainly on the material presented in Chapter 5.
2. To what extent did these parties manage to deliver on their key election pledges while in government? This will be the topic of the third section ('Policy efficacy is within the populists' reach'), which is based on the discussion in Chapter 6.
3. How was the experience of serving in government viewed by party representatives and members? More specifically, did representatives and members think that their parties were delivering on the promises made before entering government? Did they believe that government participation could, in the end, pay off? These questions, explored extensively in Chapter 7, will be addressed once again in the fourth section of this chapter ('Incumbency can be positively evaluated by populist representatives and members').

Finally, as a conclusion to our book, we will discuss possible future directions of research on populism in Europe. By reflecting on the topics listed above, we will be able to argue that the picture of populist participation in power is less bleak than has often been thought. Table 8.1 summarizes at a glance some of our key findings regarding populists in power. It shows that, albeit sometimes

Table 8.1 Populists in power

	LN	*PDL*	*SVP*
Electoral success: second-order	Yes	Yes	Yes
Electoral success: post-incumbency	No	No	Yes
Policy successes	In part	No	Yes
Members and reps: satisfaction with government participation	Yes	Yes	Yes
Members and reps: approval of party leader	Yes	Yes	Yes
Members and reps: narrative re. challenges of government participation coincides with party's	Yes	In part	Yes
Party organization keeps contact with members outside electoral/referendum campaigns	Yes	No	In part

to different degrees, these parties have often been able to achieve success on various fronts. If nothing else, therefore, we hope this book will contribute to renewed efforts to understand the trajectory of populism in Europe and help dispel the myth that populists are somehow incompatible with government.

Electoral losses are not the inevitable price of populist incumbency

In Chapter 5, we began our analysis of the electoral performance of populist parties after incumbency by recalling that governing parties of all ideological types in coalitions in Western Europe tend to pay a price for participation in office. The chapter then moved on to show that it is clearly not inevitable for populist parties to be punished by voters for taking part in governments or providing parliamentary support for them. By looking at examples from the Netherlands, Austria, and Denmark, we showed that not only is the evidence about the electoral effects of office on populists in Western Europe sparse, but what little material there is on the topic appears to have presented an overly negative view. Next, we offered original analysis of the electoral data available concerning the three parties discussed in this book for the selected periods of incumbency: 2003–2007 for the SVP and 2008–2011 for the LN and PDL. On this basis, we were able to show that a wide spectrum of results can await populists after serving in government: losing votes was one outcome, but so, too, was gaining them.

More specifically, in the cases of the PDL and the LN, we examined the pre-incumbency election which brought them into power in 2008, the two key second-order elections during their time in office and the 2013 post-incumbency general election. Having noted that 2008 was an extremely successful election for both parties, we pointed out that the 2009 EP and the 2010 regional elections also proved positive (albeit to different degrees) for the PDL and LN, particularly when seen against the backdrop of the post-2008 crisis in Europe (i.e. when governing parties almost everywhere were punished by voters). This led us to the conclusion that, during the PDL–LN government's first two years in power, there was no evidence suggesting that voters wished to 'punish' these parties due to their behaviour in office. Of course, the post-incumbency result at the 2013 general election was clearly negative for both the PDL and the LN. We showed, however, that, as far as the LN was concerned, this poor performance had not in fact been caused by its actions in government. Rather, the steep decline in its support only started in April 2012 – i.e. about six months after the party had moved into opposition following the end of the 2008–2011 Berlusconi government and its replacement by Mario Monti's technocratic executive. On the basis of opinion polling data for the years between 2008 and the end of 2012, we concluded that the very likely culprit for the collapse in LN support was an extremely damaging scandal in April 2012 involving the alleged misappropriation of public funds by the LN's founder and leader, Umberto Bossi, some of his close associates and several members of his family (this led to Bossi's replacement as leader, after two decades at the head of the LN). However, if we focus just on its time in government, the party's share in polls never fell below its result at the 2008 general election. The same was not true for the PDL as it began to lose support in the spring of 2010, i.e. one and a half years before Berlusconi's resignation, and at the same time as the economic and financial crisis started to bite in Italy. The PDL thus provides a clear-cut case of a populist party losing (a considerable amount of) support while in power.

As for the SVP, we focused on the National Council elections immediately preceding and following the election of the party's leading figure (and the man who had led the SVP's ideological radicalization and electoral rise from fourth to first place), Christoph Blocher, to Switzerland's governing Federal Council in 2003. We found that Blocher's actions and behaviour in government – which, as we have discussed in Chapter 7, arguably contributed to the other parties in parliament not reappointing him to the Federal Council – clearly did not damage the SVP at all in electoral terms. On the contrary, and despite the SVP basing its 2007 campaign around Blocher being present (and the need for him to remain) in government, the SVP vote went up, producing the best ever result of any Swiss party in a federal election since 1919. In Chapter 7, we also showed that those in his party overwhelmingly approved of Blocher's actions as a minister. It therefore appears that the SVP did not pay any price, whether at the ballot box or as far as the support of members and representatives for the party line was concerned, either during or after its participation in government between 2003 and 2007. Of course, as we noted, Blocher's (allegedly confrontational and non-collegiate) behaviour as a member of the executive *was* punished by the other main parties when they did not re-elect him to the Federal Council. This is something that could hardly be presented as a positive development, either for him personally, or indeed for the SVP. However – and this is a crucial point for us – neither the voters nor those within his party provided any sanctions. Quite the opposite, in fact. As far as electoral performances are concerned, therefore, our findings concur with those of Tjitske Akkerman and Sarah de Lange (2012), who argue that the results of radical right parties do not deviate much from those of all governing parties. As they say: 'The radical right family appears to be a normal party family in respect of the risk of electoral loss after incumbency' (ibid.: 577). In short, the evidence clearly points to these parties not being necessarily destined to lose votes because of incumbency.[2]

The finding that populists are not a 'special case' in electoral terms is interesting and supports our more general argument that, in twenty-first-century Europe, they have in many ways become more like other parties. This includes, as we discuss in the next section, their ability to deliver on their pre-electoral pledges while in government.

Policy efficacy is within the populists' reach

Reflecting on the changing circumstances in which parties in government exert their functions in post-industrial societies – including the fact that their freedom of manoeuvre is increasingly constrained by agreements made by their predecessors at the supranational level, and by decisions taken by external agencies and institutions – Peter Mair (2009) identifies a dichotomy between mainstream parties which, he says, tend to behave 'responsibly' in government (i.e. are usually willing to make 'difficult' choices, since they accept the inevitability of their hands being tied due to external pressures, global forces, etc.), and populists (who aim to be 'responsive' to popular demands, rather than 'responsible'). This is in line with Cas Mudde's view that those who are attracted by populist parties demand '*responsive* government, i.e. a government that implements policies that are in line with their wishes' (Mudde, 2004: 558, emphasis in the original). One of the consequences of this, says Mair (2009: 17), is that populists 'rarely govern, and also downplay office-seeking motives', while instead giving voice to popular discontent. Reiterating a view that, as shown below, has become widespread among academics since Reinhard Heinisch's 2003 article on the experiences of the FPÖ in government, Mair adds that:

> On the rare occasions when they [i.e. populists] do govern, they sometimes have severe problems in squaring their original emphasis on representation and their original role as voice of the people with the constraints imposed by governing and by compromising with coalition partners. Moreover, though not the same as the anti-system parties identified by Sartori (1976: 138–140), they share with those parties,a tendency towards 'semi-responsible' or 'irresponsible' opposition as well as towards a 'politics of outbidding'.
>
> (2009: 17)

As far as the populists' 'irresponsibility' is concerned, we disagree with Mair's argument. Moreover, on the basis of our findings, we consider the 'mainstream/responsible vs populist/responsive' dichotomy to be simplistic, value-laden, and possibly originating from the way many academics, and much of the media (e.g. *The Economist*, 2014), assume populists must behave while in government. In fact, both our analysis in this volume and our previous work (e.g. Albertazzi and McDonnell, 2005, 2010) show that populists can avoid being trapped by this dichotomy and instead effectively combine 'responsive' and 'responsible' approaches when in power. This is also because, since they are not simply mindless radicals only focused on 'voice' (as clearly shown in the next section), they can, and indeed do, learn from previous experiences in power (Heinisch, 2003: 119). In particular, by what we have previously termed the strategy of 'keeping one foot in and one foot out' of government (Albertazzi and McDonnell, 2005: 953), populists can act 'responsibly' in a variety of ways without laying aside their radical rhetoric. They thus gain political credit with their allies that can be 'spent' achieving progress on the issues they feel strongly about. Examples of 'responsible behaviour' by populists in government include the LN's parliamentary vote in favour of the Lisbon Treaty in 2008, despite the party's strongly Eurosceptic stance, and its approval of two large amnesties for illegal immigrants in 2002 and 2009. A further example is the decision by SVP government representatives in 2005 to support the agreements on 'free movement' that Switzerland had signed with the EU. We have thus argued – both in this book and in previous work (Albertazzi and McDonnell, 2005, 2010) – that populists are more than able to judiciously 'pick' a fight when they perceive the issues at stake to be crucial to them (thus demonstrating 'responsiveness', to use Mair's terminology), but can also act 'responsibly' when, for whatever reason, it makes strategic sense to do so. In other words, populist parties can be discerning and sophisticated political operators, just like any other party. In addition, our research has found that populists can exert influence on policy formation and deliver on at least some of their manifesto pledges (see Chapter 6). We have shown that this was clearly the case for the SVP between 2003 and 2007, particularly on asylum and law and order, and for the LN, too – although to a lesser degree, and more concretely on federalism than immigration.[3] Not only did the SVP consistently focus on the promises it had made before the 2003 election, but it succeeded in winning parliamentary backing for legislation which Blocher had put forward (notably, on asylum seekers), and which was subsequently approved by the people in a referendum. Furthermore, while in charge of the relevant Ministry of Justice and the Police, Blocher could also claim to have overseen a fall in the number of asylum applications and a reduction in the financial burden of the asylum system on the taxpayer.

As for the LN, while the legislation it managed to get approved only partially fulfilled its pre-election pledges, its impact was not irrelevant either. The party chose to focus almost entirely on its key themes of federal reform and immigration and law and order and was seen to 'own' these themes by the electorate. In the end, the LN pushed through a fiscal federal reform which could be credibly presented to supporters as constituting progress on this issue. The most interesting aspects of the reform (from the party's perspective) were the principle of fiscal federalism itself (that is, the idea that more revenue should be collected at the local level to fund essential services, in order to increase the accountability of local administrators to the electorate) and the introduction of 'standard' costs and requirements as the criteria for deciding funding levels by subnational administrations for essential services (a measure which was designed to increase efficiency). As for the Lega's other key issue of migration and law and order, the legislation championed by the LN (especially the 'security package' of 2009) and the initiatives taken by its Minister of the Interior, Roberto Maroni, mostly provided examples of purely 'symbolic' politics that did little to fulfil the pledges the party had made in 2008. Nonetheless, as we have seen, the number of reported crimes did fall during the period covered by our analysis.

The case of the PDL is quite different in this sense. Having stuck its colours so strongly to the flag of economic revival shortly before the global crisis struck in September 2008, the party failed entirely to deliver on the promises it had made before the general election. The experience of the PDL, therefore, confirms that populists do sometimes engage in a strategy of 'overbidding' with likely negative consequences. As we have argued in Chapter 6, the problem here was not only that Berlusconi had promised too much, but also that he had made the wrong kind of promises, since his pledges depended too heavily on factors over which neither he, nor indeed any other individual in Italy or abroad, had much control. Overall, however, and despite the PDL case, we have seen no evidence either that all populists *must necessarily fail* to deliver on their manifesto commitments or even that they are *more likely to fail* than others. This is also because we have found no strong indications in our research that representatives of populist parties in government are inevitably less skilled or prepared for office than those appointed by other parties. It is worth concluding this section by expanding on this issue, especially since the assumption that populists are incapable of putting forward a party elite capable of serving in government is still widespread in academia.

In an article published in 2003 and focused on the experience of the Austrian FPÖ in coalition after the year 2000 – but which also makes interesting general points about populists in power – Reinhard Heinisch (2003: 101) commented that: 'Populist parties may be severely hampered also by their complete orientation towards the leader, their lack of institutional development and, given the limited talent pool, their lack of qualified personnel'. In later work, Heinisch reiterated that the FPÖ's 'failure in government' (2008: 81) was also due to the fact that 'it lacked competent policymakers' (ibid.: 82). Repeating this claim in subsequent years, other prominent scholars studying these parties have commented on the supposed difficulty faced by populists in recruiting 'competent personnel with experience' (Akkerman and de Lange, 2012: 581). As Cas Mudde has pointed out, this has led some academics to conclude that populists are 'intrinsically incapable of governing' (Mudde, 2007: 266), and that their government representatives are usually less 'capable' than those of other parties. Indeed, it has even been said that populist representatives have 'only nominal control of policy fields' (Mudde, 2013a: 14), that they tend to hold weaker ministries in comparison with other parties (Mudde, 2007: 280) and that populist leaders, who, presumably, have more relevant political experience than neophytes, usually 'would stay outside of the government altogether' (ibid.).

Our research has found no evidence in support of these claims. We saw nothing suggesting that the LN, the PDL, or the SVP found it difficult to select and train capable representatives, including at the highest levels. On the contrary, not only did they all hold important ministries while in government, and their leaders all served as ministers (or prime minister), but the three parties dictated the agenda of government on the themes they were most interested in.[4] Claims such as those just cited concerning the alleged lack of experience and ineffectiveness of the governing teams assembled by populist parties appear to be mainly based on the experiences of such parties in government in the 1990s (specifically the first, brief and unhappy experience of the LN in 1994), or at the beginning of the twenty-first century, i.e. the FPÖ between 2000 and 2002, and the Lijst Pim Fortuyn (LPF – Pim Fortuyn List) in 2002. We argue that these three cases, interesting as they certainly are, are no longer representative of the experiences of populists in Europe today, since the three parties had no prior experience of government on those occasions. As we have said in Chapter 5, the problems they faced were thus inevitably the same as those encountered by any party in government (especially coalition government) for the first time (McDonnell and Newell, 2011: 450). This is a problem that several European populist parties will not have to face in the future. In addition, the particular circumstances of the LPF – a recently created party whose founder-leader was killed shortly before the party entered government – suggest this case is so exceptional that it can provide few comparative insights. This recalls a key point about our case selection which is worth stressing again: in this book, we are looking at examples of parties that had had previous experience of government participation. Moreover, all three parties chose as their government representatives experienced politicians who had either led them for many years and/or served in government on previous occasions. As mainstream parties across Europe are increasingly accepting the idea of having to form coalitions with populists, the latter's presence in power is bound to become more common in the foreseeable future. We believe the experiences of government we have covered in our volume are therefore more revealing of the behaviour of populists in power in contemporary Europe than the debut experiences of the LN in 1994, or those of the LPF and the FPÖ at the beginning of the twenty-first century.

Ultimately, what parties do in government obviously matters to voters. As Akkerman and de Lange (2012: 578) have said: 'Voters will judge parties on the extent to which they have kept their policy promises.' We have shown that, in Italy and Switzerland, populists focused on the 'right' issues while in government (that is, the issues their supporters cared about) because they had been able to secure the ministries that could dictate the agenda on them. Moreover, we argued that representatives from the three populist parties were not less able than those from other parties and that, in two (LN and SVP) out of our three cases, they indeed managed to deliver (to varying degrees) on the promises they had made. Clearly, therefore, policy success (in addition to electoral success) is well within the populists' reach when in office, and even in this respect populists are not necessarily different from mainstream parties. It is now time for academics and journalists to acknowledge this when reflecting on populists' experiences in power.

Incumbency can be positively evaluated by populist representatives and members

We are not aware of any comparative research which sheds light on what representatives and members of populist parties think of their parties, let alone how they assess their eventual governmental experiences. This reflects a wider tendency in political science not to conduct in-depth fieldwork examining the views of party members – a gap that has usually been justified by citing the supposed unwillingness of political parties to open up to academic scrutiny and the costs involved in such research (e.g. van Haute, 2011: 13). As regards the type of parties we have examined in our book, it is often claimed that studying their 'internal workings' is especially difficult (Ellinas, 2009: 216). And yet, after many years working on parties such as the LN, Forza Italia (FI), the PDL, the SVP, not to mention others not included in this book like the Lega dei Ticinesi (LDT – Ticino League), we are convinced of the unfounded nature of these claims. It is worth noting also that this typecasting is also usually rejected by the few scholars (see Art, 2011: 26; Klandermans and Mayer, 2006: ch. 5) who have spoken extensively to those in populist parties. If we look at the small amount of fieldwork done by social scientists among these parties, we find that some researchers have proposed 'typologies' of their activists (Klandermans and Mayer, 2006; Linden and Klandermans, 2007; Goodwin, 2011); however, there is little available even here that advances our knowledge of how the parties themselves are seen by people within them. Surprisingly, even David Art's (2011) book *Inside the Radical Right*, based on fieldwork with several parties, tells us little about the views, values, and beliefs of their grassroots and how the latter see their own parties – with the notable exception of how they view their party's organization. On this topic, too, therefore, our book has taken us into unexplored territory.

Scholars who have talked to members of parties similar to the ones covered by us have often criticized the ways in which the academic (and journalistic) literature has depicted them. For instance, Bert Klandermans and Nonna Mayer (2006: 269) find that the members of 'extreme right parties' such as the FN or the Vlaams Blok (VB – Flemish Block) are in fact 'not so extreme'.[5] As they put it: 'the first impression one gets [of these members] is at odds with the picture of marginality, pathology and violence given by earlier studies ... [since they] appear as perfectly normal people, socially integrated, connected in one way or another to mainstream groups and ideas' (ibid.). These members avoid explicitly racist statements and do not even see themselves as 'extreme right' (ibid.). Similarly, Art (2011: 6) criticizes scholars for treating the members of parties such as the LN and the SVP as 'either homogeneous fanatics or the docile followers of a powerful, and often charismatic, leader', pointing out that they 'hold different ideas about immigration and parliamentary democracy ... have different visions of their parties and different levels of commitment to them ... [and] come with different levels of education and political experience' (ibid.). Echoing the views of Klandermans and Mayer, Art also stresses 'how poorly the world of radical right activism conforms to its popular perception of an undifferentiated mass of racists and street thugs' (ibid: 31). The research presented in our volume, based on extensive fieldwork conducted among populist party representatives and members, provides further confirmation for these assertions and supports the suggestion that the latter are in fact not particularly 'extreme', as far as their approach to politics in general, and government participation in particular, is concerned. While this may not come as a surprise as far as the members of the PDL are concerned – as no scholar classifies the PDL, or its predecessor FI, as an 'extreme' or 'radical' party (see Chapter 2) – the results may be less expected in the cases of the LN and the SVP. Before summarizing our main findings on this area of our research, we wish to underline that, to a large extent, these also have implications for other kinds of parties beyond the 'populist/radical right/ extreme right' straitjacket. As we show below, the LN and the SVP appear to go against the widespread tide of mutual disengagement between party elites and voters recently discussed by Peter Mair (2013), and instead foster contact between elected representatives at all levels and grassroots members. There could thus be an important lesson to learn here for all parties that are considering whether to invest in socializing people and whether encouraging their members' active involvement in politics at grassroots level is worthwhile.

The following are the main findings of this part of the study:

1. Respondents from all parties had very realistic expectations concerning the policy gains that could be achieved through government participation, and valued the opportunity to at least make *some* progress on the issues they cared about. Importantly, none of the answers we got from any of our interviewees suggested that they may have privileged the preservation of 'ideological purity' over the possibility to move forward on key themes. In other words, members of populist parties appeared to be happy to support their government representatives, even when they were passing measures that were judged to be far from perfect, as long as these were believed to be conducive to the achievement of some kind of progress on the themes the party cared about. As one party member said to us to justify this approach (and reflecting what had emerged as the

consistent view across our whole sample): 'if you stay out of government, you cannot do anything'.

2. Interviewees from the LN and the SVP almost always sang from the same hymn sheet when justifying the compromises struck in government and the setbacks that their parties had suffered, and were able to rationalize the actions of their parties by using credible, coherent, and consistent arguments. Both these organizations thus appeared to have developed efficient channels of communication between the party elites, elected representatives at all institutional levels, and the grassroots members. Moreover, both the LN and the SVP appeared to care about what those within the party thought – although the SVP has maintained a presence on the ground and levels of activism that are not uniform across the country. Nonetheless, both parties are active in organizing activities and meetings for members (including with representatives), and rely on members for canvassing. In a word, both the LN and SVP invest in socializing those who are part of their organizations, and then use them to proselytize. We believe this must have something to do with their success and needs exploring further (see Chapters 3 and 4). The case of the PDL is different, as we have seen. PDL interviewees put forward a consistent narrative concerning the government's successes (with the exception of taxation); however, the same could not be said of their evaluation of the problems the party encountered in government. This topic generated a great variety of responses and no consistent narrative; in our view, the total lack of a PDL presence 'on the ground' and its apparent lack of interest in keeping in touch with members and supporters (see Chapter 2) may help explain this finding.

3. The members and representatives of all three parties provided very positive evaluations of their parties' experiences in power (and of the behaviour and actions of their leaders and government ministers while in power). Those within the PDL were no different in this respect, notwithstanding their party's objective failure to fulfil the campaign pledges it had made. Populist leaders thus appeared to have succeeded in convincing their members and representatives that the party had delivered, or was on course to deliver, on its most important promises and that compromises on other issues were the price to pay for this success. The great esteem in which leaders such as Berlusconi, Bossi, and Blocher were held within their parties and the considerable faith placed in them by our respondents clearly played an important role in this respect (see Chapters 2, 3, and 4). We therefore conclude that populist leaders can cultivate a framework of interpretation of events within their parties that facilitates their permanence in government. In short, *it is not inevitable* that populist leaders will fail to 'carry' their members with them when they take power. If, as Mair (2009: 12) says, 'responsibility involves an acceptance that, in certain areas and in certain procedures, the leaders' hands will be tied', then our interviewees (at all levels within the parties) came across as supportive of the need for 'their' ministers and government representatives to act

'responsibly', at least some of the time. Indeed, in our interviews, no topic was covered more eagerly by respondents than the extent to which doing politics meant accepting the idea that 'there is no gain without pain' and 'bitter pills need swallowing'.

According to Mair:

> in the past, the traditional (and lesser) incompatibility between responsiveness and responsibility could often be bridged or 'managed' by parties who were able to persuade voters on side through partisan campaigns and appeals to partisan loyalty; this is less easily conceivable today.
>
> (2009: 15)

We argue that, since the LN and the SVP foster dialogue between leaders and members within their parties – and (rightly) present this as one of the key attributes which makes them different from many other parties – their very 'responsiveness' to members creates the conditions allowing them to behave 'responsibly' when in government, despite their populism. If there is something we can take from this book, therefore, it is the suggestion that, at least for those parties able to put forward a strong and coherent ideology (and which are willing to explain to people how the world is changing), going against the widespread tide of mutual disengagement between party leaders and voters can be a profitable strategy. Either way, what is certain is that both the LN and the SVP have responded to the crises of legitimization and representation that have struck their democracies in recent decades by offering *more* participation to people, not less.[6]

As we have seen in Chapters 2 and 7, the PDL is different in this sense. Berlusconi's parties have invariably been 'personal' ones, and he has demonstrated little real interest in cultivating a strong and active party at grassroots level. Indeed, Berlusconi's strategy of communication and persuasion has entirely relied on his ability to talk directly to voters (all voters, not just those siding with him) through the skilful use of the national media (sometimes his own, of course). His has therefore been a very top-down model, based on the idea that he was the party. The evidence presented in Chapter 7 suggests that this model appeared to work during the period covered by our research. Hence, respondents were satisfied with their party's performance in government and explained this by repeating slogans – and even the very same words – that their leaders (first and foremost, Berlusconi himself) had used on national television. To what extent this model can remain effective in a rapidly changing media environment in which top-down, one-way only, non-interactive, 'twentieth-century' media such as television are increasingly becoming a thing of the past, is the matter for another book (but see Vaccari, forthcoming 2015).

Clearly, the populist parties we have covered in this book are not only interesting per se, but also because they contribute to our understanding of different organizational models which co-exist in post-industrial societies: from

Geert Wilders' 'party with no members' (Art, 2011: 186–187), to Berlusconi's parties, which have members that appear valued only insofar as they provide some kind of democratic legitimization for the organization they belong to (Chapter 2; also McDonnell, 2013), to the LN's organization, which – although never embracing internal democracy during Bossi's time as leader – in several key ways sought to replicate the traditional 'mass-party' model once found on the Left (Chapter 3; Passarelli and Tuorto, 2012). We argue that more analysis is required of how these different models work 'on the ground' and what relationships they are able to generate between leaders and members. In particular, it remains to be seen whether, by stressing the alleged homogeneity and the common interests of the 'good people' vs the 'bad elites', populist identity politics is particularly suited to encouraging the creation of closed political communities reminiscent of those fostered by the mass parties of old. In fact, as we explain below, several of our suggestions for future research focus on the need to better understand populist party organization.

Future research

For all that can be said to criticize populist parties as posing threats to fundamental liberal democratic principles in contemporary Europe (Mudde and Rovira Kaltwasser, 2012; Albertazzi and Mueller, 2013), mainly due to their 'extreme majoritarianism' (Mudde, 2013b: 4), it is arguable that they are the only ones attempting to offer solutions to intractable problems which other parties have chosen to shy away from. Elsewhere (Albertazzi and McDonnell, 2008: 5) we have said that populists are among the few political actors contending that, whatever the changes of the last decades, power can still be returned 'to the people'. In short, not only have populists not lost faith in the *redemptive* face of democracy (Canovan, 1999), but they base their appeal on the idea that they alone can make it work. Having argued that politics still matters, that the people can become sovereign again, and that governments should take initiatives which are the direct expression of the will of the majority (Albertazzi and Mueller, 2013), populists propose answers to many of the pressing issues affecting Europe today. These include the democratic deficit within the European Union's structures, the decline of the welfare state, the emerging economic and political power of Asian countries and its effects on the West, and large-scale immigration. The fact that many observers may find such answers simplistic, insufficient to address the scale of the problems, and at times even offensive, is irrelevant in this context. Voters are mostly hearing a deafening silence from mainstream parties on these themes, or at best a nebulous rhetoric that no longer cuts any ice. In addition, mainstream parties have progressively withdrawn from the spheres of engagement they once had with their grassroots supporters (Mair, 2013), while, by contrast, parties such as the LN and the SVP still strive to create a sense of community among those who join them, and help supporters make sense of the world around them and regain pride in their communities. As one of our interviewees said, being a party member was for him like 'being in a family'. For all these reasons, it is imperative for the academic community to further explore the distinguishing features of populist parties in Europe today: their ideologies and impacts on political systems (on which some literature is already available – see Mudde, 2013a), but also, and equally importantly, their different organizational models, the roles of members, representatives and leaders within them, their behaviour in government, and the consequences of government participation. We hope to have contributed to a better understanding of these topics through the work presented in this book. However, more comparative research and further in-depth analysis of specific case studies are still needed, whether of leader-centred parties with (deliberately) underdeveloped grassroots (such as FI/PDL and the PVV), or parties with organizations that have clearly been built to last (like the LN, the FN, and the SVP). Understanding how populist parties function is an urgent task now that they have inserted themselves as fixed points in the political systems of many countries across Europe, have achieved very significant electoral success in many of them, and are now more likely than ever to be part of governing coalitions. We therefore suggest the following areas as worthy of further investigation:

1. The different models, understandings, and practices concerning party organization, and the relationships between populist leaders, representatives, and members. The study of this area should also explore the circumstances in which populist leadership can be passed on (or seized), the impact that leadership changes can have on the durability of the parties, and the extent to which populist parties that rely on a party model similar to the 'mass party' are more likely to survive a change of leadership, or not. This will help us better understand how populist parties function, what the balance of power is within them, and what the prospects are for their future success.

2. The motivations of different groups of people for why they choose to become members (and, sometimes, representatives) of populist parties and the contributions that different typologies of members give to their parties. By tracing the pathways which members and representatives follow – through their socio-economic background, ideological predispositions, prior political involvement, and mode of entry into the party – such research should explain how these inform the members' motives for joining, reasons for staying, degree of adherence to the parties' ideology, and patterns of involvement in political activities (such as filling positions in the party, standing for election, canvassing). Such a study would provide us with a much more sophisticated understanding of what members *give* to populist parties (in terms of their time, contribution to campaigns, financial support, etc.).

3. What makes some populist parties effective at socializing and retaining members, and how they shape their ideology. Also, and related to this, what makes them effective at turning members into activists and

representatives. Key topics to be covered here would be: (a) what kind of 'involvement', i.e. the 'intensity of psychological identification with the party and the commitment to [...] participating in party activities' (Janda, 1980: 126), is secured among members? (b) to what extent are the party's interpretations of political events and key ideological stances shared by members, and how is this encouraged? (c) what is the role of incentives in securing participation? These may be 'material' (such as patronage, career opportunities, solutions to practical/administrative problems), 'solidary' (deriving from the act of creating communities and building identities), or 'purposive' (deriving from the stated objectives of the organizations, such as the introduction of specific pieces of legislation) (Janda, 1980: 108–109). The exploration of this area would tell us much about what populist parties have to *offer* the people who decide to join them.

4. What populist parties do once in government, how effective they are in policy terms and why – by extending the analysis beyond the countries discussed in this volume. Related to this, much still needs to be done on how representatives and members view their party's policy efficacy (in general terms) and, more specifically, how they assess their parties' experiences of either providing external support to governments or participating fully in them. It also remains to be seen whether there are differences between first and subsequent populist experiences in government in this respect. By conducting research of this kind, we would be able see how populists are adapting to the opportunities and challenges that come with government involvement, and also assess how the people within populist parties are responding to this process of adaptation and change.

5. How populists relate to other parties, what they think of them, and how they view their relationship with them (especially, but not exclusively, when they are part of the same coalition governments). This work should be carried out in parallel with the analysis of the different understandings and practices in different countries concerning the desirability, or otherwise, of mainstream parties inviting populists into government. Research of this kind would allow us to better comprehend how populist parties interact with others and how others, in turn, relate to them. This is particularly relevant now that, in many political systems, populist parties have become coalitionable.

In short, our hope is that more academics will respond to recent calls for populist parties to be 'brought (back) into the analysis and explanation' (Mudde, 2010: 1181) by focusing more on their agency, i.e. by taking a 'careful look at the parties themselves' (Art, 2011: 5), as we have done in this book. Despite populist parties often being far more open to academic scrutiny than is commonly believed, and notwithstanding the ever-growing number of scholars working on populism, studies of populist party organizations, let alone comparative studies of them, are still very much an exception. In other words, while populist parties have increased greatly in importance, their inner workings and the views of those who join them have remained largely a mystery. Not only have some of these parties now been around for decades, but many seem clearly 'built to last' and have already survived changes (or seizures) of leadership (e.g. the LN in Italy, the FPÖ in Austria, and the FN in France). In addition, the issues populists focus on (and are often alone in talking about) are quite obviously not going to disappear any time soon. These parties' relevance can be expected to translate into electoral success across Europe in the foreseeable future (witness the results of the 2014 European elections). The time has therefore come to take populists more seriously as builders of organizations, creators of communities, givers of identity, shapers of political agendas, and, increasingly, as parties in power.

Notes

1 These were: Prawo i Sprawiedliwość (PiS – Law and Justice), Samoobrona Rzeczpospolitej Polskiej (SRP – Self-Defence of the Republic of Poland) and the Liga Polskich Rodzin (LPR – League of Polish Families).

2 Akkerman and De Lange include the LN and the SVP in their 2012 study, but not the PDL. This is understandable, since they are looking at what they define as the 'radical right' (which would not be a fitting definition for the PDL). However, as discussed in Chapter 2, the PDL easily fulfils the criteria to be defined as 'populist', hence its inclusion in our book. Here we will again refer to the work of scholars who write on the 'radical right' (e.g. Art, 2011), or the 'extreme right' (Klandermans and Mayer, 2006). These categories only partially coincide with our own, as we have discussed at some length in Chapters 2–4; nonetheless, the cited studies are among the few available that provide data and analyses which can be used for a better understanding of populism, and therefore need to be taken into consideration here.

3 Our findings are in line with Tjitske Akkerman (2012). Having assessed the impact on immigration legislation of 'radical right' parties which had served in government in various Western European countries, she concludes that the SVP's influence was the strongest of all (during the 2003–2007 period). 'In all the other cases', she argues, 'the direct influence of radical right parties on policy change was rather marginal' (Akkerman, 2012: 523). Although the author is here assessing the performance of the LN between 2001 and 2006, her conclusions are consistent with our assessment of the government in which the LN participated between 2008 and 2011. The influence exercised by the party on immigration legislation has in fact always been modest throughout the years. However, the picture changes somewhat if one also considers the legislation the LN managed to get passed on federalism, as we have done in some detail in Chapter 6. Here some success was achieved by the party, albeit partial. Moreover, we cannot agree with Akkerman that the LN should exclusively be viewed as an 'anti-immigrant' party since northern autonomy (whether called devolution, secession, or federalism) has always been at the very core of its ideology (McDonnell, 2006). The success (or otherwise) of the LN's performance in government should therefore be assessed by considering *all* of its key themes. The same point, of course, applies to other populist parties, something we have constantly kept in mind in this book (see Chapter 6).

4 To recall just a few of those who served in government during the periods covered by this book: the LN's Roberto Maroni (a former minister and future party leader) and the SVP's leading figure Christoph Blocher held the ministries responsible for immigration and law and order in Italy and Switzerland, respectively; the LN's party

leader Umberto Bossi was his country's Minister for Federal Reform; the prominent PDL member Giulio Tremonti served as Italy's Minister of Finance; and last,
but obviously not least, the PDL's founder and leader Silvio Berlusconi served as
Italy's PM.
5 The 'Vlaams Blok' changed its name to 'Vlaams Belang' (VB – Flemish Interest)
in 2004; however, it is still referred to as 'Vlaams Blok' in this book, presumably
because the fieldwork was conducted before the party changed its name.
6 As we have noted already, levels of engagement and activism vary more widely
within the SVP than the LN (see Chapter 4). These geographical differences are not
surprising, since Swiss parties are networks of cantonal organizations which maintain strong autonomy from the centre, both in organizational and ideological terms.
Nonetheless, the model of the 'new' SVP, as redefined by Blocher in the 1980s,
values territorial roots, the involvement of members in electoral and referendum
campaigns, and the organization of social events – by following the model set by
Blocher's successful Zurich branch (see Chapter 4).

Bibliography

Akkerman, T. (2012) 'Comparing Radical Right Parties in Government: Immigration
and Integration Policies in Nine Countries (1996–2010)', *West European Politics*, 35
(3), 511–529.
Akkerman, T. and de Lange, S. (2012) 'Radical Right Parties in Office: Incumbency
Records and the Electoral Cost of Governing', *Government and Opposition*, 47 (4),
574–596.
Albertazzi, D. and McDonnell, D. (2005) 'The Lega Nord in the Second Berlusconi
Government: In a League of its Own', *West European Politics*, 28 (5), 952–972.
Albertazzi, D. and McDonnell, D. (2008) 'Introduction: The Sceptre and the Spectre',
in Albertazzi, D. and McDonnell, D. (eds), *Twenty-First Century Populism: The
Spectre of Western European Democracy*, Basingstoke: Palgrave Macmillan.
Albertazzi, D. and McDonnell, D. (2010) 'The Lega Nord Back in Government', *West
European Politics*, 33 (6), 1318–40.
Albertazzi, D. and Mueller, S. (2013) 'Populism and Liberal Democracy: Populists in
Government in Austria, Italy, Poland and Switzerland', *Government and Opposition*,
(48) 3, 343–371.
Art, D. (2011) *Inside the Radical Right: The Development of Anti-Immigrant Parties in
Western Europe*, Cambridge: Cambridge University Press.
Canovan, M. (1999) 'Trust the People! Populism and the Two Faces of Democracy',
Political Studies, 47 (1), 2–16.
Economist, The (2014) 'Europe's populist insurgents', 4 January 2014.
Ellinas, A.A. (2009) 'Chaotic but Popular? Extreme-Right Organisation and
Performance in the Age of Media Communication', *Journal of Contemporary
European Studies*, 17 (2), 209–221.
Goodwin, M. (2011) *New British Fascism. Rise of the British National Party*, London
and New York: Routledge.
Heinisch, R. (2003) 'Success in Opposition: Failure in Government: Explaining the
Performance of Right-Wing Populist Parties in Public Office', *West European
Politics*, 26 (3), 91–130.
Heinisch, R. (2008) 'Austria: The Structure and Agency of Austrian Populism', in
Albertazzi, D. and McDonnell, D. (eds), *Twenty-First Century Populism: The
Spectre of Western European Democracy*, Basingstoke: Palgrave Macmillan.

182   *Conclusions: populists and power*

Janda, K. (1980) *Political Parties – A Cross-National Survey*, New York and London: Free Press.

Klandermans, B. and Mayer, N. (eds) (2006) *Extreme Right Activists in Europe: Through the Magnifying Glass*, New York: Routledge.

Linden, A. and Klandermans, B. (2007) 'Revolutionaries, Wanderers, Converts, and Compliants: Life Histories of Extreme Right Activists', *Journal of Contemporary Ethnography*, 36 (2), 184–201.

Mair, P. (2009) 'Representative versus Responsible Government', MPIfG Working Paper 09/8. Cologne: Max-Planck-Institut für Gesellschaftsforschung.

Mair, P. (2013) *Ruling the Void*, London: Verso.

Mény, Y. and Surel, Y. (2002) 'The Constitutive Ambiguity of Populism', in Mény, Y. and Surel, Y. (eds), *Democracies and the Populist Challenge*, London: Macmillan.

McDonnell, D. (2006) 'A Weekend in Padania: Regionalist Populism and the Lega Nord', *Politics*, 26 (2), 126–132.

McDonnell, D. (2013) 'Silvio Berlusconi's Personal Parties: From Forza Italia to the Popolo della Libertà', *Political Studies*, 61 (S1), 217–233.

McDonnell, D. and Newell, J.L. (2011) 'Outsider Parties in Government in Western Europe', *Party Politics*, 17 (4), 443–452.

Mudde, C. (2004) 'The Populist Zeitgeist', *Government and Opposition*, 39 (3), 541–563.

Mudde, C. (2007) *Populist Radical Right Parties in Europe*. Cambridge: Cambridge University Press.

Mudde, C. (2010) 'The Populist Radical Right: A Pathological Normalcy', *West European Politics*, 33 (6), 1167–1186.

Mudde, C. (2013a) 'The 2012 Stein Rokkan Lecture. Three Decades of Populist Radical Right Parties in Western Europe: So What?', *European Journal of Political Research*, 52 (1), 1–19.

Mudde, C. (2013b) *Are Populists Friends or Foes of Constitutionalism?*, Oxford: The Foundation for Law, Justice and Society.

Mudde, C. and Rovira Kaltwasser, C. (eds) (2012) *Populism in Europe and the Americas. Threat or Corrective for Democracy?*, Cambridge: Cambridge University Press.

Passarelli, G. and Tuorto, D. (2012) *Lega & Padania – Storie e luoghi delle camicie verdi*, Bologna: Il Mulino.

Taggart, P. (2000) *Populism*, Buckingham: Open University Press.

Taggart, P. (2004) 'Populism and Representative Politics in Contemporary Europe', *Journal of Political Ideologies*, 9 (3), 269–288.

Vaccari, C. (forthcoming 2015) 'The Features, Impact and Legacy of Berlusconi's Campaigning Techniques, Language and Style', *Modern Italy*, 20 (1).

van Haute, E. (2011) 'Party Membership: An Under-Studied Mode of Political Participation', in van Haute, E. (ed.), *Party Membership in Europe: Exploration into the Anthills of Party Politics*, Brussels: Editions de l'Université de Bruxelles.

Appendix 1: Summary of relevant political events in Italy, 2008–2011

2008

Following the defeat of Romano Prodi's centre-left Unione (Union) in a Senate confidence vote on 24 January, Parliament was dissolved on 6 February and a general election called for 13–14 April. The main changes in the electoral offer compared to 2006 were as follows: on the centre-left, the Partito Democratico (PD – Democratic Party) ran with Italia dei Valori (IDV – Italy of Values), but not with any of the radical left parties and smaller partners from the ill-fated Unione coalition. On the centre-right, Silvio Berlusconi's new party, the Popolo della Libertà (PDL – People of Freedom), stood with the Lega Nord (LN – Northern League) and several other minor allies. The general election was a triumph for the PDL–LN alliance, which gained large majorities in both the Chamber of Deputies and the Senate. The PDL received 37.4 per cent of the vote, while the Lega increased its share considerably, from 4.6 per cent in 2006 to 8.3 per cent in 2008. Overall, the centre-right coalition was well ahead of its main rival, taking 46.8 per cent compared to the centre-left's 37.6 per cent. At subnational level, the centre-right easily won the Sicilian regional and provincial elections in April and June. More surprisingly, at the end of April, the PDL's Gianni Alemanno (formerly known for his radical right-wing views) defeated Francesco Rutelli for the mayoralty in Rome – thus ending 15 years of uninterrupted centre-left control of the capital.

The new government was made up, in addition to Berlusconi as PM, of 12 former Forza Italia (FI) ministers, which included four who had been in Alleanza Nazionale (AN – National Alliance), four from the LN and one from a minor post-Christian Democratic party. The former AN leader, Gianfranco Fini, became president of the Chamber of Deputies. The major difference in terms of portfolio allocations compared to the 2001–2006 centre-right government was that this time the LN gained two ministries of particular importance for its main themes – Interior (Roberto Maroni) and Reforms (Umberto Bossi). As for the other key positions, Giulio Tremonti (perceived as the closest PDL member to the LN) was again Finance Minister and Franco Frattini (PDL) returned to his old post at Foreign Affairs. New entries included Angelino Alfano (PDL) at Justice and Mariastella Gelmini (PDL) at Education.

Overall, the LN enjoyed a reasonably good start to the new legislature. The bill on fiscal federalism was approved by the cabinet on 3 October while, as regards another of its big issues, criminality (strongly linked to immigration for the LN), the 'security package' (Law 94/2009) was passed in the Chamber on 15 July. It was not all plain sailing, however: in June and July, representatives of the Council of Europe said that Maroni's proposal to fingerprint Roma children living in nomad camps was in violation of human rights law. Finally, despite its Eurosceptic stance, the LN had to swallow the bitter pill of voting with the PDL in favour of the Lisbon Treaty in the Chamber on 31 July.

Once in government, the PDL quickly set about tackling the issues it had promised to resolve during the campaign. The cabinet's first meeting was held on 21 May in Naples, where in addition to approving the 'security package' and abolishing property tax on people's primary residences (ICI), it passed measures to tackle the rubbish crisis in the city. On 18 July, it again met in Naples, with Berlusconi claiming that the rubbish crisis had been resolved. The administration's early months in power also saw the launch of two high-profile reforms: the first presented by Renato Brunetta in June to make the public administration more efficient (but framed in terms of tackling 'wasters'), the second presented by Gelmini in August/September, introducing a major reform of schools and universities (including 87,000 jobs to be cut in schools over three years). Gelmini's reform provoked large street protests during the last four months of the year.

Berlusconi's fractious relationship with the judiciary continued in 2008. During the year, he made several strong statements condemning magistrates on the grounds that they were 'politically motivated' and harmful to democracy. Such comments appeared to relate in particular to his ongoing legal problems. So too did the cabinet's approval of a bill on 27 June which would grant immunity while in office for the President of the Republic, the PM and the presidents of the two houses of parliament. This was seen primarily as an *ad personam* measure to protect Berlusconi from the cases against him. Another emerging problem for the PM in 2008 was his relationship with Fini, with the latter stating in November – in a clear reference to Berlusconi's leadership style – that 'the PDL needs strong internal democracy in order to avoid Caesarism'.

As regards the economy, it is worth noting that the signs were discouraging even before the worldwide crisis hit in mid-September 2008. On 15 July, the Bank of Italy reduced its forecast for gross domestic product (GDP) growth in 2008 and 2009. Meantime, inflation rose to its highest levels since 1996 (4.1 per cent by the end of July). Once the crisis struck, the Milan stock market dropped steeply, with bank shares in particular plunging in value. In October the government introduced emergency measures guaranteeing deposits and bank liquidity. In response to the effects of the crisis on the general population, the cabinet approved a package of measures in late November. These included a 'social card' worth €40 per month for the poorest citizens, other one-off payments for families in need and steps to aid those without fixed-rate mortgages.

Another significant event in 2008 was the Alitalia crisis, which, during the election campaign, saw Berlusconi oppose the company's sale to Air France on the grounds that it should remain in Italian hands. This would eventually lead to Alitalia being taken over by an Italian consortium, but not before the government had to bail it out to the tune of €300 million at the end of April. In the same period, Alitalia announced that it would cut up to 70 per cent of its flights from the Lombardy airport, Malpensa – a move which was bitterly opposed by the LN.

2009

Considering the economic crisis and problems encountered by sitting governments in Europe, the coalition parties did well in the 2009 European Parliament (EP) elections held on 6–7 June. The PDL result of 35.3 per cent was only two points down on its general election result (37.4 per cent). In addition, the June local elections delivered the best results for the centre-right at that level for many years. Among the provinces that held elections, the centre-right increased the number it governed from 9 to 34 and large city councils from 5 to 14. The LN EP result of 10.2 per cent was its best ever in a national-level election: almost two points higher than its vote share in the 2008 general election (8.3 per cent). These results were seen as increasing the pressure on the PDL to agree to support Lega representatives as the alliance's candidates for at least two of the 2010 northern regional presidential elections.

Generally, 2009 was an excellent year for the Lega. In addition to its EP performance, it achieved important results on its key themes of immigration and federalism. The fiscal federalism bill was approved by the Chamber on 24 March and the Senate on 29 April. The 'security package' – which criminalized illegal immigration and legalized local patrols – was approved by the Chamber on 14 May and the Senate on 2 July. Also concerning immigration, the policy known as *respingimenti* (that is, turning back boats from Africa carrying immigrants), which began in May, was seen as an important LN success (particularly for Interior Minister Roberto Maroni).

Other than the elections, 2009 was a mixed year for the PDL. Its inaugural conference took place on 27–29 March and Berlusconi was elected party president by acclamation. However, in the ensuing months, tensions between him and Fini were apparent (and much discussed in the media). In particular, Fini was said to be dissatisfied with Berlusconi's dominance of the party and his closeness to the LN. Their rift was widened in December by the release of footage in which Fini could be heard saying to a magistrate at a conference that Berlusconi 'confuses popular support with a sort of immunity'.

These were not the only problems for Berlusconi: it emerged on 29 April that he had attended an 18-year-old girl's birthday party and there was much subsequent speculation about the nature of their relationship. On 3 May, Berlusconi's wife announced she was seeking a divorce. Revelations about the PM's sex life continued: in July the magazine *L'Espresso* published a recording of a conversation between Berlusconi and an escort, Patrizia D'Addario. In September, the *Corriere della Sera* released details of Berlusconi's friendship with a businessman, Gianpaolo Tarantini, who was said to have paid dozens of girls to attend parties with the PM and, in some cases, to sleep with him. Berlusconi's response to the scandals was usually to shrug them off. For example, on 22 July, he said: 'there are lots of pretty girls around. I'm not a saint. You've all realized that'.

Berlusconi faced other judicial troubles in 2009: in October, the appeal trial of David Mills – a British lawyer who was said to have lied to protect Berlusconi and his Fininvest group – confirmed his sentence of four and a half years (although he would still be able to make a final appeal). Berlusconi claimed the decision was the product of 'political hatred and envy'. In October, he went further, accusing 'certain judges' of wanting to 'overturn the popular will'. He also cast doubt on the impartiality of Giorgio Napolitano (on the grounds that the President of the Republic was a former member of the Italian Communist Party).

Economic indicators in 2009 all pointed to a worsening of Italy's position. Data in March showed that 2008 GDP had fallen by 1 per cent. On 15 January, the Bank of Italy estimated that GDP would fall that year by 2 per cent. In April, the International Monetary Fund forecast was much worse, estimating a 4.4 per cent Italian GDP fall in 2009. Confirmation of this very negative trend came with Istat figures in May, showing that GDP in the first three months of 2009 was down 5.9 per cent, the worst result of its kind since 1980. In response, the government launched an 'anti-crisis decree' in June. This was intended to provide tax breaks for firms reinvesting profits and to reduce energy bills for families. It also proposed an amnesty (upon payment of a 5 per cent penalty) for those declaring capital hidden from the taxman in foreign bank accounts. Parliament approved these measures at the end of September. In October, some members of the PDL pushed for the government to abolish the regional business tax IRAP, but Tremonti opposed this. Berlusconi's response to the crisis was generally to play it down. For example, on 6 March, he stated: 'it is a serious crisis, but not a tragic one' and criticized the media for its portrayal of it.

On the opposition front, 2009 was 'the year of the 3 PD leaders'. On 17 February, Veltroni resigned following a regional election defeat in Sardinia (Berlusconi had been heavily present during the campaign in support of the local PDL candidate). Dario Franceschini was elected Secretary by the PD national assembly on 21 February, until such time as full leadership primaries could be held. These took place on 25 October and were won by the former minister, Pierluigi Bersani.

A final significant event in 2009 was the 6 April earthquake in l'Aquila, (Abruzzo) in which over 300 people died, with many more left injured and homeless. In response, Berlusconi decided that the July G8 meeting would be moved from Sardinia to l'Aquila. During the summer, he claimed the reconstruction work so far had been conducted in 'record time'. He also said he was looking for a house in Abruzzo in order to personally supervise work in August that year. This did not happen and Berlusconi instead spent his holidays, as usual, at his mansion in Sardinia. In the ensuing years, the merits of the l'Aquila reconstruction – and the legality surrounding the rebuilding contracts – would be strongly contested.

2010

Once again in contrast to governing parties elsewhere in Western Europe during the crisis, the PDL and LN did well in the regional elections on 28–29 March. The centre-right won four large regions – Piedmont, Lazio, Campania, and Calabria – from the centre-left and held both Lombardy and Veneto. Apart from Basilicata and Puglia, the centre-left only retained control of those regions in the centre and North which were its traditional strongholds. The centre-right also won all four provincial elections, while the municipal election results were more balanced.

In particular, 2010 was another excellent year for the Lega. In negotiations with the PDL, it was able to secure the regional presidential candidatures for Roberto Cota in Piedmont and Luca Zaia in Veneto. Given that the PDL was far stronger electorally in Piedmont and already held the regional presidency in Veneto, these were significant concessions. In the elections, Zaia took 60 per cent while Cota won narrowly against the centre-left incumbent. Across the North, the LN achieved its best ever results at regional level. It also continued to make progress on its key themes. In October, the cabinet approved the final decrees required to introduce federalism while, throughout the year, the Interior Minister Maroni – seen as the face of the fight against immigration and crime – was constantly the highest-ranked minister in public approval surveys.

Two key features of the PDL's year were its focus on curbing the power of magistrates and the involvement of senior party figures in scandals. At the beginning of 2010, Berlusconi announced there would be reforms on justice, schools, and tax. However, the first two of these seemed to occupy the government's attention more than the third. In particular, much effort was spent devising and debating bills restricting phone wiretaps and the introduction of a 'legitimate impediment' law which politicians could use to avoid attending court trials. This was passed in the Chamber in February and in the Senate in March. While both the PDL minister Claudio Scajola and party coordinator Denis Verdini were the subjects of corruption allegations during 2010, it was again Berlusconi who faced the worst accusations. Most notably, at the end of October, the 'Ruby' scandal broke – with Berlusconi accused of having paid for sex with an underage Moroccan escort and of having also used his influence to get her released from police custody following her arrest for theft.

In the case of the latter incident, Berlusconi claimed he believed Ruby was the granddaughter of Egyptian President Hosni Mubarak and so he acted in order to avoid a diplomatic incident. As regards his personal life, his response was generally to shrug off criticism with jokes about his liking for women in the same manner as with the D'Addario scandal the previous year.

By far the most significant event concerning the PDL in 2010, however, was the split it suffered. The tensions between Fini and Berlusconi, already present in 2009, quickly escalated in 2010. In early March, Fini said he did not like the PDL in 'its current state'. On 16 April, he went further by raising the possibility of forming a separate parliamentary group (which would, however, support the government). This led to a highly charged televised meeting of the PDL National Executive on 22 April in which, having criticized one another, Fini and Berlusconi openly argued, with Fini asking 'are you going to throw me out?' The party executive overwhelmingly approved Berlusconi's stance by 171 to 12 votes.

In the ensuing months, the breakaway of Fini and his supporters became a question of 'when' and 'how' rather than 'if'. The end came on 29 July when the PDL expelled several members close to Fini and, the following day, Fini responded by holding a press conference in which he called Berlusconi 'illiberal' and claimed that he had been effectively expelled from the party. He and his supporters – including over 30 deputies – formed a new group, Futuro e Libertà per l'Italia (FLI – Future and Liberty for Italy), which pledged to support the government on most, but not necessarily all, issues. Given the coalition's now reduced majority, there was media speculation about the possibility of the former member of the centre-right coalition, the Unione di Centro (UDC – Union of the Centre), entering government. This suggestion was strongly opposed by the Lega.

Those ministers who had joined FLI remained in place for a few months, but resigned in mid-November. During that month, FLI began to vote with the opposition on some issues. In the first half of December, it looked as though the government would be brought down when FLI, together with a series of other small parties, proposed a motion of no-confidence. However, to some surprise – and thanks to the last-minute return of two FLI members to the PDL – the government survived in the Chamber on 14 December with 311 deputies voting in favour, 314 against and 2 abstaining. The following day, Fini announced the creation of a new alliance with the UDC and some of the minor groups in parliament.

The crisis continued to bite in Italy, with the government blaming it on several occasions for the failure to cut taxes. At other times, Berlusconi promised that tax reform and reductions were on the way, but these never materialized. Although the government was forced to introduce a budget which made cuts to large public works projects, some pensions, and hiring rounds in state enterprises, Berlusconi claimed that Italy was better off than other European countries and that his government had the merit of protecting the public purse without raising taxes.

Two other relevant pieces of news in 2010 were, first, the re-emergence of the rubbish crisis in Naples in November – with the EU saying the situation had not fundamentally changed since 2008, and, second, the passing of the Gelmini university reform by the Chamber on 30 November and by the Senate on 23 December. This was marked by a series of large protests across the country, some of which led to violent clashes with the police.

2011

Following its narrow survival in the December 2010 no-confidence vote, the Berlusconi government spent much of 2011 clinging to power before finally succumbing in November to the combined pressures of the financial crisis, the erosion of its parliamentary majority, and the loss of confidence in its abilities – particularly among elites – both inside and outside Italy. For our purposes, however, it is important to note that, while the mid-2011 crisis determined the timing and manner of the government's collapse, the preceding months were also difficult and unproductive ones for the PDL and the LN.

Both parties performed poorly in the May 2011 local elections. In the two biggest contests, the centre-right lost the mayoralty of Milan, having held it for decades, and also failed to win in Naples, where it had been strongly tipped to replace a centre-left administration damaged by scandals and bad management. Instead 'outsider' Left candidates won in both cities. Elsewhere, the mainstream centre-left held most of those councils it previously controlled and gained several medium-sized cities. The defeat of the PDL's mayor in Milan, Letizia Moratti, was a particularly hard blow for Berlusconi not only because it was his home city, but also because he personally intervened in the campaign with a series of public and television appearances, which sought to portray the elections as yet another crucial 'choice of sides' between good and evil.

The local elections were shortly followed by referendums on 12–13 June on water privatization, nuclear power, and the 'legitimate impediment' law, all of which the governing parties had first opposed and then depicted as 'irrelevant' (encouraging their supporters not to vote). The referendum, however, became the first in over a decade to reach the turnout quorum (with 55 per cent voting) and resulted in overwhelming victories (over 94 per cent on all issues) for the 'yes' camps against the government positions.

While the Lega vote in the local elections was up slightly on the same elections in those cities five years previously, it dropped considerably compared to the party's performances in the 2008–2010 period. On its key themes of federalism and immigration, there was little for the LN to celebrate in 2011. While parliament approved a number of decree laws on federalism, the financial crisis made it apparent that little would happen in concrete terms. On immigration, the main issue was the arrival of migrants due to the 'Arab Spring' uprisings in Tunisia and Libya. Maroni strongly criticized the EU for supposedly leaving Italy alone to deal with the arrivals. Tensions between the government and the EU were exacerbated by a European Court of Justice ruling on 28 April that illegal immigration could not be punished by a prison sentence. 2011 also saw disagreements emerge first between the Lega and the PDL and, second, within the Lega itself. Concerning the former, the party's relations with Berlusconi and Tremonti worsened due to the government's failure to cut taxes and Tremonti's proposals for pension reform. Italy's participation in the bombing of Libya from late April onwards was also a source of strong discord between the two parties, as the LN was opposed to it. As regards the LN internally, it became clear from the middle of the year onwards that there were problems between Bossi and Maroni. These could be seen particularly regarding key appointments in the party (such as the confirmation of the Bossi loyalist, Marco Reguzzoni, as the party's group leader in the Chamber of Deputies).

As mentioned, the 2011 local elections went badly for the PDL and its vote declined heavily. Despite the economic and financial crises, much of the party's attention in 2011 seemed devoted to overhauling the legal system. Indeed, even at the height of the financial crisis in mid-September, Berlusconi met Napolitano to discuss a decree blocking the publication of wiretap transcripts. As for his own problems with the law, Berlusconi said in May that the magistrates investigating him were 'a cancer' and told Barack Obama at the G8 meeting the same month that in Italy there was 'almost a dictatorship of left-wing judges'. Within the PDL, there were two important developments: first, Berlusconi's announcement that Justice Minister, Angelino Alfano, would take on the newly created role (by Berlusconi) of party secretary. This was ratified 'by acclamation' at the PDL's National Council on 1 July. Second, there was a clear and public breakdown in the relationship between Tremonti and Berlusconi, especially during the summer and autumn crisis.

There is not the space here to deal with each step of the severe financial crisis which began in July other than to note that it led to shares on the Milan exchange dropping heavily on many occasions, the spread between Italian and German 10-year government bonds widening rapidly, with yields for Italy's bonds soaring through the 7 per cent ceiling that had previously signalled the need for Greece, Ireland, and Portugal to be bailed out, and agencies downgrading Italy's credit rating. These events in turn raised serious questions as to whether the state would be able to continue servicing its massive public debt. At the heart of the sustained pressure on Italy was the seeming inability of its government to take any decisive measures to get the public purse under control and relaunch the economy. The government had promised tax reforms and significant growth packages during the first half of 2011, but these never materialized. Even during the height of the crisis in August and September, it talked about tough measures (e.g. on pensions, increasing VAT, making big local authority cuts, abolishing provinces), but was never able to deliver any of these fully or quickly enough to reassure the markets and Italy's EU partners. In October, the European Council formally asked Italy to confirm that it would keep to its promises on reforms. However, it was clear by this time that elites in neither Europe nor Italy (e.g. the main business leaders' association Confindustria) had faith in the government.

As mentioned, even before the crisis, the government enjoyed only a slim parliamentary majority in 2011. However, this evaporated entirely when five deputies left the party on 3 November, with others following in the ensuing days. On 8 November, in a vote on the financial accounts, it became apparent that Berlusconi could no longer count on a majority of deputies. He met with Napolitano and announced he would resign on 12 November once the stability bill (which contained a series of measures concerning privatizations, the reduction of bureaucracy, and various incentives for business) was passed. The President of the Republic reacted by first appointing the former European Commissioner, Mario Monti, as Life Senator and then asking him to form a government. Although the PDL was initially divided about how it should react, Berlusconi agreed to support the new administration. So too did the PD and the UDC. On 17 and 18 November, Monti's government – containing only technocrats and not a single party representative – won confidence votes in the Chamber and the Senate. It was supported by all parliamentary parties, with only the LN opposing it. This difference of opinion brought a temporary end to the LN–PDL alliance which had lasted for over ten years. The Monti government began its time in office by immediately passing a series of austerity measures, most notably pension reforms and the introduction of property tax. Although he expressed doubts about it, Berlusconi and almost all the PDL MPs voted for the package, as did the PD and the UDC. The Lega, by now the main parliamentary opposition force, voted against.

Appendix 2: Summary of relevant political events in Switzerland, 2003–2007

2003

The most significant political event of 2003 was the success of the Schweizerische Volkspartei (SVP – Swiss People's Party) in the October federal (general) election. Having achieved 26.7 per cent of the vote in the lower chamber, the National Council (+4.2 per cent on the 1999 election), and thus become the largest single party, the SVP was able to claim a second seat in the seven-member Federal Council (the Swiss governing executive). The two main left-wing parties – the Sozialdemokratische Partei der Schweiz (SPS – Swiss Social Democratic Party) and the Grüne Partei der Schweiz (Greens – The Green Party) – also gained votes, increasing the polarization of the party system. Their combined electoral strength rose by 3.2 percentage points, reaching 30.7 per cent overall.

The members of the Federal Council enjoy equal powers and are elected individually for four-year terms by the two chambers of parliament sitting in common session. Executive seats have traditionally been distributed in accordance with parliamentary strength, by means of a 'magic formula' in place since 1959. For four decades, this consistently assigned two seats each to the SPS, the liberals of the Freisinnig-Demokratische Partei der Schweiz (FDP – The Free Democrats) and the Christlichdemokratische Volkspartei der Schweiz (CVP – The Christian Democrats), with the remaining seat going to the SVP. Because the SVP was the only party to have steadily (and rapidly) increased its share of the vote and parliamentary representation since 1991, it was increasingly difficult by 2003 to resist claims that the party should be given an additional seat in government. Moreover, the SVP demanded that this second seat should go to its chosen candidate: the president of its Zurich branch and de facto leader of the party nationally, Christoph Blocher. If successful, Blocher would thus enter government alongside the party's existing federal councillor (i.e. minister), Samuel Schmid, who had been elected to the executive in 2000 and represented the SVP's more moderate Bernese branch. On 10 December 2003, parliament elected Blocher to government, in place of the CVP's Ruth Metzler. Not only did this change the 40-year equilibria between the parties in the executive, but it was also the first time a sitting federal councillor who was willing to continue in office had failed to be re-elected.

The SVP's federal election campaign had focused prominently on the following themes: (a) opposing 'excessive' immigration and the 'abuse' of the asylum system; (b) defending Switzerland's exceptionalism, known as the 'Sonderfall Schweiz' (based on the country's unique combination of three-tiered federalism, neutrality in foreign affairs, and direct democracy); (c) opposing closer ties with the EU; and (d) ensuring the welfare of Swiss citizens (by focusing on pensions and health care).

As for public opinion trends in 2003, a survey during the summer showed that pensions, the economy, health care, asylum, and public finances were the main issues concerning voters. The prominence of the asylum issue could in part be explained by the fact that in 2002 the electorate had rejected an SVP-sponsored popular initiative entitled 'Against the Abuse of Asylum Rights', which had dominated public debates for months. This initiative had been rejected by the narrowest of margins: only 50.1 per cent of voters had opposed the hardening of asylum legislation proposed by the SVP, while a majority of cantons (15 vs 11) had in fact supported it (although this was not sufficient to carry it). Although it declined in salience during the year, asylum was still ranked fourth among the issues concerning voters in autumn 2003.

In September – one month before the federal elections – two popular initiatives were announced by the SVP: the first demanded a tougher stance on asylum seekers, while the second aimed at allowing municipalities to continue deciding the naturalization of foreigners through local ballots (a practice that had been outlawed by the Federal Tribunal on 9 July). As for foreign policy, in May 2003 the SVP petitioned the government to withdraw its application for EU membership (made in 1992) and demanded a halt to all further bilateral treaties with the EU. However, a majority of 116 to 61 rejected the motion in the National Council. The powerful Conference of Cantonal Governments also expressed its support for the Swiss government's European policy, and a manifesto signed by prominent figures from the cultural, scientific, and economic milieux called for the opening of full accession talks with the EU by 2004. The Neue Europäische Bewegung Schweiz (New European Movement of Switzerland) acted as the sole non-parliamentary counterweight to the SVP's policy of withdrawing from all bilateral treaties with the EU. In other matters of foreign policy, there was broad consensus among the parties (a prominent example being Switzerland's refusal to allow the United States to use Swiss airspace during the Iraq war since military action had not been authorized by the United Nations).

As for the economy, it recovered slightly in the second half of the year, although unemployment rose to 3.7 per cent (from 2.5 per cent the year before). In September, Finance Minister Kaspar Villiger (FDP) announced that he would resign and Hans-Rudolf Merz (FDP) was elected to succeed him on 10 December.

2004

The year began with the inauguration of Christoph Blocher as Minister of Justice and the Police (which includes responsibility for asylum matters). Blocher's first year in office was marked by what was seen by many as a refusal to play by the rules of concordance and collegiality, including the principle that ministers should defend all decisions taken by the Federal Council, regardless of whether they agree with them or not. Blocher's reluctance to abide by this principle was shown on two occasions in 2004: an initiative launched by the SVP for the introduction of 'life imprisonment for non-treatable extremely violent criminals and sex offenders' (opposed by the government) and two referendums (supported by the government) aimed at facilitating the naturalization of second-generation foreigners and making the naturalization of third-generation ones automatic. In both cases, Blocher decided not to tour the country in support of the government's position (as ministers usually do) and confined himself to neutral statements when forced to speak on these matters. On 8 February, 56.2 per cent of the people (and the vast majority of cantons) accepted the initiative on life imprisonment. As a result, a provision was inserted into the Federal Constitution removing the possibility of early release and prison leave for certain categories of offenders. Moreover, on 26 September, the two referendums on naturalization were rejected by the electorate, providing another victory for the SVP. It is worth noting here that, when reforms to the SVP's liking were to be decided by the people (e.g. a popular vote on a tax reform held in May), Blocher did not refrain from expressing his views. Blocher's participation in the executive also led to increased media focus on supposed disagreements between ministers. As Blocher continued to give the impression of being both in government and in opposition, tales of interpersonal animosities were reported by the media more often than had been the case in the past.

In May, the SVP launched a popular initiative (entitled 'In favour of democratic naturalization') to give Swiss municipalities the option to maintain local ballots when deciding on the naturalization of foreigners, without the possibility of appeal. It was eventually rejected in 2008.

In August, Blocher merged two administrative divisions within his ministry – the Federal Office for Immigration, Integration and Emigration and the Federal Office for Refugees – into a new Federal Office for Migration. While those on the Left and some non-governmental organizations (NGOs) criticized the move as further blurring the distinction between asylum seekers, migrants, and foreign residents (including temporary ones), the centre-right praised the synergies and cost savings that this streamlining was supposed to bring.

On 26 October, the Swiss government signed the second batch of bilateral treaties between Switzerland and the EU. These covered issues such as the taxation of bank deposits; anti-fraud measures; media, pension, and education matters; the Schengen/Dublin agreements (including the abolition of ID checks at the common borders of the Schengen member states, along with security and asylum co-operation), and many others. The SVP claimed that the Schengen/Dublin agreements posed a threat to Swiss security and independence. The party therefore supported a referendum launched by the Aktion für eine unabhängige und neutrale Schweiz (AUNS – Campaign for an Independent and Neutral Switzerland) to repeal Switzerland's participation in the agreements, following parliament's approval of them on 17 December. On the same day, parliament had also approved the extension of the first batch of the bilateral treaties signed in 1999 to the ten countries (mainly from Central and Eastern Europe) that had joined the EU in May 2004. While trade unions and left-wing parties had secured the introduction of several measures aimed at avoiding a 'dumping effect' on salaries caused by the arrival of foreign workers, the SVP attacked the very principle of European integration. Outvoted in both chambers, the party then launched two referendums on these matters (see next section).

The economy continued to improve, with GDP growing by 1.7 per cent. However, unemployment remained high by Swiss standards at 3.9 per cent. In September, two Swiss soldiers who were part of the multinational force based in Afghanistan were injured in an attack on a German military camp at Kunduz. Nevertheless – and despite opposition from the SVP, the Greens, and some SPS deputies – in December the National Council agreed to Switzerland contributing a small contingent to a 'European Union Force' based in Bosnia-Herzegovina.

2005

The political agenda of 2005 continued to be dominated by Blocher and Swiss–EU relations. Unlike the previous year, in 2005 Blocher reluctantly supported the official government stance on EU matters, although he openly stated that there were divisions within the government on the matter. At the SVP delegate assembly in January, he spoke in favour of freedom of movement within Europe and said it would ultimately benefit the Swiss economy. However, the assembly disagreed and only 94 delegates out of 297 supported Blocher's position. On 5 June, the Swiss electorate voted on a referendum launched by the SVP and AUNS to reverse the government's decision to sign up to the Schengen/Dublin agreements. The vote was lost by the SVP, as 54.6 per cent of voters followed the recommendation of the executive (including both SVP government members, Blocher and Schmid). A few months later, on 25 September, a second popular vote was held on a referendum launched by the small right-wing party Schweizer Demokraten (SD – Swiss Democrats) and supported by the SVP. This aimed to block the extension of free movement rights to citizens of countries that had recently joined the EU. In the end, 56 per cent of voters rejected the proposal and sided with the government and all major parties (except the SVP).

During the autumn parliamentary session, however, the SVP achieved some important victories. First, parliament accepted several amendments proposed by the party to the laws on foreigners and asylum seekers (introduced by Blocher's ministry). These aimed to (1) introduce tighter criteria for the right of family reunion; (2) set the ability to speak the local language as an essential requirement for proof of successful integration; (3) require asylum seekers to show an official identification document (ID or passport) to apply for asylum; and (4) introduce cuts to state aid for asylum seekers. The Left, backed by various NGOs, announced that they would launch a referendum to repeal these measures (see next section).

As for the themes the SVP focused on in 2005, the party combined its core ideas – i.e. defending the independence and well-being of Switzerland and opposing 'excessive' immigration and asylum applications – with the defence of Swiss jobs (shown by a survey in August to be the main issue voters were concerned about). On this topic, the SVP said it was opposing the EU in order not to import 'unemployment through Schengen' (as one of its slogans stated) and warned of the risk of Eastern Europeans 'migrating en masse' to Switzerland.

As for the economy, unemployment decreased only slightly (to 3.8 per cent), while GDP grew by 1.9 per cent. In March, Lufthansa bought Swiss International Air Lines – formerly Swissair – without any opposition expressed to Switzerland's only 'national' airline being taken over by a German company.

2006

Three important referendums (on asylum, foreign residents, and the EU) generated much debate throughout the year. On 24 September, 68 per cent of voters rejected two referendums supported by the Left that were aimed at repealing the modifications to the asylum law and the law on foreigners introduced by parliament and sponsored by the SVP and Blocher's Ministry of Justice and the Police (see previous section). The SVP claimed that – as a result of this victory – the asylum system would become cheaper and that the party was thus fulfilling its electoral promises, mainly thanks to Blocher being the minister in charge of asylum matters. Second, on 26 November, 53.4 per cent of voters rejected a referendum backed by the SVP which sought to revoke Switzerland's pledge that it would contribute one billion francs to a fund set up to facilitate the economic development of the ten countries that had joined the EU in 2004. While all major political parties and business organizations were in favour of making this contribution (formally detached from the bilateral treaties, but the de facto price which Switzerland had to pay for access to the single market), the SVP had opposed it. The vote was the third held on the EU in the 2005–2006 period – and the third victory for the government.

As for Blocher's relationship with his government colleagues, a minor scandal erupted during his visit to Turkey in early October. While abroad, Blocher criticized article 261bis of the Swiss criminal code (which punishes racist expressions) and announced that a revision of the law would soon be undertaken. This announcement broke protocol, as Blocher had apparently failed to consult his government colleagues first. Also in October, the SVP published its electoral manifesto for the 2007 federal elections. This was entitled 'Mein Zuhause – unsere Schweiz' ('My Home – Our Switzerland') and emphasized the traditional core issues of the party: the fight against higher taxes and the alleged abuse of the welfare system, criminality, immigration, and the defence of Switzerland's independence.

On 18 December 2006, the SVP tabled four law-and-order parliamentary motions. These comprised measures designed to (1) expel not only foreign residents who committed certain crimes but also their parents in the case of underage offenders; (2) cut welfare benefits to foreigners convicted of crimes; (3) increase the penalties for rape. Because none of the motions achieved the necessary support, the party decided to launch a popular initiative for their introduction (see next section).

As far as the economy was concerned, unemployment decreased from 3.8 per cent to 3.3 per cent, exports rose by 10 per cent and investments went up by 7.1 per cent. Overall GDP grew by 2.8 per cent. The government was thus able to achieve a surplus of 2.5 billion Swiss francs in the public finances. Despite the improved figures, 66 per cent of respondents in a national survey during the summer still cited unemployment as their most pressing concern. Other issues cited by respondents were health care, pensions, and asylum seeking.

2007

The October federal elections dominated Swiss political life in 2007. On 27 January, the SVP delegates' assembly in Payerne voted almost unanimously in favour of the party moving into opposition in the event that Blocher and Schmid failed to be re-elected to the Federal Council after the election. It was also decided that if any member of the party accepted support from other parties in order to take Blocher's or Schmid's place in the executive, he or she would be expelled. This reflected the fact that, apart from the FDP, it was clear none of the other three main parties wanted Blocher to stay on. In particular, the SPS was categorical that it would not vote for him, and offered his seat to the CVP instead. Meanwhile, the Greens claimed they should be given Blocher's seat, given their recent electoral growth.

On 17 March, the SVP delegates' assembly in Lugano debated criminality and the alleged unwillingness of many young foreigners to fully integrate into Swiss society. It was decided that the party would launch a popular initiative aimed at ensuring that 'whoever lives here has to obey our laws'. The following month, the party again criticized the Federal Tribunal for 'overstepping its competences' by not allowing naturalization procedures to be decided through local ballots. On 30 June, party delegates agreed on a text for the popular initiative mentioned in the preceding section – which was designed to allow the expulsion of foreigners who committed crimes in Switzerland (the 'expulsion initiative') – and began collecting signatures for it. Moreover, in August the SVP published its 'Contract with the People' (which in its style and graphics very much recalled the Swiss Confederal Pact of 1291/1315, through which Switzerland had been founded). This document promised that the party would: (1) oppose any plans to join the EU; (2) fight to expel foreign criminals; (3) endeavour to reduce taxes for everybody. The SVP also insisted that it was crucial to vote for them in order to keep Blocher in government.

As part of its campaign for the 'expulsion initiative' the party produced a poster which caused an international outcry and was widely criticized as racist since it depicted three white sheep kicking out a black sheep against the backdrop of the Swiss flag. The poster prompted the 'UN Special Rapporteur on contemporary forms of racism, racial discrimination, xenophobia and related intolerance' to protest to the Swiss government.

In an August 2007 survey, 57 per cent of citizens cited unemployment as their most pressing concern (a drop of nine percentage points on the previous year), 45 per cent listed pensions (−6 points) and 38 per cent health care (−17 points). Compared to 2006, more people (+8 points) expressed concerns about 'foreigners, migration, and asylum seekers' (35 per cent in total), while 30 per cent feared for their personal safety (an increase of 17 percentage points on the previous year).

In early September, a major controversy erupted when a parliamentary subcommittee criticized Blocher for having undermined the independence of the federal prosecutor, Valentin Roschacher (CVP), who had stepped down at the end of 2006. The report did not discount the possibility that Blocher might even have been involved in a conspiracy to remove the prosecutor (who is elected by the whole government but is responsible to the Ministry of Justice). In a specially convened, televised parliamentary debate on 3 October, SVP deputies argued that Blocher was being victimized by the other parties.

In the federal elections on 21 October, the SVP achieved the best electoral result ever by a Swiss political party, gaining 28.9 per cent of the vote (+2.2 percentage points on 2003). The second-strongest party, the SPS, was almost 10 points behind, with 19.5 per cent (−3.8 points). The FDP received 15.8 per cent (−1.5 points) and the CVP 14.5 per cent (+0.01 points). With 62 seats in the National Council, the SVP now had as many MPs as the two centrist parties (FDP and CVP) combined. However, since the Greens had also increased their seat tally (from 13 to 20), the overall Left–Right balance in parliament remained unaltered. In the upper chamber (the Council of States), the SVP lost one seat and the FDP two seats at the expense of the Greens (+2) and the new Green Liberal Party (+1 seat).

On 12 December, Blocher was not re-elected to the Federal Council. This caused a lot of controversy for two reasons: first, it is extremely uncommon for the Swiss parliament not to re-elect a member of government, although this had happened for the first time in over a century four years earlier, when

Blocher himself was elected; second, the SVP had again increased its support at the election and was now the strongest party in the country by an even larger margin. A more moderate SVP member was chosen by parliament to replace Blocher in government – the Finance Minister of Graubünden Canton, Eveline Widmer-Schlumpf – and she accepted the job. This enabled the other parties to claim that the seat had still been awarded to the SVP, albeit against its will.

Following the strategy agreed before the election, the SVP asked Widmer-Schlumpf's cantonal branch, SVP Graubünden, to expel her (since this decision could not be taken by the party in central office). When this request was refused, the party expelled the entire cantonal branch. In mid-2008, the Berne and Glarus branches of the SVP joined the former SVP Graubünden and created a new party, the Bürgerlich-Demokratische Partei (BDP – Conservative Democratic Party), which vowed to act as a less extreme, centre-right version of the SVP. As for the SVP, it announced at the end of 2007 that it would 'join the opposition', by which it meant that it would make even more frequent use of direct democratic methods – the referendum and the popular initiative – to oppose government policies.

As regards the economy, for the first time in five years, unemployment figures fell below 3 per cent, reaching 2.8 per cent.

Index

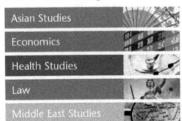
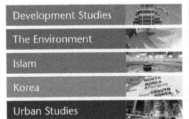

Lightning Source UK Ltd.
Milton Keynes UK
UKHW021848171218
334166UK00008B/140/P

9 781138 670440